FROM GODS
TO BAD BOYS

FROM GODS TO BAD BOYS

A HISTORY OF THEATRE IN TWELVE LIVES

Giles Ramsay

GILES RAMSAY

FROM GODS TO BAD BOYS

A History Of Theatre In Twelve Lives

Copyright © 2023 by Giles Ramsay

All rights reserved. No part of this publication may be reproduced, distributed or transmitted in any form or by any means, including photocopying, recording, or other electronic or mechanical methods, without the prior written permission of the publisher, except in the case of brief quotations embodied in critical reviews and certain other noncommercial uses permitted by copyright law.

Printed in the United States of America

For my parents - wot brung me up.

FROM GODS TO BAD BOYS

PROLOGUE	1
DIONYSUS: *God of Many Forms*	5
AESCHYLUS: *A Soldier in Society*	15
EVERYMAN: *Escaping from God*	29
CHRISTOPHER MARLOWE: *Poet and Spy*	43
WILLIAM SHAKESPEARE: *Building Show-business*	57
A DIGRESSION ON SHAKESPEARE: *The Alchemy of Acting*	71
APHRA BEHN: *Agent 160 - Punk Poetess*	81
DAVID GARRICK: *Actor and Impresario*	101
A DIGRESSION ON VICTORIANS: *Shakespeare and Elephants*	121
OSCAR WILDE: *A Well-Polished Paradox*	127
GEORG II, DUKE OF SAXE-MEININGEN: *The Maker of Modern Theatre*	149
TERENCE RATTIGAN: *Part One - Passion Restrained*	167
LILIAN BAYLIS: *Acting for God - Praying for Lust*	175
TERENCE RATTIGAN: *Part Two - Passion Released*	183
JOE ORTON: *Part One - Bring on the Bad Boys*	207
JOE ORTON: *Part Two - Bad Boys Blazing*	235

PROLOGUE

We often end up in the theatre as a punishment. On a birthday or an anniversary some loved one surprises us with dinner and just when the food and the wine have lulled us into a comforting reverie they announce that, on top of everything, we are now going to a show. Into the dark box of dubious delights we go. A place where the interval wine wouldn't have been used for cooking by the chef of our now much pined for restaurant and the seats were designed by a limbless architect with spite in his heart. As for the entertainment? It's all so hit and miss. So many two or three star shows instead of five star fireworks guaranteed every time.

Well, I'm afraid that's the nature of the beast. However those five-star velcro moments that stick in the mind for life do come around every now and then and thus we keep going. The prize for enduring all those semi-forgettable matinees and evenings is that we are occasionally rewarded with an event so captivating that it becomes a tiny part of who we are. We connect and we are changed.

But to connect is often easier said than done and sometimes to know a little bit about the world the play sprang from might help us move closer to it and understand it a little more. Context can clarify. So for those of you that have persevered in the perverse habit of theatre-going here is a little book that might just make the process of connecting a little easier.

It is not a book for experts and is in no way comprehensive. All this book attempts to do is act as a refresher to what most people already know - nothing comes from nothing. All playwrights lived in the world before they wrote plays. These are their little worlds.

GTR London, September 2021

DIONYSUS

DIONYSUS
God of Many Forms

People often talk glibly about the birth of theatre but theatre wasn't born, it didn't spring from some godhead fully formed - it was assembled. Theatre is an ungainly golem of a thing made up of multiple disparate parts stuck clumsily together over thousands of years. Amorphous and unfinished. Work in progress.

Theatre, also, in no way resembles real life. It is a shadow of reality bringing the mystical and the material together almost within our reach. Theatre at its best gives us a momentary corner-eye glimpse of who we are or might be before, fugitive art form that it is, darting away into the dusk.

More prosaically, around 64,000 years ago in western Spain a Neanderthal man decided to crawl into the darkness of a cave. What motivated him is impossible to know. Perhaps it was raining. Once there he mixed water and pigment in his mouth, placed his hand firmly on a rock and began to painstakingly spit around it creating a stencil that can still be observed today. Similar images can be found all across the world from Europe to Australia to Africa - temporal moments, the placing of hands, made permanent through pigment. Human fragility projected forever onto the solidity of stone. In some caves we see the hands of children - did these tribesmen revisit the caves as adults and place their larger hands over the shadows of their previous, smaller selves and remember? If you can ponder the past you can ponder the future, consider human time against geological time and your place in the universe.

Later, such caves would become filled with startling images of horses, deer and bulls. Such paintings, created around 36,000 years ago in Altamira in northern Spain, are so beautifully rendered that Picasso observed that after their creation 'all is decadence'– in other words it was downhill for art from that point on.

Picasso also said 'art is a lie that makes us realise truth'. Sometimes the allegorical can be more revealing about reality than the literal. Perhaps these cave paintings were more than merely early hunting manuals but instead reflected something of the awe early man felt towards the life force of the great beasts. A life force they sought to control, dominate and incorporate into themselves. Perhaps in these images we see early man trying to make sense of living amongst aliens; aliens that swim and fly, aliens that he ate and who in turn ate him.

These images could only be seen by firelight and in its flickering glow the beasts of the field would have appeared to charge across the curves of the rocks. Some of the figures were painted with eight legs as if to enhance the affect of motion. Life recreated by man on rock. Flutes and whistles crafted from bone have been found in these caves so we can project a soundscape onto the action taking place. I have no doubt that there was also movement and drumming and the sound of the human voice. Something we can properly refer to as ritual.

All societies have created rituals to mark events that matter to them - the beginning, the middle and the end of seasons and of lives. Over time a sequence of actions involving gestures, sounds and objects, repeated in a selected, 'sacred' space (a cave perhaps), form a tradition. What began as something instinctive and spontaneous became a formalised part of the community's autobiography. Thus, the ritual elevated itself into an art form, where the *form* will thereafter dominate the *content*.

But the form must be perfectly enacted, or the magic will simply not work. Which led, all those millennia ago, to the rise of something our present day media is so suspicious of - the expert. Some members of the tribe were simply better at cave painting than others. Some were better players of bone flutes; some were more convincing at imitating the movement of bulls or deer. Some even had the heightened skill and charisma to lead the tribe in the ritual, acting as their shaman or priest, thereby connecting the community most effectively to the spiritual, the super-natural - to the gods.

Whilst we do have records of religious presentations dating back to 2500 BC in ancient Egypt we cannot be certain that the Abydos Passion Play (performed each November for 2000 years until 250 BC) resembled anything that we can fairly call drama. It is likely that this re-telling of the story of the slaughter of Osiris and his followers by his brother Seth was more of a public spectacle or a re-enactment of a royal funeral than traditional theatre. Our only piece of primary evidence for these ritualistic events is a stela or stone tablet written in approximately 1868 BC by the courtier Ikhernofret who was a participant in the ritual that year. Through whatever means Ikhernofret was remembering his gods at this annual Khoiak festival it wasn't in the form of a scripted play.

It was not in Egypt but around the Aegean that the most relevant gods to our story emerged about 5,000 years ago. They became the foundation stone for everything that we recognise as Western civilisation. The Olympian gods and their deeply human tales of sex, valour and woe provided a multitude of allegories for the meaning of life as well as a star-studded series of bodice-ripping sagas to keep the tribes of Greece and Turkey occupied for generations. A latecomer to this panoply of the gods was Dionysus.

It is fitting that Dionysus, the god of duality, has two birth stories. The first relates that he was the child of Zeus and Persephone - the Queen of the Underworld. The second, that he was the progeny of Zeus and the mortal Semele. In the latter myth Semele asked to see the face of Zeus and when he appeared to her was duly burned to a husk. Zeus seized the foetus from her combusting womb and preserved it by sewing it into his thigh until it came to full term and Dionysus was finally born again. Twice born Dionysus is the god of paradox.

Holding in his nature the divine and the mortal and encompassing the heights of Olympus to the depths of Hades, Dionysus is the epitome of Heraclitus' observation that 'everything always has its opposite within itself'. From the pain of childbirth springs the gift of life.

It is as the god of life, fertility and the harvest that Dionysus fulfils his most potent role. He is the renewer of life, the re-birther, the bringer of bright spring out of darkest winter. Forever associated with the gift of the vine, the grape and of wine Dionysus, like alcohol, can enhance or destroy; bring serenity or frenzy. Dionysus reveals to us the dual nature of life - we are both man and beast and we can suffer the horrors of the night just as we can rejoice in the heights of bliss. Indeed, to be truly alive we need to embrace both the dark and the light or, as President Richard Nixon grudgingly put it, 'only if you have been in the deepest valley can you ever know how magnificent it is to be on the highest mountain'.

Bringing in the harvest is a time for celebration in any rural community. It is a time for thanking the powers-that-be for providing sustenance for another year. Once, through threshing, we have separated the wheat from the chaff we are left with a circle of beaten earth on the ground. What better space on which to dance out our thanks to our gods.

Over time this celebration became ritualised into a choric dance called the dithyramb - a dance with songs in praise of Dionysus for his gifts of fertility. To the Greeks Dionysus was undoubtedly real having been made manifest in the harvest just as the absolute existence of Poseidon could be seen in the rolling of the waves and felt in the tremors of the earth. As for Aphrodite - have you never been aroused or in love? Natural forces existed and so the gods existed. They lived and dwelt among the mortals who could see and engage with them.

But while all mortals are equal, some are more equal than others. Re-enter the experts. As the ritual of the dithyramb became more established, professionalised, we begin to hear the names of those talented men who helped it evolve. Archilochus (680 - 645 BC) is credited with the first mention of the dithyramb. "I know how to lead the fair song of the Lord Dionysus, the dithyramb, when my wits are fused with wine."

Archilochus was a lyricist from the Aegean Island of Paros who set the tales of his community - tales of war, of famine, of feast - to music. He was like Demodocus, the blind bardic singer in Homer's Odyssey, who sung of the Trojan War and provoked a catharsis in Odysseus thereby causing him to reveal his true self. The transformative power of art.

But Dionysus also stands for the transformative power of wine. People today talk about 'getting out of their heads' and dancing themselves into trance-like states on drugs like Ecstasy. Human beings have always needed occasional moments of frenzy and dis-order. It is only by stepping over the boundary into licensed chaos that we can release communal tensions and enjoy a communal catharsis before stepping back into the safety and order of everyday life. This is the transformative path gifted to us by Dionysus. He allows us to be 'other', to push ourselves into super-natural states, to become as one with the deer, the buffalo, with nature and with the gods.

The Romans recreated these Dionysian rituals in the Saturnalia when masters would wait on their servants and society would inject a bit of topsy-turviness into their lives. In the medieval period this human need manifested itself through The Feast of Fools with the cross-dressing Lord of Misrule and The Boy Bishop. For these moments only everything that kept society stable was turned on its head. The valve on the pressure cooker of human society was temporarily released. This was carnival, this was Mardi Gras, this was a rave. And then, with a communal sigh of relief, the valve was re-closed and order and safety restored.

Arion of Lesbos, who lived fifty years after Archilochus, was a professional citherode - a player of the lyre or harp. He took the dithyramb a step further and is credited by Herodotus as being 'the first of men we know to have composed the dithyramb and named it and produced it in Corinth'.

The lyre is the instrument of Apollo, the god of order, of mathematics and of architecture. As Shakespeare wrote in *Troilus and Cressida* 'untune that string and, hark, what discord follows'. You cannot play the lyre if its strings are out of tune or broken and as such it is the instrument of the rational. The other instrument integral to the dithyramb was the aulos, a twin-reeded wind instrument not unlike a clarinet or oboe and forever associated with Dionysus. If the cithera provided classical order then the aulos provided jazz-like frenzy.

Equally important to the performance of the dithyramb was the element of dance. We can catch glimpses of it frozen forever under the glaze of ancient pots depicting the elaborate costumes and stylised movements of the chorus. This interaction between a solitary singer or narrator and the all-singing, all-dancing chorus accompanied by bands of cithera, aulos and drums was clearly, by the sixth century BC, a very potent mix.

In the late sixth century BC a man called Thespis was born in Icaria in Greece. He trained to become one of the professional singers/narrators in the dithyramb and later in his career is credited with an innovation that radically transformed the ritual. Previously the chorus had simply sung of the acts of warriors and kings. Thespis stepped out of this throng and identified directly with the subject of the story giving him or her a living, spoken voice - he *became* them. 'Here is' became 'I am'.

As the first actor, he bequeathed us the word 'thespian' and by painting his face or donning a mask he was able, in a large open space, to differentiate himself as individual characters separate from the chorus. Now the audience could see and hear a god or a warrior act and speak for himself and watch the chorus respond accordingly thereby creating a new dramatic dialogue. This new art form was called Tragedy.

Tragoidia translates as 'the song of the goat' and no-one really knows why. Perhaps a goat (a useful symbol of fecundity) was sacrificed as part of the increasingly elaborate festivities? Perhaps a goat was the prize for the best dithyramb? (Greek society was fantastically competitive, hence the Olympic Games). Perhaps a chorus of boys with their unbroken voices sounded like the bleating of goats? There are many possibilities, but all we are left with is the word.

As the originator of this dance-drama it is fitting that in the spring of 534 BC Thespis won the first competitive presentation of this new art form at the recently instituted City Dionysia in Athens. Subsequently he bought himself a chariot and travelled around the Aegean capitalising on his celebrity status thereby introducing theatrical touring. Not just the first actor; Thespis was the first impresario.

From his mythical, rural beginnings Dionysus was now at the very heart and centre of Athenian religious and social life. As the city state evolved so Dionysus evolved with it; he was urbanised - the first metrosexual. Originally represented by a crude image of the phallus, Dionysus gradually morphed into the androgynous figure of a beautiful young man; sometimes with horns on his head, always with vine leaves in his hair. Man and beast, beauty and horror, summer, and winter - no wonder this inexpressible paradox, this god of many forms, so captured the imagination of mankind. In 1888 Friedrich Nietzsche wrote: "The saying Yes to life even in its strangest and hardest problems; the will to life … that is what I call Dionysian."

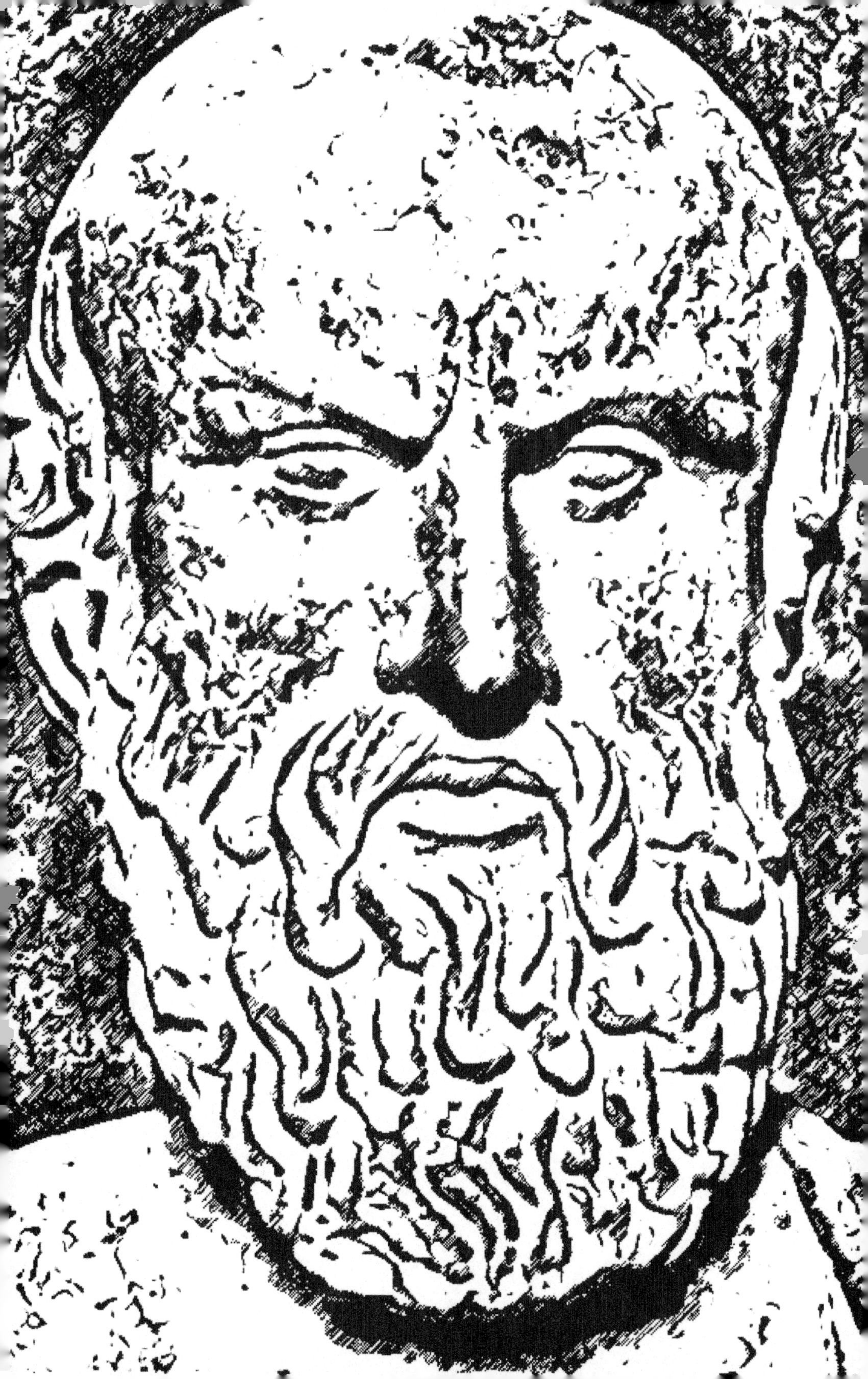

AESCHYLUS
A Soldier in Society

Aeschylus was the father of modern tragedy who fought at the Battle of Marathon and was killed by a flying tortoise. Born in 525 BC at Eleusis about ten miles north-west of Athens he came of age at a time of astounding social and political change that would profoundly affect his life and his art. Art never forms in a vacuum - it is always a response to something. Nothing comes from nothing.

The Greek Dark Ages - the age of Homer, The Illiad and The Odyssey - came to a close around the ninth century BC with the first glimmerings of the city states. This transition ended the unquestioned rule of hereditary kings. The aristocratic elites who took their place were in their turn usurped in the seventh century BC by a new breed of opportunistic and populist noblemen - the tyrants.

Tyranny simply meant 'rule by one man' and was not altogether viewed as a negative thing. Some tyrants were good, others not so good. Draco, who seized power in the early 600s, despite his draconian reputation, was a rather efficient and positive legal reformer replacing the old system of oral law and blood feud with a written code overseen by a court of law. Such reforms brought a level of equality into society that was not always to the taste of the remaining aristocrats.

To calm the simmering tensions between the nobility and free citizens that was dragging Athens towards chaos, the statesman and poet Solon (630 - 560 BC) successfully instigated a series of further reforms to even out the constitutional, economic and moral playing field. For the first time in human history the peasant classes (the thetes) were given the right to participate in politics and the creation and application of the law. To have a voice in Athens no longer depended entirely on your birth.

By the time Aeschylus was a young man the Athenian body-politic was once more in dire need of renewal and in 508 BC the recently installed leader of the city, Cleisthenes, embarked on the most radical reforms of all. To end the strife and rivalry between the four dominant aristocratic clans that had delivered nothing but tension and disorder for decades he abolished them, replacing them with ten brand new tribes. These new groupings were delineated by place of residence not by blood.

These 'demes' were in turn sub-divided into three territories - the city, the rural areas, and the coastline, thereby ensuring a level of balanced representation for all regions. As an Athenian your loyalty was now to a *location* not to a family and the dominant power of the nobility was duly broken. Democracy had arrived – at least for the 50% of the population who were neither slaves nor women.

Cleisthenes also introduced the system of ostracism to the city whereby over-mighty and potentially dangerous citizens could be voted down and expelled from Athens for ten years; a pretty efficient way of pre-empting the ambitions of aspirant tyrants and a political tool well overdue for renewal.

Whilst the threat from within had been calmed the threat from without was ever-present in the form of the Persians. King Darius the

Great, from modern Iran, ruled an empire that already encompassed the Balkans, the Indus Valley and North Africa (it is often forgotten that the Persian Empire was larger than the future Roman Empire covering more than ten percent of the planet) and the time had now come for him to subjugate the Aegean. In August or September 490 BC Darius sent tens of thousands of men to destroy the Greeks at Marathon. This should have meant certain defeat for the Greek army as they were massively outnumbered but, at the end of the day, the battlefield was strewn with the corpses of 6,400 Persians compared to 192 Athenian dead. Standing alive that late summer's day and surveying the carnage was a thirty-five-year-old Aeschylus. Amongst the Athenian fallen was his brother Cynegirus.

Ten years later, in 480 BC, Aeschylus was to witness another great victory when the outnumbered Greeks saw off the mighty Persian navy at the Battle of Salamis. With the reforms of Cleisthenes providing stability within and two crushing defeats of the Persians neutralising the enemy without it most certainly was a glad confident morning for the Athenians. A golden age, the Classical Age, had dawned.

It is fitting that the man who was going to dominate the theatre world for the next two-and-a-half thousand years began his career following a visitation from Dionysus. Whilst sleeping in a vineyard, the god whispered in the youthful Aeschylus' ear that he should dedicate his life to the fledgling art of tragedy and once he awoke the boy dutifully began to write. By the age of twenty-six Aeschylus was presenting his plays at the City Dionysia, but he failed to win the prize until 484 BC. He would go on to win it a dozen more times in his lifetime.

By the early fifth century BC, dramatic competitions had become an integral part of the spring festival dedicated to Dionysus. Events would begin with a procession or leading-in ritual where an image of the god was presented to the crowds and placed upon an altar. This was followed by a dancing competition made up of boys' and men's dithyrambs involving up to a thousand participants.

Then the major dramatic competitions commenced. The primary competition was between three separate playwrights each presenting a series of three tragedies linked by a common theme. Each of these culminated in a work known as a satyr play which was a form of cathartic comic burlesque in which the heroes of the tragedies were portrayed as cowards and buffoons. These were essential light relief after the intensity of the tragic trilogies just as Kyogen plays are used in Japanese Noh drama or the roles of drunken Noah and his nagging wife lighten the mood in medieval mystery cycles.

It was Plato who described the Bacchic dancing that lies at the core of the satyr plays as being 'not of the polis'. By this he meant that they were not representative of the sophisticated Athenian city state but rather something that harked back to a more primitive and rural past. Originating in the Bronze Age culture of Minoan times, Bacchic dancing had developed into the more carefully structured rite of the dithyramb which was in turn incorporated into Tragic drama. Finessed beyond recognition the primitive fertility rites of the past had been civilised, tamed and controlled. But their potency had not been forgotten.

The satyrs themselves were the chief followers of Dionysus and represented the natural passions and extremes of human emotions. According to mythology they were the spawn of water nymphs and were represented as hairy beasts with upturned, pig-like noses, pointed ears and two small horns growing out of their heads. Long horse-like tails adorned their rumps whilst an impressively large phallus protruded from their front. Obsessed by wine and other sensual pleasures they spent most of their lives sleeping, dancing, drinking and fornicating, whilst also being confirmed cowards with a distinct propensity for mischief.

The older satyrs were called Sileni whilst the younger ones Satyrisci. They also had individual names such as Ivy, Revel, Fun, Lustful and Dithyramb proving to be the ancestors of Oberon's entourage in Shakespeare's *A Midsummer Night's Dream*. Their leader and father is Papa Silenus who is jovial, paunchy and bald-headed; the sort of lovable drunken rogue who will always let you down. Not unlike Falstaff.

The content of a Satyr play was largely the same as that of tragedy although the meter of the verse was usually freer and the mood coarser. Heroic figures from the great myths clashed with the vulgarity of the satyrs and graceful language was juxtaposed with bawdy humour. The genius of the genre was, as the Victorian classical scholar A E Haigh observed, 'to combine in a single performance the dignity of tragedy with the the boisterous licence of the primitive dithyramb'. If tragedy was a rational expression of man's position in the world the satyr plays were an expression of the irrational elements of man's being.

In *Cyclops* by Euripides, which is the only fully extant satyr play we have, Papa Silenus and his sons have become the slaves of the Cyclops, Polyphemus, on the island of Sicily into which world arrives the heroic figure of Odysseus. Realising that he and his fellow sailors are in danger they are determined to leave as soon as possible but not before they have re-stocked with food for the rest of their journey. Encountering Papa Silenus, Odysseus foolishly offers to swap wine for vittles, much to the gluttonous satyr's delight, who immediately resolves to steal the necessary supplies from the Cyclops by getting him drunk. Once Polyphemus is inebriated (and after he has enjoyed a furtive sexual encounter with Silenus) he is famously blinded by Odysseus who has introduced himself by the name of 'No-one'. Screaming that he has been attacked by 'No-one' the Cyclops is mocked by the drunken satyrs and Odysseus makes good his escape.

Throughout this jaunt Papa Silenus maintains an amiable disrespect for the gods (even for Dionysus) berating them in a style that would have been familiar to Tevye in *Fiddler on the Roof* some 2,500 years later. In the same way the haughty Cyclops boasts that 'if Zeus thunders at me, I wank in his face'. In the satyr plays man was nearer to the beasts than the gods and it is this primitive realisation of man's baseness that is at the core of the genre - a genre that was important enough to make up a quarter of all the writings of Aeschylus, Sophocles and Euripides. The satyrs reflected the childish and bestial elements of the audience who understood that when people are contained in a city they sometimes need to re-connect with elements that are not of the city. Much as the Athenians might have striven to serve Apollo they recognised their need to dance with Dionysus.

The Persians was written by Aeschylus in 472 BC and was the second play in a trilogy of which parts one and three are now lost. The satyr play was about Prometheus' theft of fire of which only a few comical fragments remain. However, we have the full text of *The Persians* making it the oldest extant play in the world and the only surviving tragedy to deal with historical events rather than myths and legends.

Eight years before presenting this play Aeschylus had faced death in the battle of Salamis as, presumably, had many of the men sitting in his audience. In this context *The Persians* is an astoundingly contemporary play which was daringly written, without enmity, entirely from the point of view of the Persians. This was no piece of theatrical propaganda or nationalistic jingoism but a subtle analysis of the fortunes of empire and war, provoking sorrow for the defeated foe and pride for the

Athenian victors. The stark fact Aeschylus lays bare is that even the mothers and widows of the vanquished grieve.

If *The Persians* is the earliest full play in existence, Aeschylus' *Oresteia* is the earliest full trilogy to survive. Winning all the laurels at the Dionysia of 458 BC it tells of the aftermath of the Trojan War beginning with the return of King Agamemnon who ten years previously had set off in hot pursuit of Helen of Troy. To placate the gods and benefit from favourable winds he had sacrificed his daughter Iphigenia to them - without consulting his wife Clytemnestra. Sometimes what may please the gods goes down less well with the mother.

We should remember that before the paternalistic pantheon of the gods of Olympus there had been the Titans and before them the maternal chthonic (of the underworld) nature gods who had never really gone away. These fecund entities still existed deep below the strata of the earth, ancient in their power and in their fury. Woe betide the man or woman who forgot them.

Part One of the trilogy, *The Agamemnon*, opens after the Greeks have finally won victory over the Trojans and a long-suffering watchman announces that Agamemnon is coming home. Clytemnestra awaits him having had ten years to brood over her loss and take another lover, Aegisthus. She welcomes Agamemnon back into his home, the cursed House of Atrius, and takes her long-planned revenge by slaughtering him in his bath. Blood must have blood; that is the ancient Greek way. Natural law. Don't get mad, get even. Thus, Iphigenia is avenged.

It is worth considering at this point that all of the great female roles of Greek theatre such as Clytemnestra, Antigone and Medea were parts written by men to be acted by men in front of an, almost certainly, entirely male audience. When Medea bewailed the lot of a married woman and cried 'yet I would rather stand three times in the front line of a battle than once give birth to a child' certain members of the male military elite watching must have scratched their heads and pondered the veracity of her ideas. Woman might have been excluded from the theatre and from the body politic but their thoughts and concerns were certainly on Athenian men's minds. After the actions taken by Clytemnestra against her husband perhaps one should not be surprised.

Into *The Oresteia's* cycle of vengeance Aeschylus injects more than one major coup de theatre. When Clytemnestra invites Agamemnon from his chariot to enter his palace she will not have 'the foot that stamped out Troy' touch mere earth again. Her maid-servants strew his path with crimson tapestries and robes and 20,000 members of the Athenian audience watched transfixed as Agamemnon marched towards his death along a path stained blood red.

Technically the Theatre of Dionysus in Athens could physically seat 17,000 people (and for 'people' read 'men') just as the present British House of Commons can physically seat 437 worthy backsides. However, the British Parliament has 650 members to seat which means that during major political events the chamber is crowded with MPs sitting buttock to buttock, crammed in on the steps and in the aisles. The Great Dionysia, for the Athenians, was a major event in entertainment, social, religious and political terms. We thus need to imagine an intense, tightly-packed crowd sitting in the Teatron (the viewing space) staring down upon the vast 85-foot diameter Orchestra (the dancing space). From here, in the spring sunshine, the intensity of seeing a king striding through red to enter the house where he will die must have been intoxicating.

In Part Two, *The Libation Bearers,* we see the titular handmaids of Dionysus coming to anoint the tomb of Agamemnon several years after his murder. Orestes, the son of Agamemnon and Clytemnestra, has secretly returned to Argos from exile where he had been sent during the war for safe keeping. He has returned to avenge the slaughter of his father, as is right and proper. Blood must have blood. The dilemma of course is that the blood he must honourably take is that of his mother.

And herein lies one of the fundamental themes of Greek tragedy. Where do our loyalties lie? The family or the gods? The individual or the state? The 'I' or the 'We'? As Sophocles will make extremely clear in his work *Antigone,* sometimes there is more than one valid source of authority. The eponymous Antigone is morally right as a sister to demand to bury the body of her brother but Creon, as a political leader, is equally obliged to maintain the laws of the state and forbid the burial. The centre cannot hold and tragedy ensues.

In the same way another great work by Sophocles, *Oedipus Rex*, is about far more than sexual taboo. Tom Lehrer sums up the overt plot rather magnificently as 'he loved his mother and she loved him and yet his story is rather grim' but the play is about far more than accidental incest. Firstly it's a whodunnit. Oedipus became King of Thebes for saving the city from plague by solving the riddle of the sphinx. Now that the pestilence has returned Oedipus is naturally convinced he can save the day again. On realising that the citizens never discovered who actually murdered their previous King Laius he is determined to put matters right. He will detect the murderer. Of course the knowing audience of fifth century Athenians are writhing in their seats squealing (spoiler alert) "Don't go there! Whodunnit? Youdunnit!". And this is exactly what the blind prophet Tiresias tells Oedipus to his face very early on in the play when he cries 'you are the man, the unclean thing, the dirt that breeds disease'. Now this technically should mess up the dramatic tension for the rest of the show. Oedipus has been told what the problem is. Him. So game over?

Not at all, for Oedipus can in no way accept such an accusation. "I heard but I did not believe my ears," he argues and, from his point of view, he is being sane, logical and correct. He knows that he is a good man, a bit of a hero in fact, who has saved the city before. So, of course, Tiresias must have ulterior motives, must be plotting against him with others. Utterly convinced of his own righteousness Oedipus cannot accept any other version of events and paranoia sets in. Truth has been spoken to power and power was deaf to it. So what do we do? What do we as a citizen of fifth century Athens or twenty-first century London or Washington or Moscow do when a leader calls it wrong? Thank goodness we will never be put in such a situation.

Anyway, back to Mycenae. Orestes faces his predicament with resolve, slaughtering Clytemnestra alongside her lover Aegisthus. This might be within the honour code of the Greeks but it is also clearly against nature and consequently, rising up from the bowels of the earth, appear the ancient, vengeful chthonic forces - the Furies.

The last episode in this Aeschylus boxset is *The Eumenides*. This commences with Orestes being pursued by the Furies to the temple of Apollo at Delphi which is 75 miles from Athens. From there he is sent into the City of Athens itself to consult with the goddess Athena. Aeschylus is bringing the drama home! Sitting in that theatre in 458 BC the audience would have watched a scene set in the Acropolis which was standing on a rocky outcrop just behind them. The drama draws to its close with Athena selecting a jury of twelve Athenian citizens to decide between Orestes and the Furies. His argument follows the interesting logic that mothers do not really matter - they are merely pods that incubate the all-important male seed. Clytemnestra was in fact a glorified chicken and, after a cliff-hanger of a hung jury, Athena finds in favour of Orestes. He is freed of the guilt of blood and the curse of the House of Atreus finally comes to its end.

Then, remarkably, Athena invites the defeated Furies to stay in Athens and become the city's lucky spirits, the kindly ones, the Eumenides. With such benevolent inclusivity the trilogy concludes.

The audience have in one day been taken on a journey populated by the myths and heroes of their own cultural past, travelled from Argos to Athens in their minds and pondered the transformation of their own society from kingship to the rule of aristocrats and tyrants, and on to the rationality of their new democracy. The archaic age of vengeance, of vigilante justice, has been superseded by the rule of law and Athena has placed the majesty of Persuasion above the sledgehammer of Revenge; justice is to be tempered by mercy.

The Oresteia was Aeschylus' last work. In his lifetime he is estimated to have written around ninety plays, winning the first prize at the Dionysia thirteen times. Above the clarity of his language and his deep understanding that contradiction lies at the very heart of what is dramatic stands his remarkable sense of the power of the visual in the theatre, of spectacle. However, Aeschylus' greatest contribution to the evolution of drama was purely technical. It was Aeschylus who introduced a second actor to the action.

By stepping out of the chorus, Thespis had presented a living character on the stage for the first time thereby revolutionising the process of storytelling. In the same way Aeschylus' second actor, by physically turning in and standing face-to-face with the first, allowed for dialogue, for interaction, for opposition, for conflict. The possibilities for storytelling were not just doubled by a second actor but increased a hundredfold.

In the same year as his triumph with *The Oresteia* in 458 BC Aeschylus made a return visit to Sicily. While he was sitting on a hillside outside the city of Gela a flying eagle dropped a tortoise onto his head mistaking his bald pate for a rock that would crack open the tortoise's shell. Aeschylus, the father of tragedy, was mortally wounded. Why make it up?

On his deathbed he composed his own epitaph:

"Beneath this stone lies Aeschylus, son of Euphorion, the Athenian,
who perished in the wheat-bearing land of Gela
of his noble prowess the grove of Marathon can speak,
and the long-haired Persian knows it well."

No mention of his theatrical career at all. Just of Marathon. Aeschylus wanted to be remembered as a soldier, a man who had fought for the new freedoms his society valued so highly.

It was in 405 BC, fifty-three years later, that the great writer of comedies, Aristophanes finally gave Aeschylus, the man who had 'first decked out tragedy with magnificence', the honour he truly deserved. In his satire *The Frogs,* Dionysus, disgusted by the shoddy state that Athenian theatre had fallen into, descends into Hades to bring back the recently deceased tragedian Euripides for the greater good of Greece. The god of theatre returned with Aeschylus instead.

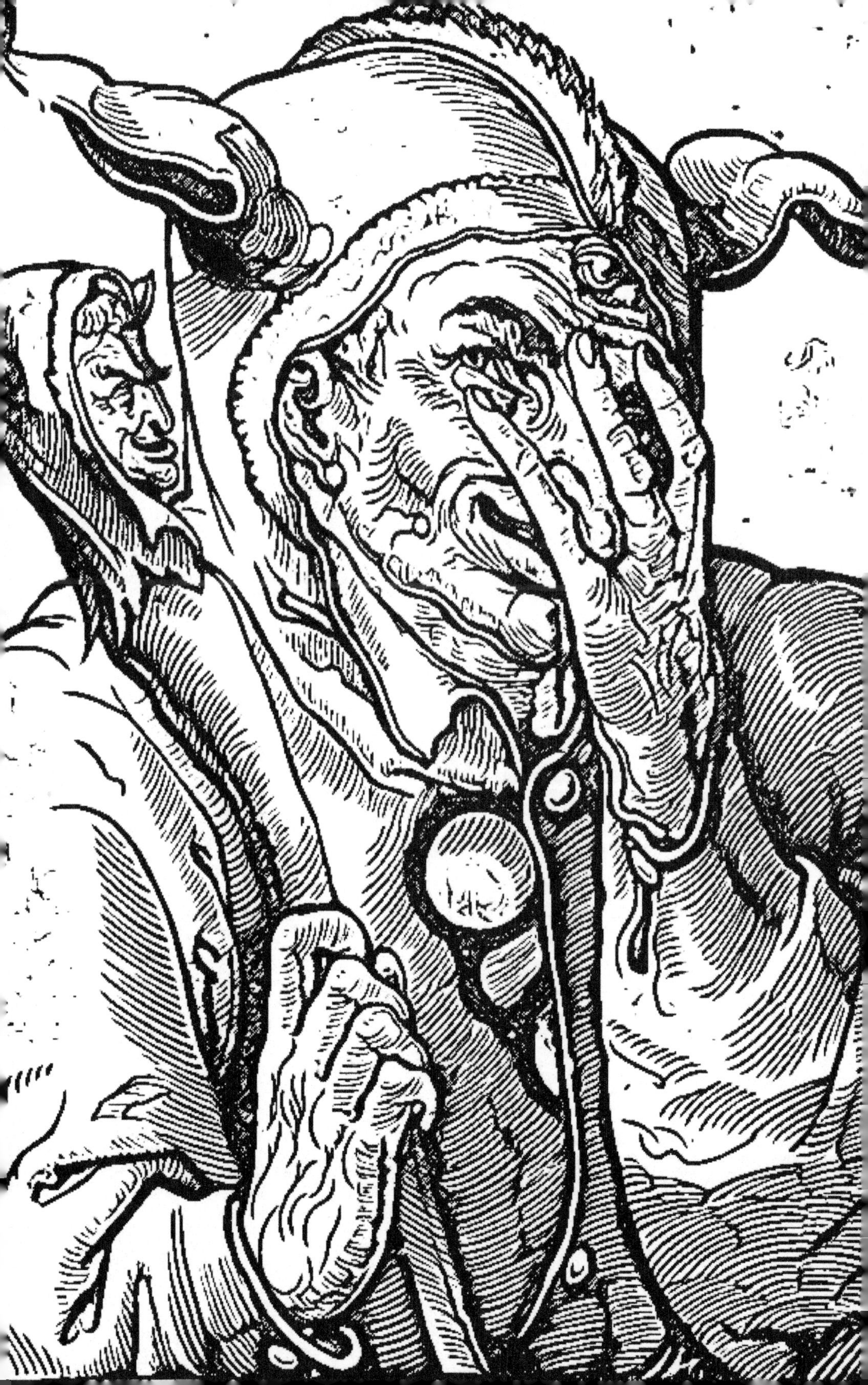

EVERYMAN
Escaping from God

All civilisations rise and fall and are replaced. The Golden Age of Pericles in fifth century Athens was superseded by that of Alexander the Great whose vast and extraordinary empire was, in its own turn, absorbed by the mighty Roman Empire. With military imperialism came cultural imperialism as the recognisable imprint of the Greek and Roman amphitheatre was stamped across the known world from Syria to Spain and from Germany to Jordan.

For almost seven hundred years these theatres rang with the roar of everything from Aeschylus to gladiatorial combat until they fell into disuse following the slow decline and final collapse of the Roman Western Empire in the sixth century. In trying to appeal to the new Christian mistrust of entertainment and spectacle, the Emperor Justinian ordered the closure of the public theatres in 526 AD and the last reported performance of a play occurs in a letter in 533 AD. The last recorded games took place in Rome in 549 AD. The rest is silence.

Except it wasn't. In 692 AD the Christian church convened the Trullan Council during which they banned both clergy and laity from attending theatrical performances which clearly suggest that they were still taking place. These proto-puritans also banned prostitution, pornography, and transvestites - which puts theatre in pretty good company.

Who knows what really happened during these purported dark ages? State-sponsored entertainments might have been officially banned but the human race has a knack of circumventing the constraints of the moral majority. One suspects that there was always a professional storyteller, ballad-singer, acrobat, pornographer, jongleur or jester to be found somewhere if you needed one. And these ages were also not quite so dark if you happened to live in southern Spain.

Moorish Cordoba rebuilt its great cathedral/mosque in 600 AD and the city luxuriated in three hundred public baths, seventy libraries, running water and public street lighting. Toledo was equally advanced and the oldest continually operating university in the world is at Fez. It was founded in 859 AD by a woman, Fatima al Fihiri. Tell that to the Taliban!

The Islamic universities became the unrivalled repositories of the ancient texts discovered in the great libraries of Egypt and the Mediterranean, such as the Alexandrian Library. The syllabus texts of the Greeks, from Aeschylus to Aristotle, were preserved there and carefully translated into Arabic until the twelfth and thirteenth centuries.

When the Johnny-come-lately scholars of Oxford and the Sorbonne finally connected with their confrères at Cordoba and Toledo they were able to discover an astonishing, pre-Christian world. This injection of philosophical and scientific Viagra was augmented by a second shot in the arm following the fourth crusade and the acquisition of Constantinople in 1204. Here were found the much copied and re-copied ancient texts of the Byzantine Empire (Aeschylus' *The Persians* had been re-copied in Greek as late as 900 AD). Ancient ideas were sexy again.

So the renaissance was simmering away nicely, waiting for us to whip it out of the petri dish via the printing press a few hundred years later. Meantime Western Europe needed to get its act together - which brings us to Charlemagne.

He was born in 742 AD and crowned Emperor of the Romans on Christmas Day 800 AD and subsequently proceeded to expand his usurping father Pipin's illegitimate empire into what we would now recognise as the bulk of modern, continental northern Europe. With ancient Imperial Rome as his political and cultural model, and the western Christian church providing his bureaucracy, this all-crushing juggernaut bulldozed the dark ages out of existence. By attempting to regenerate a magnificent Roman past, Charlemagne created a catholic, universal future.

Imposing Roman basilica lookalikes were constructed, such as the Imperial chapel at Aachen, which was built in 806 AD and based on the ground plans of San Vitale erected some four hundred years earlier. In Charlemagne's re-invented world, Christ was Emperor. A Divine Roman Emperor looming down from above over an ever-descending snakes and ladders hierarchy of archangels, angels, saints, popes, bishops and clergy down to the very dregs of the laity.

The only desired direction of travel for the average human being at the bottom was up: up to the dream of Christian salvation. The only way to achieve this sacred aspiration was through the Christian hierarchy. Climb the ladders, avoid the snakes.

Keeping an illiterate population on the straight and narrow was harder than it looked. It did not help that the sung liturgy (or spiritual guidebook) was in a language nobody understood - Latin. One must have a modicum of pity for the lower medieval clergy in implementing a near impossible task. However, necessity is the mother of invention.

At some point a poor priest or monk must have looked at a blank wall, blinked back at the souls eagerly awaiting salvation behind him and bingo - a theological eureka moment - that priest or monk began to draw.

He began to cover the walls of the church with elaborate murals depicting the central tenets of Christendom. The Bible stories, lives of the saints, a primary-coloured roadmap to salvation complete with angels and devils. Envisage a priest with a long stick - talking and pointing - explaining the scriptures to his illiterate congregation through visual aids. Show and tell salvation!

Pope Gregory had said in the sixth century that 'a picture is displayed in churches…in order that those who do not know letters may at least read by seeing on the walls what they are unable to read in books'. These images would have been painted in the brightest of colours and, with the accompaniment of chanting, incense and bells, they must have made a dazzling impression on the parishioners in contrast to their otherwise drab world.

John Lydgate of Bury (who we will meet properly later) remembered in the early 1400s a mural he had seen as a child:

Which now remembering in my later age
Time of my childhood, as I rehearse shall,
Within 15 holding my passage,
Mid of a cloister, depicted on a wall
I saw a crucifix, whose wounds were not small.
With this word 'vide' (see) wrote there beside
Behold my meekness, O child, and leave thy pride.

Here the man re-meets the boy - just as his Neolithic forebears had returned to their caves to look at the stencilled handprints they had made in their own childhoods. Past and present frozen together on a wall.

The fact that there was a text to accompany the mural that the young John Lydgate contemplated reveals the multi-purpose nature of these wall paintings. In the Benedictine Monastery at Milton Abbas in Dorset there used to be a mural augmented by extensive Latin texts for the literate monks and simple English labels for the less literate laity. These images could be all things to all men.

By the tenth century another innovation had arrived. The sung liturgy took the form of chanting. Onto this chanting could be added a second layer of content in the form of a trope. A trope is the adding on of an extra section of words and music which makes specific reference to a particular occasion or festival. The addition of a trope means you can say two things at one time like the ticker tape of headlines that runs along the bottom of your TV screen during the evening news. Tropes are breaking news - 'It's Easter!'.

Originally the tropes would be sung in descant to the main plainchant. Then in the eighth century some monks decided that it would be more effective to act them out. Show and tell had just gone three-dimensional and the liturgical playlet had been invented. Souls were saved and the monks got to dress up as women. Everybody won.

The earliest of these performances was for the Easter liturgy and is known as the *Quem Quaeritis* or *For Whom Do You Seek?* It refers to the three women called Mary who had gone to anoint the body of Jesus in the tomb following his crucifixion. There they are intercepted by the gardener who is in fact an angel. He tells them that Christ has risen:

Interrogatio: 'Quem quaeritis in sepulchro, o Christicolae?'
Responsio: 'Jesum Nazarenum crucifixum, o caelicolae.'

Angeli: 'Non est hic; surrexit, sicut praedixerat. Ite, nuntiate quia surrexit de sepulchro.'

This translates as:

Question by the Angel: 'For whom do you seek in the sepulchre, O followers of Christ?'
Answer by the three Marys: 'Jesus of Nazareth, the Crucified, O heavenly one.'
The Angel: 'He is not here; he is risen, just as he foretold. Go, announce that he is risen from the sepulchre.'

Now this is all very exciting. The medieval instructions of 965 AD are clear - three priests should 'costume themselves' and be secreted at the back of the church in preparation for walking up the nave 'as if' (Quasi in Latin) they are the three Marys looking for something. Another priest should secrete himself up by the altar so that he can represent the role of the angel. By default, of course, the nave has now been transformed in the congregation's imagination into the garden and the altar is no longer an altar but a tomb.

If you can do it for Easter why not for Christmas? Priests as shepherds stumbling up the aisle, which is now a field, towards an altar which is now a manger. Epiphany? Priests as wise men marching majestically up the aisle as they follow a star being winched up the nave by a pulley system. It actually happened.

By the twelfth century in France we have a play called *Adam* that ranges from the Fall of Man to the Days of the Prophets by way of Cain and Abel as well as renditions of the tale of Christ and the *Wise and Foolish Virgins*. In this cornucopia Christ and the virgins speak in Latin and French whilst the angel speaks only in French. This drift towards the vernacular gradually distanced the presentations from the Church.

When the common language began to dominate the dramas, they departed the precincts of the sanctuary entirely and ceased to be purely liturgical dramas at all.

Perhaps over time the plays became too long or complicated to be staged easily within the confines of the church. Perhaps renditions of Bible stories such as *The Slaughter of the Innocents* were too violent. Perhaps characters such as Herod or drunken Noah and his scolding wife were just too non-Christian (and fun) for the Church to bear. No longer part of the central worship the religious drama burst through the west doors of the church and went feral.

Once out on the street the religious element was not forgotten but their enactment was passed on to the secular community who, at this time, were controlled by the guilds. These were early trade unions in a community where skilled craftsmen were essential. Whether you were a butcher, a baker or a candlestick-maker you had to learn your craft and thereafter stick to the union rules. Advertising, for example, was verboten by the guilds who viewed it as creating unfair competition.

Young boys were duly apprenticed to a craftsman who would teach them the tricks of the trade – such as silver-smithing. The boy would eventually present his masterpiece and be inducted as a full member of the guild. Once he had learnt this skill he was highly unlikely to want to share it with all and sundry since it was the mystery of his craft from which he made his living. Thus, when the guilds began managing the religious dramas for the great church festivals throughout the year, they were referred to as Mystery Plays. And so, in this way, the guild plays helped reveal the mystery of faith.

We can divide Mystery Plays into two sorts. Firstly, Miracle Plays which are the Bible stories and the lives of the saints. Secondly, Morality Plays which are more abstracted, self-help dramas. These guide the community on how to avoid the temptations of the world and the devil, such as lust, greed and sloth, and thus make it to the bosom of Christ on the Day of Judgement.

The Miracle Plays would eventually run the gamut from the creation of the world and Adam and Eve to the crucifixion and resurrection of Christ and each individual guild would take responsibility for a particular play. Traditionally the plasterers got the job of presenting the creation of the world (up to the fifth day) whilst the shipwrights got the building of the ark and would then hand over to the fishers and mariners to tell the tale of Noah and his wife. The goldsmiths got the Adoration of the Magi and the bakers handled the Last Supper. All very logical, although quite why the capmakers got *The Woman Taken into Adultery* is above my pay grade.

When the dramas were performed in the church, the actors (for that is what they now were) and the congregation would move from side-chapel to side-chapel. Each chapel contained a custom-built set that was appropriate to the tale being told. These sets were called mansions. Once the storytelling had moved into the street the guilds began to use wonderful theatrical juggernauts called pageant wagons. These were vast stages on wheels, like the modern float in a parade, with a canopy and an under-stage which allowed for the full bells-and-whistles of special effects to create fantastical representations of heaven and hell, angels and devils, the world and his wife.

We can only imagine the level of competition between the guilds to produce the best wagon and the best pageant as, once again in history, the ritual was formalised and became an art form. We know from their financial accounts that they rehearsed in the early morning (so as not to interrupt the working day) and therefore had to provide, and budget for breakfast to keep the company happy. They were also able to take a deposit from the performers which they would forfeit if they turned up late or drunk, failed to learn their lines or let the reputation of the guild down in any other way. Which contemporary theatre director would not be just a tiny bit jealous of this element of control?

Drama had come a long way from the three Marys simply visiting Christ's tomb. With all these new elements combining in increasingly complex ways, it was important that someone had an overview and unified the production into one coherent whole. Consequently, it is at this juncture we begin to get the first glimpse of what will become the professional theatre director. A new expert had arrived.

John Lydgate of Bury (1370-1451) wrote and presented court entertainment for Kings Henry IV, V and VI and has some right to be considered as the first English director of drama. Over in Italy, Leone de Sommi (1525 - 1590) was another of these orchestrators. He wrote a handbook of stagecraft in which he made the pertinent observation that 'it is far more essential to get good actors than a good play'.

There is a painting called *The Martyrdom of Saint Apolonia* painted by Jean Fouquet around the 1450s. Here you will see the cheery depiction of a woman being tortured by having her teeth pulled out (St Apolonia remains the patron saint of dentists). But all is not as it seems. Look again and you will see her torture is taking place on a raised platform and people are seated all around gawping at her death. This is not a martyrdom Fouquet has painted but a Mystery Play production retelling the final moments of this saint's life.

Look yet once more and you will see a man in the middle of the action wearing something like a bishop's mitre and holding a conductor's baton. This is the Maitre de Jeu, or Master of Play, appearing in the performance itself like some sort of ringmaster or prompter. Perhaps this is not a painting of the play at all but the rehearsal of the play about the martyrdom of Saint Apolonia.

Whichever way the smoke and mirrors of this painting are interpreted, we are clearly observing a man at the very centre, with a script in his hand, orchestrating the action. That such orchestration was necessary is made clear when you look at Denys van Alsloot's 1615 painting of *The Ommeganck Procession in Brussels*. Whilst no longer in the medieval period this extraordinary painting captures the essence of that world. The sets, or mansions, are clearly in no way amateur (or cheap!) and when you consider everything from the costumes of the devils to the sheer volume of people involved you must surely recognise the need for an auteur of some kind, as well as for a special effects designer (who was quaintly known as the Conducteurs des Secrets). A third painting from 1547 - *The Valenciennes Passion Play* - displays some wonderful pyrotechnics emerging from hell's mouth. Google and peer at these three pictures for a little longer. You have just got as close as you ever will to watching a medieval play in production.

A final painting that reveals something of the essence of medieval drama is *Christ Carrying the Cross* by Hieronymus Bosch (circa1515). At the painting's centre is the pious and pained face of Christ as he drags his cross to Calvary, eyes closed in resignation and acceptance. All around him though are the grotesque, gargoyle-like faces of grimacing thieves, monks and voyeurs, each peering and leering or simply ignoring the man on his way to death. There is a human truth in this image and this simultaneous combination of the divine and the bawdy is at the core of the Miracle Plays.

The medieval mind had a very deep and personal relationship with death - not unlike that in modern day Mexico with its Day of the Dead. The dead are dead, but they are also with us, lying in the churchyard at the centre of the community rather than in graveyards outside the town walls. This concept is best summed up in the old French fable where three living aristocrats bump into three rotting corpses. The cadavers, by way of a memento mori, point out the unmistakable truth that 'such as I was you are, such as I am you will be'. At a time when death and disease were routine and plague was an ever-lurking threat, it was not an unreasonable observation.

Between 1346 and 1350 the Black Death stormed through the European continent and carried away up to half the entire population; high and low born alike. As Shakespeare observed in *Richard II*:

> [death] Comes at the last, and with a little pin
> Bores through the castle wall, and farewell king!

The murals covering the church walls and the devils in the dramas made it quite clear to everyone what was at stake - life, death, judgement, and the hope of salvation. In this fearful time, it is hardly surprising that, when there was the opportunity for light relief in the form of a truly good villain such as Herod or a great comic rogue like drunken Noah with his nagging wife, the community would grab at it for dear life. There was always room for humour, even when staging the Bible.

Around 1470, a play simply called *Mankind* was staged somewhere in Norfolk. It is remarkable for its juxtaposition of salvationist theology and 'Carry On' smut. Wearing its serious hat, the play piously demonstrates the fall and redemption of a man as he struggles against the temptations of the world ranging from lust to fashion. In its smut mode, it presents the audience with a communal singalong. All together now...

> It is written with a coal, it is written with a coal ...
> He that shitteth with his hole, he that shitteth with his hole.

The song concludes with some decidedly un-divine references to analingus.

There is also a splendid moment when the audience are prepared for the arrival of the demon Titivillus. This disciple of Lucifer was thought to prowl the earth with a sack on his back to collect the loose words of gossips and blasphemers. These words are to be used as evidence against them on the Day of Judgement. The audience are told that Titivillus is about to make a no-doubt extravagantly costumed appearance on the stage but that they will first have to make a donation if they wish to see his 'abominable presence'. A hat is duly passed around and the performers earn their keep.

Equally the *Second Shepherd's Play* of the same period is the companion piece to a worthy rendition of the shepherd's visit to the Christ child. However, this drama is a bawdy antidote to piety, not unlike the Satyr plays of the Greeks. Lazy Mak steals a lamb from some good shepherds and hides it in a cradle at his home. When the shepherds come looking for the lost lamb, Mak and his wife Gill pretend that the bleating of the swaddled lamb is in fact the crying of a newborn baby and Gill states boldly that if she is lying, she will eat the baby herself - as she has every intention of doing. Eventually the ruse is discovered and Mak is beaten and tossed in a blanket before he is thrown out of his own cottage. In this vignette we have a petit secular comic drama that parodies a Bible story. Whilst the play ends with a frightfully grown-up angel appearing and getting things back on the theologically straight and narrow, this is a godless play. The Churches grip is weakening.

Not so with *Everyman*. Also written in the late fifteenth century, this play is purely focused on the salvation of mankind and opens with the lines:

> Here begins a treatise how the high Father of Heaven sends Death to summon every creature to come and give account of their lives in this world and is in the manner of a moral play.

Everyman believes that he can enlist the help of his earthly companions to support him on his journey towards death. This motley crew of friends includes Fellowship, Good Deeds, Knowledge, Beauty, Strength and the Five Wits and each of them promises to stand by him through thick and thin until they realise the destination of the trip. Then they each turn their back on Everyman who discovers that he is essentially alone in this life and all the seemingly important things of the world will desert him by the end. All apart from Good Works which, when he finally faces Death, is all he really has.

> O all thing faileth, save God alone;
> Beauty, Strength, and Discretion;
> For when Death bloweth his blast,
> They all run from me full fast.

For five hundred years the early and late medieval dramas depicted the battle between virtue and vice for Man's soul. Their legacy was a long one. In the early 1600s Shakespeare borrowed the plot of *Everyman* as his theme for *Timon of Athens* and their influence on John Bunyan is clear. The full title of Bunyan's 1678 moral guide is *The Pilgrim's Progress from This World to That Which Is to Come; Delivered under the Similitude of a Dream*. I cannot think of a better summary of *Everyman*.

In a time of faith these plays connected the average man and woman to their community and to their god. Both serious and silly, sacred and secular, they made the population of Europe think and they made them laugh. God and farts - what a great combination.

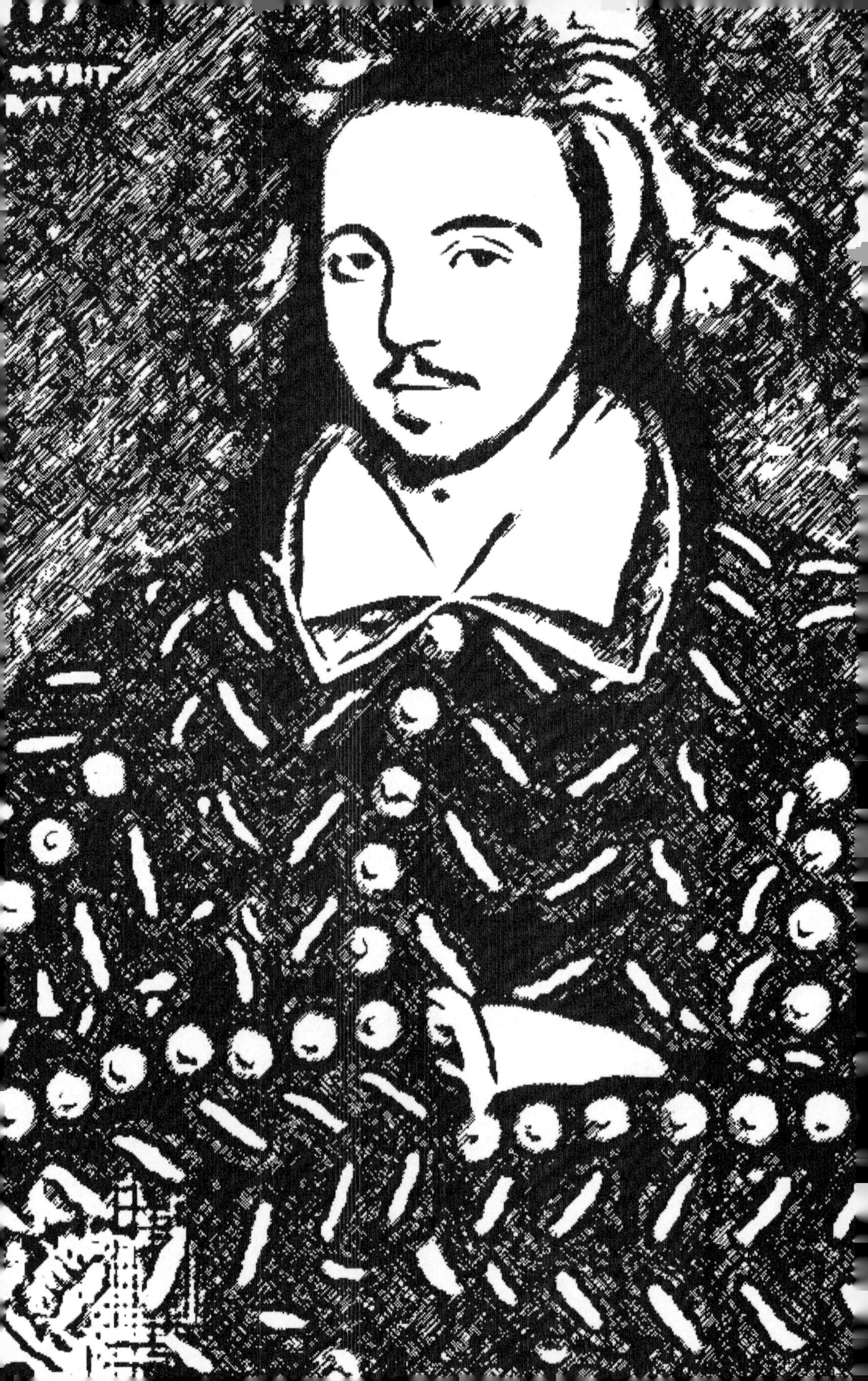

CHRISTOPHER MARLOWE
Poet and Spy

The famous portrait of Christopher Marlowe that hangs in the dining room of his old Cambridge college, Corpus Christi, was found in a skip in 1953. Painted on board it had been propping up a chimney lintel until college renovations began and it re-saw the light of day. Of course, there is no evidence that the person staring at us from that portrait is in fact Christopher Marlowe - but, if it is not Marlowe, it should be. The youthful face is surrounded by flaming red hair, has a sensuous mouth and sports a beautiful, slashed doublet of black and gold. This is exactly what the author of *Tamburlaine* and *Dr Faustus* should look like. And the motto in the corner? 'Quod me nutrit me destruit' translates as 'What feeds me will destroy me'. Appetite! That is the force that through the green fuse drove the flower of Kit Marlowe and his extravagant and dangerous Golden Age.

Marlowe was born in 1564 - the same year as his contemporary William Shakespeare. But whilst Shakespeare was born in rural Warwickshire, Marlowe was raised in Canterbury. Canterbury was the seat of the archbishop and was within a day's travelling time of London. It was also the refuge for the largest number of Protestant Huguenots outside the capital itself. Shakespeare grew up with the sound of bird-song;

Marlowe grew up with the buzz of French accents and the chatter of continental politics. For this was a time of intense international politics. This was an age when men were willing to murder or be martyred for their religious faith. This fractured Europe meant the stakes were high, crowns were at risk and the newlyformed English security services were zealously gathering intelligence on their militant Catholic enemy, at home and abroad, on behalf of their Protestant Queen. This was Marlowe's world.

And that world had been forged on the battlefield of Bosworth when, in 1485, the voice of Richard III called across the wasteland: "A horse, a horse. My Kingdom for a horse." No horse? No Kingdom. For the next 527 years a tarmacked Leicester car park was to become the uncomfortable resting place of the last of the Plantagenets.

Richard's ambitious replacement was Henry Tudor who, facing the inevitable instability caused by his contested claim to the throne, understood what Bill Clinton understood: "It's the economy stupid." With steadfast efficiency the newly-crowned Henry VII began to put the finances of England back in order. Economic stability encouraged political stability on which strong foundations he began to establish a dynasty.

Henry's first-born son was named Arthur, thereby forever associating the new regime in the minds of proud Englishmen and suspicious continental observers alike with Camelot. An alliance was struck in 1501 with a newly-united Spain under Ferdinand and Isabella, when young Arthur was married off to their daughter Catherine of Aragon. In celebration of their wedding Henry re-minted the entire coinage of England and had himself portrayed not wearing the standard open crown but an imperial closed crown instead as worn by historical winners such as Henry V. England was re-branding itself as an empire and aiming to punch above its weight on the international stage. And then, just six months later, Arthur carelessly died.

This generated two problems; how to maintain the Spanish alliance and what to do with Catherine. For eight years she lived under semi house-arrest at Durham House on the Strand - later the home of Sir Walter Raleigh and the venue for his secretive salon, the School of Night. But in 1509 the new king, Henry VIII, chose to make her his queen. This was no arranged marriage. Henry had known her as his brother's wife and had continued to know her for eight further years as his brother's widow. Clearly there was genuine affection, even love, at play here; they were a team. Following a discreet wedding at Greenwich Palace the pair shared a spectacular joint coronation at Westminster Abbey on 24th June 1509. This was presided over by twenty-eight bishops and, as Sir Thomas More erroneously observed:

> This day is the end of our slavery, the fount of our liberty; the end of sadness, the beginning of joy... Such a King will wipe the tears from every eye and put joy in the place of our long distress.

Alas, it wasn't to work out quite like that.

A daughter was born, Mary, but at this early stage in the new Tudor dynasty it was a male heir that was required, and it was a son that Catherine fatally failed to provide. Henry knew that he could sire sons successfully, doing so in 1519 via his mistress Elizabeth Blount in the form of Richard Fitzroy. The fault that continued over the next sixteen years therefore surely lay at the feet of the ageing Catherine - and the wrath of God.

Inexorably Henry's roving eye turned to the younger and feistier Anne Boleyn and 'the King's Great Matter' had begun. A divorce from Catherine needed to be arranged and the man to fix it was the king's loyal servant Cardinal Thomas Wolsey. Wolsey has been likened to P.G. Wodehouse's stately butler Jeeves - but a Jeeves with attitude.

The consequences of Wolsey's failure to deliver the divorce were manifold - not least the unilateral declaration of independence from the papacy that became the frenzied dance of one step forward, two steps back that was the English Reformation. The Henrician reformation had no road-map. If the Continental reformation began with theology and later became political in England it was the other way around. Across the entirety of Europe what was at stake were the eternal souls of all mankind and whether they were best preserved by the snakes-and-ladders of the ancient Catholic angelic hierarchy or by Martin Luther's revolutionary new DIY salvation through faith alone. What was certain was that, on such an important matter, there could be no middle way. Each side must annihilate the other to satisfy the will of God.

To get a feeling for how hot tempers became we need to turn to a diatribe written against Martin Luther by Sir Thomas Moore - the Man for all Seasons:

> Someone should shit into Luther's mouth, he farts anathema, it will be right to piss into his mouth, he is a shit devil, he is filled with shit, dung, filth, and excrement; look, my own fingers are covered with shit when I try to clean his filthy mouth.

Behold the words of a Saint!

Henry VIII died in 1547 bequeathing the throne to his Protestant son Edward VI. On Edward's death in 1553 the realm (and all the souls of its population) passed to the Catholic daughter of Catherine of Aragon, Bloody Mary, and on the succession of Elizabeth I in 1558 all those souls flipped back to being Protestant again. For those born as good

Catholics in the coronation year of Henry in 1509 their official religion was to fundamentally change five times before they had reached the age of forty-nine. These turbulent times led some to become extremists while others observed that, whichever way the sacred weathervane was spinning, the skies had not actually fallen in. Religious indifference was quietly on the rise as exemplified by the changing nature of the way people laid out their wills. In the early 1500s wills were overtly Catholic in their referencing of saints and the Blessed Virgin. By the middle of the century Protestant references were abundant. By the end of the century people were writing their wills without reference to God or any overt theology at all. The seeds of non-conformism and individual agnosticism were starting to germinate.

Elizabeth I realised that religious instability could easily lead to political instability and initially stated that she 'would not make windows into men's souls'. You *will* go to the Protestant service in the morning but if you choose to go to a quiet Catholic Mass in the afternoon (to be forgiven for going to the Protestant church a few hours earlier) so be it. This 'don't ask, don't tell' policy might have worked had Pope Pius V not escalated matters by placing a fatwa on Elizabeth through his Regnans in Excelsis in 1570. In this, Pope Pius decreed that Elizabeth was 'the pretended Queen of England and the servant of crime' and ordered all good Catholics that it was their duty to assassinate Elizabeth and restore England to the Catholic faith.

The time for turning a blind eye to people's individual faith preferences was over. Now that the safety of the realm was in real and present danger Elizabeth needed to see all and hear all and the man doing the watching and the listening was Sir Francis Walsingham. The founder of the first professional English security services, Walsingham was a man who believed that 'there is less danger in fearing too much than too little'. As the English Ambassador to Paris in August 1572 he was present at the St Bartholomew's Day Massacre when, with a nod and a wink from the Medici, the Catholic French turned on their Protestant neighbours and butchered them in the streets. This violence spilled out of the city and over a long hot summer somewhere between 10,000 and 30,000 protestants were slaughtered. This was a Rwandan moment, a 9/11, and Walsingham had seen it with his own eyes and knew exactly what Catholics were capable of. Consequently, he set up agents across the known world from Moscow to Algiers, from Venice to the New World and was able to garner quality intelligence faster than anybody else in the game. It was Walsingham who, with the help of two agents - Robert Poley and Nicholas Skeres - brought down Mary Queen of Scots through the Babington plot and it was Walsingham who recruited Christopher Marlowe as a spy and sent him on undercover missions to Catholic Europe.

Marlowe was obviously a bright boy. Born the son of a shoemaker and baptised as a good Protestant in the Canterbury church of St George, he attended King's School Canterbury which had been founded in 957AD and still operates as a school today. Marlowe was talent spotted (not for the last time) and was awarded an Archbishop Mathew Parker scholarship to Corpus Christi College, Cambridge. There, alongside his studies, he dabbled in writing poetry and plays, breathing new life into the works of Ovid and Lucan and theatrically reinventing exotic characters such as Dido Queen of Carthage and Tamburlaine the Great.

By 1587 he had also succeeded in alienating the university authorities who mandated that he should not be awarded a degree due to his unauthorised absences and his indiscreet public support for Catholic causes to the extent of allegedly planning to attend a Catholic training camp at Rheims on the continent. However, on 29th June 1587 a letter arrived at Cambridge signed by, amongst others, the Archbishop of Canterbury John Whitgift and the Lord Treasurer Lord Burleigh. In it they stated that Marlowe 'had done Her Majesty good service' and that 'he had been (employed) in matters touching the benefit of his country'. Marlowe it seems had been laying 'deep-cover' as an agent for Walsingham's secret state. His degree was reinstated.

1587 was a busy year for Marlowe in other ways, for it was in that year his first major play, *Tamburlaine the Great*, made its appearance on the London stage with the title role played by the leading actor of the day, Edward Alleyn. Charting the inexorable rise to power of the Scythian shepherd, the first part of the play ends with Tamburlaine marrying the Sultan of Egypt's daughter and crowning her Empress of Turkey and Persia. This was heady stuff for an Elizabethan London audience who could easily connect with this exotic tale of vaulting ambition for beauty and power. But it was not just the larger-than-life character of Tamburlaine himself or the fantastical foreign settings that drew the public to this production - it was the very passion and vigour of the language that Marlowe brought to the stage. 'Marlowe's Mighty Line', as Ben Jonson would later describe it, captivated audiences with its fresh and dynamic use of blank verse. Post-renaissance theatre suffered from an over sufficiency of 'tiddly-pom, tiddly-pom' rhyming which Marlowe would robustly dispense with. He was certainly neither the first nor the only utiliser of blank verse, but in 1587 he was the best.

To sense the vitality and freshness that Marlowe brought to the theatre, one could compare it to the sudden usurping of comforting 1950's crooners such as Perry Como ('Oh, hot diggity, dog ziggity, boom what you do to me, It's so new to me, what you do to me') by the lip-curling, pelvis-twirling young rock-and-roller from Mississippi - Elvis Presley. After *Heartbreak Hotel* and *Hound Dog*, twentieth century music jumped onto different tracks and the same cultural leap occurred after Tamburlaine.

On the back of this first major theatrical success, Marlowe shrewdly followed it up with *Tamburlaine Part Two* in which he introduced such visual coup de theatres as the scene when Tamburlaine enters the stage with a whip in his hand riding on a chariot drawn by the Asian kings he has conquered crawling on their knees with the horse bits in their mouths.

His next play *The Jew of Malta*, (1588) opens with the controversial figure of Machiavelli appearing on the stage to declare:

"I count religion but a childish toy
And hold there is no sin but ignorance".

This at a time when all of Europe was rent by religious discord. In this play Marlowe introduces us to Barabas, one of the most brazen and boisterous villains of any age (created four years before Richard III and sixteen years before Iago!). Barabas is the eponymous Jew who will slaughter all the nuns of a convent, including his own daughter, before, in another fantastic coup de theatre, being boiled alive on the stage in a vast cauldron. It is sweet to note that the prop list for the company that presented Marlowe's work included 'a cauldron for the Jew'. An indication of the play's popularity was that it was performed thirty-six times between 1592 and 1596 - a record for the period.

A further sign of his growing success was Marlowe's patronage by fellow Kentish man Sir Thomas Walsingham (first cousin removed of spymaster Francis) of Scadbury Manor. Sir Thomas supported a retinue of artists at Scadbury, including Thomas Nash and George Chapman. He also played host to some slightly less reputable figures including Nicholas Skeres (the spy and sidekick to Mary Stuart's and Sir Anthony

Babington's nemesis Robert Poley) as well as a splendidly dubious spy and rogue notorious for running extortion rackets called Ingram Frizer. These gentlemen must have made for some heady weekend parties.

Doctor Faustus is the work for which Marlowe is best known in modern times. Tackling the major theme of the worth of the individual against the worth of authority figures like kings or even God himself, Marlowe is tearing up the Elizabethan corner stone of The Tree of Commonwealth. This decreed that all human affairs should be ordered by rank and degree. But this is not for Faustus who will directly challenge the hierarchy of God whilst knowing that this challenge will drag him down to Hell. Here, in *Doctor Faustus*, the medieval mind meets the renaissance mind, old ways clash with new thoughts. This craving for individual power, this over-reaching as it is often described, once again reflects living characters of the age from Henry VIII to Montezuma, from Drake to Raleigh. These huge men of the sixteenth century no-longer knew their place and were fixated on self-determination at any cost, and Marlowe reflects their appetites in his magus. It was also rumoured around the streets of London at one time that the Devil himself appeared on the stage during a performance of *Doctor Faustus*. But here I smell the sixteenth century marketing department of the Rose Theatre at work rather than sulphur.

Doctor Faustus might be Marlowe's best-known work, but *Edward II* is undoubtably his finest. Written around 1590 it is both a morality play and a history play as, once again, medieval and renaissance ideas combine in Marlowe's theatrical world view. If his earlier plays can sometimes be criticised for being merely a series of vividly striking scenes, in *Edward II* he achieves an integrated drama with extremely perceptive character portrayals. This includes the character of a king who will lose his crown and his life over an arriviste favourite for whom his fondness was somewhat 'undue' - as the medieval Lanercost Chronicle decorously puts it. The hypocrisy of the barons is obvious. Their resentment of Piers Gaveston is motivated more by his being 'basely born' than by his being the King's bawd. In England it is always about class. Marlowe, as the ambitious son of a shoemaker mixing in aristocratic circles, would have known all about that. In *Edward II* we see Marlowe deftly shifting perspectives on his central characters as he turns the wronged Queen Isabella into an adulteress, the noble Mortimer into a scheming villain and an immature and selfish king into a sacrificial and sympathetic victim.

In January 1593 the Company Manager of the Rose Theatre, Philip Henslowe, scheduled four plays: *The Jew of Malta* and *The Massacre at Paris* by Marlowe and *Titus Andronicus* and *Henry VI* by Shakespeare. For just a moment in a cold, dank Tudor January we have the two great men working in the same building at the same time. They must have gone for a pint! But by the end of May Marlowe was dead.

On 5th May 1593 an anonymous document known as the Dutch Libel appeared in the churchyard by St Paul's Cathedral encouraging English Protestants to rebel against their Huguenot neighbours on the timeless premise that these immigrants were stealing their jobs. The last thing the Elizabethan state needed at this time were riots or pogroms that might escalate into a full-scale rebellion. The authorities needed to know who had published this act of sedition. Unfortunately for Marlowe the name of Machiavelli was mentioned in the text as was the Paris Massacre (his latest play) and the signature at the end was Tamburlaine.

On 10th May, the Lord Mayor of London offered a reward of one hundred crowns for information leading to the apprehension of the culprit and on 11th May Marlowe's old flat mate, author of the record-breaking play *The Spanish Tragedy*, Thomas Kyd, was arrested. By 12th

May Kyd was being tortured at the Bridewell Prison and, with the encouragement of the rack, Kyd began to conveniently remember the heretical and disreputable table-talk of his erstwhile friend. By 20th May Marlowe had been summoned from the recreational comforts of Scadbury Manor in Kent to appear before the Council. Here he was subsequently bailed thereby leaving him free to accept a generous invitation to lunch down in Deptford to the east of the city.

Before this lunch could take place a fellow spy from Marlowe's past in Rheims, Richard Baines, suddenly emerged from the shadows and, like Kyd, conveniently started to remember all the inappropriate thoughts that Marlowe had ever dared to express. It is from Baines' letter of 26th May that we, and the government of the day, shockingly gleaned that Marlowe had said all the following terrible things:

That all protestants are Hypocriticall asses.
That the woman of Samaria & her sister were whores & that Christ knew them dishonestly.
That St John the Evangelist was bedfellow to Christ.
That all they that love not tobacco & Boies were fooles.

What a Janus-faced, atheistic rogue Marlowe clearly was. Mad, bad and dangerous to know. So who, and why, had someone invited him to lunch?

It was a Sunday, as it happened, when Christopher Marlowe made his way down the River Thames by boat to the Deptford Watergate where he joined three other men for lunch in a private house owned by a lady called Eleanor Bull. She just happened to be a cousin of the Walsinghams. Two of the party were Robert Poley and Nicholas Skeres - 'the men of doubtful credit' who had set up Mary Queen of Scots. The third was Ingram Frizer from the Scadbury Manor clique. Four spies in a room eating and drinking the day away. What could possibly go wrong?

Whatever did happen in that room as the twilight came in has been puzzled over and disputed for over four hundred years. However, the consequence was that by end of that day Christopher Marlowe was lying dead with a dagger wound to the brain just above his right eye. Perhaps it was a cock-up and three living, drunken spies were suddenly left looking down at one recently deceased drunken spy with a great communal cry of *'oops!'* Perhaps it was a conspiracy, a wet job by the security services to take Tamburlaine out. What might independent-minded Marlowe have said in the dock or on the rack? Or perhaps, of course, it was a cover-up and Marlowe in fact fled the country, settled in Venice and continued writing plays under pseudonyms for the rest of a long and happy life.

Dismissing the third option, what is disturbing is that Marlowe was hastily buried in an unmarked grave by Deptford parish church, and the coroner's court met and filed their report (found in the 1920s) with extraordinary and unusual speed. The three amigos, Poley, Skeres and Frizer, all received pardons and pensions from a grateful state until each in their turn faded from history. Furthermore, Kyd and Baines continued to remember negative table-talk from Marlowe over the next few weeks and months in a clear attempt by the government to rubbish Marlowe's reputation posthumously.

However, in swift retaliation as part of an equally clear attempt to set the record straight, Marlowe's friends rallied round to defend the reputation of the man whose over-reaching appetites so mirrored those of his age.

George Peele dubbed him 'the Muses' darling'. George Chapman referred to his 'deathless memory' and Henry Petowen wrote of 'still-admired Marlowe' and said of him:

Marlowe, late Marlowe, now framed all divine,
What soul more happy than that soul of thine!

Michael Drayton added verses of praise with:

Neat Marlowe ....
Had in him those brave translunary things
That your first poets had; his raptures were
All air and fire, which made his verses clear.

But all these words are in praise of his professional skills as a poet and a playwright. Perhaps the anonymous author of *The New Metamorphosis* in 1600 takes us nearer to the gentler, warmer man when he refers to 'kind Kit Marlowe' and maybe Thomas Nashe, the friend who knew him best, was spot on when he mourned the loss of 'one of the wittiest knaves that God ever made'.

Whatever the truth, flaming-haired, sensuous, magnificent Marlowe was dead in a ditch in Deptford, which left a gap in the market for a young, aspirant, actor/playwright from Warwickshire.

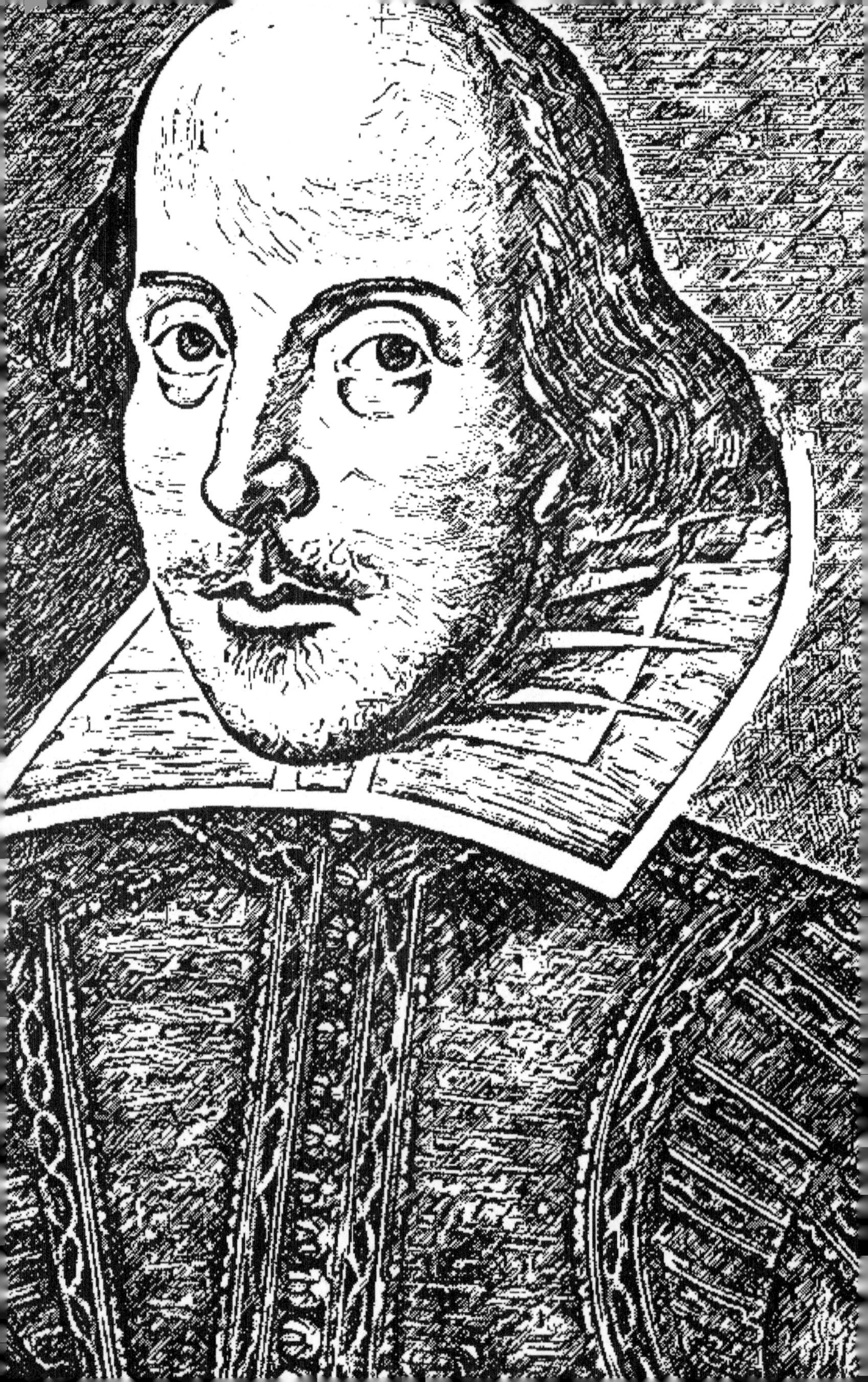

WILLIAM SHAKESPEARE
Building Show-business

Shakespeare divides the world. When some people hear his name they go all misty-eyed, lean forward and whisper reverently – 'the Bard'. For the rest of the population he brings back tedious memories of long-drawn-out afternoons at school, reading aloud, mind-numbing boredom and complete incomprehension. So let us start somewhere in the middle and neither react to Shakespeare with revulsion nor place him on some unreachable pedestal.

To take a fresh perspective and shake away our prejudices, consider the fact that on 5th September 1607 *Hamlet* was performed in Sierra Leone, a third of the way down the west coast of Africa. Two English ships owned by the East India Company, the Red Dragon and the Hector, were moored offshore so that the crew could recuperate from a bout of scurvy. To boost morale during these citrus-sipping days their Captain, William Keeling, arranged for the crew to perform *Hamlet* and then on 29th September he gathered them together again to perform *Richard II*. These occasions were also used to invite some local West African dignitaries on board ship, thereby probably making this the first true attempt at 'audience diversity'.

That these performances of Shakespeare raised the spirits of the crew rather than instigated a mutiny tells us how accessible and popular his work was across the social classes both in London and throughout the world within his own lifetime. For Shakespeare was not some erudite poet dying in penury in a garret whose work would only be found and appreciated by future generations. Rather he was an above the title celebrity, a millionaire populist artist and entrepreneur in his own lifetime. Not unlike like Andrew Lloyd Webber.

Two years later in 1609, on the other side of the world, *Hamlet* was performed on another ship in Indonesia; a trick that was repeated there in 1619. Shakespeare went global in his own lifetime and all without the help of the British Council. As an aside, I should observe that the Chief Merchant of the Hector enjoying *Hamlet* and *Richard II* in the tropical sunlight of 1607 was a man named Marlowe. Now there is one for the conspiracy theorists!

William Shakespeare was born in Stratford-upon-Avon in April 1564, where his father was a successful glove-maker and a respected member of the community. He, in fact, rose to become Mayor of Stratford in 1568. Whilst the records of the local grammar school are lost, it seems almost certain that young William attended the new King Edward VI's School as was the right of sons of local council members. It would be extraordinary if the aspirant John Shakespeare had not availed himself of this perk on behalf of his son. Having had Latin and a little Greek duly beaten into him, William Shakespeare left school around 1578 and shortly after managed to successfully impregnate a local older woman called Anne Hathaway. A shotgun wedding in 1582 was followed by three baptisms - Susanna in 1583 and twins Hamnet and Judith in 1585. With an older wife and three children it is perhaps unsurprising that by 1589 Shakespeare moved to London.

Between 1550 and 1600, London's population had doubled from around 100,000 to 200,000. Shakespeare arrived in the capital at a time of growth and change and the entertainment business was no exception. In the year of his birth the most common places for theatrical entertainment in the country were churches or village greens whilst in the towns and cities it was the coaching inns. These transport hubs were extremely performance-friendly venues with their large courtyards and galleried balconies providing generous sight-lines. The merchants could come in and park their horses and carts ready for the market on the following day and the entertainers could come in, erect their stage in the central courtyard and play to a captive audience. This captive audience would then move on the next day and be replaced by another crowd of merchants and travellers equally eager for distraction.

In today's modern London Bridge Railway Station there are fifteen platforms. If you are a regular commuter to the south-east you know which platform to join in order to get home, whether you are returning to Dover, Ramsgate or Sevenoaks. The Elizabethan equivalent of London Bridge Station was Borough High Street where, from the medieval period onwards, there were twenty-three platforms, or coaching inns, each serving a different part of southern England. These included the Bear, the Queen's Head, the King's Head, the Catherine Wheel, the Tabard, the White Hart, and the George - part of which still stands and is now a magnificent pub owned by the National Trust. The site of the Tabard lies at the far end of the High Street, and we know which part of southern England this coaching-inn/platform served because Chaucer told us in his aptly named *Canterbury Tales*.

One problem with this business model, from the entertainer's point of view, is that they could only charge their audience by passing the hat after they had seen the show. Then, as now, not everybody paid up.

However in 1567, when Marlowe and Shakespeare were just three years old, a man called John Brayne had a bright idea. He took over a coaching inn called the Red Lion in London's Whitechapel, and invested £20 (£5,000 in modern money). He transformed it into a purpose-built entertainment venue with a raised three tier acting space, a backstage and dressing rooms and ran it as a receiving house, subletting it to the various entertainment companies. He thus became one of the first English theatre producers.

One of the performers there would almost certainly have been his brother-in-law James Burbage who had married Ellen Brayne in 1559. Originally trained as a joiner Burbage had diversified into property development and acting, the latter career going well enough for him, by 1572, to end up as the leader of the Earl of Leicester's Men - the paramount private theatre company in the land. This situation had come about as an unintended consequence of the fatwa Pope Pius V had placed on Queen Elizabeth in 1570.

At times of plague London's places of entertainment were closed to help prevent the spread of the contagion thereby forcing the actors to leave the capital and tour the countryside to make a living. Once the Queen's life was placed in jeopardy, freedom of movement was severely curtailed in England via the 1572 Vagrancy Act. Travelling players might be exactly what they said they were, but they could just as easily be under-cover Catholics threatening the safety of the realm. The servants of the higher nobility were exempt from this legislation which is clearly what inspired Burbage on 3rd January 1572 to apply for his company of actors to become the 'household servants' of the Earl of Leicester, one of the mightiest aristocrats in the land.

On 10th May 1574, the Queen awarded the company a Royal patent which gave them the freedom to play 'comedies, tragedies, interludes, stage-plays and other such like… throughout our Realm of England'. It was a licence to perform and a licence to tour. Burbage was now literally playing at the highest level.

By 1576 he was ready to go into business with his brother-in-law, but this time the project was not just to convert a coaching-inn to theatrical purposes, as Brayne had done with the Red Lion, but to construct a theatre from the ground up. Around the same time another actor, Jerome Savage, had built a theatre called the Newington Butts near a drainage ditch in what is now the Elephant and Castle in Lambeth. It was disputed then and is disputed now which theatre opened first but what we do know is that for the first time since Roman times professional theatres were being built in London as viable business concerns.

Burbage and Brayne located their theatre in Shoreditch outside the London city walls and out of the control of the local puritan-leaning politicians. As part of their research these two entrepreneurs went down to the Mortlake house of Dr John Dee, the Queen's magician and alchemist. Dee's private library was larger than those of the universities of Oxford and Cambridge and whilst there they poured over the architectural plans of Greek and Roman theatres, even taking the name The Theatre to lend their business venture classical respectability.

Their investment was the vast sum of £700 (£150,000 in modern money) and now the aim was to create a production house with a resident theatre company - the Earl of Leicester's Men. In the 1580s the Earl of Leicester's Men was replaced by the Admiral's Men. James Burbage remained the leading management figure with his son Richard fast becoming the leading actor alongside Marlowe's star performer, Edward Alleyn. Following a theatrical tiff around 1591 Alleyn and the Admiral's Men moved south of the river to work with another impresario, Philip

Henslowe, at the Rose. From 1594 the resident company at the Theatre was called the Lord Chamberlain's Men by which time a young William Shakespeare had joined them.

Shakespeare's early plays such as *Richard III*, *Romeo and Juliet* and *A Midsummer Night's Dream* would have premiered at the Theatre or in Burbage's second space, The Curtain, which he opened two hundred yards down the road in 1577. The public response to these offerings was clearly positive and financially rewarding enough to justify such expansion.

By 1594 Shakespeare had established himself as the leading scriptwriter for the company and was earning enough money to be able to buy into his own business and become a Sharer in the Acting Company - the first playwright in England ever to achieve this. The only other Sharers up to this point had been actors and that was clearly not where Shakespeare was making the bulk of his money. His investment allowed him not just to be paid as the author and occasional actor but to take a cut of the day's box-office as well. Such newfound independence was not just financial but also creative. It is from this date that Shakespeare ceased to collaborate with other writers. In his apprenticeship years it made perfect sense for Shakespeare to work with others (George Peele was the co-author of *Titus Andronicus* for example) but in his heyday the increasingly independent Shakespeare worked as a solo writer. Only in his very last years did he collaborate again and work as senior pen to the next generation of up-and-coming playwrights such as John Fletcher, with whom he openly worked on his last play *Henry VIII*.

Collaboration in the creation of plays was the norm at this time. Like the Hollywood script-writing system, the philosophy was that many hands make light work and light work got more plays onto the stage more quickly. The potential theatre capacity had grown from around 5,000 per week in the 1580s to around 15,000 per week in the 1590s but theatre companies needed a swift turn-around of product to keep audiences coming through the doors. Shakespeare's contemporary Thomas Dekker wrote some seventy plays of which fifty are collaborations and in 1598 Dekker worked on sixteen collaborations for which he was paid £30. This averaged twelve shillings a week which was twice the average artisan's wage of one shilling per day. Thomas Haywood claimed 'an entire hand, or at least a main finger' in 220 plays. Collaboration worked.

So, from 1594 onwards Shakespeare was the in-house writer for the most esteemed company of actors in England; a company he worked with, ate with, drank with and whose voices and individual skills he knew well. For the long-forgotten but famously skinny John Sincere he created the role of Starveling in *A Midsummer Night's Dream,* and it was the company lead Richard Burbage whose unique voice he heard in his inner ear when he created most of his major roles ranging from Richard III to Hamlet to King Lear.

Other men Shakespeare knew well were his clowns. Richard Tarlton had set the gold standard in comedy for the previous generation but he had died in 1588 (perhaps Yorick (your Rick), 'a fellow of infinite jest' in Hamlet's grave-digger scene was a small homage to the great man). Tarlton's position was eventually taken by William Kemp for whose acrobatic, broad comic style Shakespeare created Dogberry, Bottom and Lancelot Gobbo. When he left the company in 1598 Robert Armin's more cerebral, melancholy kind of clown inspired the creation of Touchstone, Feste, and the Fool in *King Lear*. Shakespeare cut his theatrical cloth according to the talents of the individual men around him and it should be noted that you would not bother to create Lady Macbeth or Cleopatra unless the individual boy actors who originated those roles were fully up to the task.

The dream of businessmen like James Burbage was to have an indoor theatre as well as an open-air playhouse so that they could present entertainments all year round. Thus in 1596 Burbage bought the old refectory in the dissolved monastery of Blackfriars for £600 (£105,000 in modern money). Between 1576 and 1584 another part of the Blackfriars had been home to a boys' company made up of choristers of the Chapel Royal and Windsor Chapel. Under the latter's Choir Master, Richard Farrant, the boys rehearsed plays for the Queen but also 'accidentally' allowed paying members of the public to be admitted. Control of this project eventually slipped into the hands of the writer John Lyly but by 1584, following a dispute over the original lease, the boys' company was dissolved.

When Burbage started work on the first permanent, purpose-built indoor theatre in 1596 he was optimistic. However, he had not factored in the nimbyism (not in my back yard) of the residents who petitioned the Privy Council against allowing something as tawdry as a theatre to open in their neighbourhood. Clearly it would 'lower the tone' and perhaps the house prices. Burbage would never see his adult company move into the Blackfriars from the Shoreditch Theatre for he died early in 1597 leaving his theatrical empire to his sons Cuthbert and Richard.

Two months after Burbage's death, the lease on the Theatre in Shoreditch expired and the landlord, Giles Allen, refused to renew it. Litigation ensued and Allen v Burbage Jnrs rumbled on in the courts for two years. By December 1598 the Burbage brothers finally realised that, whilst they might not own the land, they did own the building, so they took the unorthodox step of dismantling the Theatre beam by beam until Giles Allen was the proud owner of a hole in the ground. They stored these timbers at Blackfriars (still owned by the family) and in the spring ferried them across the River Thames and began building a new theatre on Bankside. The resulting Globe Theatre opened in the summer or early autumn of 1599.

To fund this radical move Richard and Cuthbert Burbage had to raise capital from the company members themselves (at least those who could afford to invest) and so it was that Shakespeare stepped up from being an Author-Sharer to becoming a Housekeeper as well eventually owning 12.5% of the whole Globe project. From this point on he was paid as the author, took a cut of the box office and part-owned the building - another first in English theatre history. As the years went on Shakespeare continued to invest, mostly in land around Stratford: £320 in May 1602 and £440 on a lease of tithes in July 1605. These sums were the equivalent of over £100,000 in modern money and, according to The National Archives, had a purchasing power in the early 1600s of ninety-two horses, 408 cows and 15,200 days' work.

In March 1603 Queen Elizabeth I, against her better judgement, finally died. The theatres were duly closed out of respect and then remained closed throughout Lent. But around this same time people in London also began to mysteriously die. By May it was around twenty people a week, by July a thousand and by August three thousand people were losing their lives every seven days. The plague had returned to the city and, apart from a brief re-opening in April 1604, the theatres were to remain shut for eighteen long months.

Shakespeare was no stranger to the Black Death. In 1564, the year of his birth, a quarter of the population of Stratford-upon-Avon was carried away by the pestilence. He would have grown up in a world where sisters had lost brothers and husbands had lost wives. From his earliest days there were poignant gaps in his community and memories of loss are long. Between 1603 and 1604 30,000 Londoners perished out of a population of 200,000. How many were Shakespeare's friends or colleagues? Ben Johnson's son - 'his best piece of poetry' - was taken. How alien a place had his adopted city suddenly become with the church bells continuously tolling for the dead? Strict rules of quarantine were enforced within the city walls, marshals paraded the streets with three-foot wands to encourage social-distancing and funerals were limited to six people. Crosses marked the doors of the afflicted, where the living had to co-exist with the dead and physicians (believing the infection was airborne) wore beak-like masks filled with herbs, spices and fragrant oils as they patrolled the desolate streets.

Pre-pandemic there were 20,000 theatre visits in London every week, making it the primary source of public entertainment. All this abruptly stopped, not just for the audiences but also for the actors, the theatre-managers and the playwrights. Yet it was out of this literal wasteland that plays such as *Macbeth, King Lear, Measure for Measure* and *Timon of Athens* began to germinate in Shakespeare's mind. *Macbeth* was first performed in 1606 with Richard Burbage playing the title role, Robert Armin playing the drunken porter and Shakespeare himself playing the doomed King Duncan. Beyond the inspiration of the blasted heath *Macbeth* is of special interest being a Scottish play for a Scottish King.

King James had to postpone his coronation twice due to the Plague. When he descended on London to start his reign he made two major decisions that were to affect the theatre. Firstly, he banned them from opening on Sundays and secondly he elevated the Lord Chamberlain's Men to become his personal company, the King's Men. (We sometimes forget that Shakespeare, as the in-house writer, was as much a Jacobean playwright as an Elizabethan one.)

Macbeth also centres around witchcraft, which is fitting for a monarch who was obsessed with the subject. James personally attended the north Berwick witch trials and published a book on the subject called *Daemonologie* in 1597. *Macbeth* was also a gunpowder play, part of a very contemporary genre of plays referring to the recent Catholic assassination attempt on James' life - the Gunpowder Plot of 1605. The papal fatwa of 1570 had passed on from Elizabeth to the new King and he had just escaped death by the skin of his teeth.

If somebody says the words 'grassy knoll' most people think of the assassination of JFK rather than a mound of earth. In the same way all the references to 'blow, blast and scatter' in *Macbeth* would have been interpreted as relating to the bomb that had not gone off. Shakespeare's contemporary audience would have also heard the drunken porter's speech rather differently from the way we do. To them the opening of 'hell's gate' to a farmer, an equivocator and a tailor would have been direct references to the Jesuit conspirator Henry Garnet who had been put on trial and executed earlier that year. The Jesuits were famous for their equivocation (their use of ambiguous language to conceal the truth). Farmer was the alias used by Garnet when he was working undercover and it was a tailor who was found to be in possession of a rather grisly holy relic - a straw husk stained with the blood of Garnet after he had had been hanged, drawn, and quartered.

Another way Shakespeare adapted to fit in with the tastes of the new court was the inclusion of masques. James and his wife, Queen Anne, were major supporters of these visual extravaganzas and employed the leading architect of the day, Inigo Jones, to design them and the playwright Ben Jonson to write them. Jonson penned twenty-three of the thirty-seven masques performed during James' reign. *The Masque of Blackness* performed at the Banqueting House on Twelfth Night 1605 had a budget of £3,000 which is half-a-million pounds in modern money (or 1,612 cows!).

The star of the show was Queen Anne herself, blacked-up with body paint to resemble an African exotic and the rest of the company was the duchess of this and the countess of that. This was entertainment for the court by the court and it employed all the cutting-edge technology of the day. Chariot-and-pole machinery had been developed in Italy during the previous century and was an extraordinary system of winches and pulleys that enabled scenery and props to appear and disappear. Queen Anne made her entrance in one of these masques standing on a gigantic seashell that trundled into the hall on invisible trucks. The use of this technology had not been particularly available to the old public playhouses due to the absence of a roof but in the Banqueting House or the Palace of Whitehall all sorts of special effects were now possible.

In 1608 Richard Burbage finally achieved his father's dream and was given permission to present plays at the Blackfriars and so, finally, Shakespeare and the King's Men moved into an indoor theatre. Basic admission to the Globe was one penny; admission to the Blackfriars was six pennies. This made the latter the preserve of a more privileged audience and provided commensurately larger profits for the company shareholders. Also, having a solid roof allowed for greater use of chariot-and-pole machinery. In the opening scene of *Henry V* the chorus beseeches the audience of 1598 'let us … on your imaginary forces work'. By the time we come to *The Tempest*, which premiered at Whitehall Palace on 1st November 1611 and was subsequently performed at the Blackfriars, we find Shakespeare incorporating a full masque within the play and filling the action with spectacular visual effects. At one point Ariel claps his wings upon a table and 'with a quaint device the banquet vanishes'. And in Act IV, there is a 'most majestic vision' as the goddesses Ceres, Iris and Juno descend. The court must have been heartily satisfied. How the master wordsmith William Shakespeare felt about all this razzle-dazzle is a matter for conjecture.

Shakespeare's last play was *Henry VIII* and it was written in collaboration with the young up-and-coming playwright John Fletcher. It was performed at the Globe and the production called for the sound of cannons to be fired which, in 1613, was duly provided by firing a cannon. Unfortunately the wadding from the cannon set the thatched roof of the theatre alight and burned the Globe to the ground. One audience member's breeches caught fire but his neighbour put out the flames by pouring a bottle of ale over him. This fact tells us that audience members were allowed to eat and drink throughout the show as does the contemporary complaint from some actors about being distracted by the hiss of beer bottles and the cracking of nuts. Excavations of Elizabethan theatres have revealed vast quantities of shells from oysters, mussels, periwinkles and whelks.

It is at this point that shareholder, housekeeper, actor, author and well-rewarded celebrity William Shakespeare chose to retire from the theatre. At the age of forty-nine perhaps he just could not face the rebuild. Perhaps the continuing fascination with masques and special effects were not to his taste and the master-builder of London's show business felt it was his time to quit that particular stage. It does seem that from as early as 1610 he had been spending more time in Stratford and in September 1611 his name appears on a list of subscribers to promote local highway maintenance, which seems a very parochial concern.

Nicholas Rowe, who was to be the first editor of Shakespeare's plays in 1709, had a particularly bucolic view of William's last years:

> The latter part of his life was spent, as all men of good sense will wish theirs may be, in ease, retirement and the conversation of his friends. He had the good fortune to gather an estate equal to his occasion and, in that, to his wish; and is said to have spent some years before his death at his native Stratford.

Whatever the truth of his last years may be, death came in 1616. It was Ben Jonson, his friend and rival, who gave him the kindest of epitaphs: "He was not of an age but for all time." Which, as with so much that Ben Jonson said, was to turn out not to be strictly true.

A DIGRESSION ON SHAKESPEARE
The Alchemy of Acting

"This is nonsense" a sullen actor groaned despairingly at me down the phone when I rang to ask about their work on Shakespeare. "Would you ask a top surgeon to write about his or her expertise in cardiac surgery or brain surgery? No, they would expect to be speaking to a peer on the subject and thus that the pertinent things are a known given. Just so, when an actor broaches one of the most complex and vivid poets in the history of dramatic literature you want simple answers. Why? Oh Giles, why are you suddenly being so stupid?".

I was quite flattered by the word 'suddenly' carrying, as it does, the implication that my stupidity is not viewed as a permanent state of affairs – even by actors.

It was Laurence Olivier who archly observed that he loathed talking about theatre in the abstract. "It bores me," he said. I knew I was on a hiding to nothing as I set out to try and get some of the best Shakespearean actors in Britain to reflect on the magic behind their art; for there is an element of magic in it. Something happens in the theatre when the right actor meets the right text at the right time in front of the right audience. Something changes. That alteration, that alchemy, is why we, as audience members, wade through all those terrible and unmemorable productions in the hope of discovering the gem; the transforming production or performance that is pure gold.

For the magicians of the Middle Ages the aim of alchemy was to turn base metals into gold. For Shakespearean actors the sorcery is more complex. They must take words, which in the wrong hands can be leaden, make them light and sinewy and fresh and cast them generously over an audience. If they weave the right spell then it is we the audience who are transformed.

But how? And what was it about unravelling the process of preparing Shakespeare for production that made my actor friend so edgy? I smelt fear. Could it be that even for someone with decades of experience on the stage, asking someone to articulate how one approaches Shakespeare is still a daunting task? That by talking about the actors' alchemy they might somehow break the spell and risk being revealed as pretentious or, worse, dumb? Perhaps it was time to get away from abstract generalisations and ask some specific questions about craft? I picked up the phone again.

Daniel Evans is currently the Artistic Director of the Chichester Festival Theatre on England's south coast. He trained at the Guildhall School of Music and Drama from 1991-1994 but joined the Royal Shakespeare Company before completing his course.

Camouflaging my stupidity as best I could, I asked him where, as an actor, he started with the development of a character. He answered:

> The words on the page. I draw a list of undeniable facts about each role - facts which are spelled out in the text. For example: my name is Hamlet; I am the Prince of Denmark; my mother is called Gertrude etc. I ignore any interpretative information (e.g. what other

characters' impression of me might be). Then I hope to draw a timeline of each event in the character's life - again, entirely based on the textual evidence. Where there might be gaps, I eventually try and interpret what might have happened and test these surmises against the flow and requirements of the play. This way I feel like I have a good foundation on which to build a character which can be a real person.

Inevitably, my own personality and the character will converge - even in the most difficult of roles. It's an actor's job to imagine the connection between the two, to put himself or herself into another's shoes. Some actors like to think that they play the character. Others think that the character plays them - that they are the puppet, and the character is the hand that moves them. I like this latter approach.

Guy Henry, who has played a multitude of roles for the RSC ranging from King John to Sir Andrew Aguecheek to Malvolio, feels much the same way:

Very often one line in a part will sing out to you, strike a chord and it'll make you believe instantly that - eventually - you *will* be able to play the part! For instance, in *All's Well* it was Parolles' line 'Simply the thing I AM shall make me live' - and with *King John* it was the very stark simplicity of his only soliloquy, being left alone for a brief moment on the stage having played a whole scene of political manipulating just after hearing the news: 'My mother dead!'

Shakespeare can seem dense and remote to us now but it's the shining demonstrations of simple human expression such as these that, I find, hold the key and remind us that he is probably the finest chronicler of human behaviour that we've yet had!

Now this was much more like it. Feeling I was starting to get somewhere I went back and quizzed Daniel Evans a bit more on how he managed to bring something new to a Shakespearean role that has been performed by some of the finest actors in history without resorting to gimmickry:

> In one sense, any interpretation will be new, simply because there is a new actor playing the role. Each actor is unique, and each actor brings his or her personality to match the part. So, while the thought of famous actors playing the same role can be intimidating, each actor must concentrate on how they connect to the part. It can be difficult to ensure you start with a blank sheet of paper and be completely unhindered by past interpretations but it's essential. One must start and end with the text.

> As Shakespeare's plays are text-based, the language becomes everything. It's a mistake to think that Shakespeare's language (because it's archaic) is the same for each character. It's not. It's entirely different. Take Othello, for instance. Othello often speaks in regular, beautiful, rhetorical verse which is peppered with metaphor or imagery. Iago, on the other hand, speaks with little metaphor. His vocabulary is coarse, he speaks in prose often, only reaching to metaphor in extremely heightened situations. In Shakespeare language *is* character, so it's impossible to divorce the two.

But how does Daniel make Shakespeare's verse accessible, understandable and spontaneous to audiences four hundred years after Shakespeare's own day?

> Clarity becomes essential. There are so many schools of thought regarding verse-speaking that it sometimes becomes stifling to listen

to them all. One thing is certainly true: Shakespeare's language requires vast muscularity and athletic ability. One must have a sense of the iambic rhythm which underlines the verse but not stick slavishly to it. In fact, the best advice comes from Shakespeare himself through Hamlet's advice to the players. All we need to know lies there.

This observation reminded me of an interview I did with Sir Derek Jacobi in 2003 when he was playing Prospero to Daniel's Ariel in Michael Grandage's production of *The Tempest* that played at the Old Vic in London. Sir Derek Jacobi is one of Britian's most distinguished actors, with over four decades of stage and screen performances to his credit.

Sir Derek's view was that the art of acting Shakespeare is to make the words appear as though they have been plucked out of the air "…as if they've entered your brain at that moment and you've just decided to say them. The actor must get rid of any hint that the lines have been written down on a page. With Shakespeare this can be particularly difficult due to the weight of history and scholarship that accompany his words. They must be the words you have chosen to say. You have to psych yourself out of the fact that the words have been said many, many times before."

Sir Derek was also very revealing about how the actor's personality and character converge. He first played Prospero in 1982 when he was forty-four years old. At the time he was learning the script he was in Austria making a movie in which he was playing Hitler. "I was reading *The Tempest* in full Nazi garb, so I was in a 'hard' mood," he told me. "The forgiveness is wrenched out of Prospero at the end. He hasn't become a kind of Jesus." In this way Sir Derek was able to reveal that Prospero is not actually embracing his enemies at the end of the play but accepting them knowing them for what they are and what they might still do. "'Every third thought shall be my grave' is not Prospero's way of saying he is getting old and is going to die soon rather it is him saying 'here's my brother who is obviously not repentant so I'm going to be more wary when I get back. I'm going to be watching him'. In this way instead of being just a famous scene it became a situation. Something that has to be resolved by Prospero."

For both Sir Derek and for Daniel Evans the text is the starting point, the key, to everything else. Sir Derek concluded by saying that his aim was to try to discover a way to share the play with the audience as if it were a modern play whilst also retaining the verse. For Daniel:

> One has to be ready intellectually, emotionally, physically and spiritually to meet the demands of the text. Speed of thought, emotional availability, intellectual nous and a free voice and body are all required. Again, the text should guide the actor. For me, the text is the ultimate guide.

This opinion is one shared by Dame Janet Suzman who also very kindly gave me some insights into her process:

> Any ordinary literate person when they read a play by William Shakespeare will be struck by the complexity of the writing and will have to do the text the honour of working out what is being said. I say 'said' advisedly, as these are plays and therefore are to be spoken out loud. And just as you try to read the intentions of anyone you come across in life by the tone of voice, the attitude of the speaker, the temperature of the context etc so you try to assess the same dangers to you in fictional life.

> Shakespeare is deep English, not superficial English, and we all should know by now the difference in the profound use of language

and the use of language for mere ease of communication. The trouble with English is that everybody thinks they can use it well enough. It is the lingua franca of the world. But it has another life altogether, which poets and actors and novelists and philosophers ignore at their peril.

Dame Janet is an extraordinary force who, with great charm and intelligence, takes her art immensely seriously and is rightly one of the most respected Shakespearean actresses working today. After training for the stage at the London Academy of Music and Dramatic Art she became a member of the Royal Shakespeare Company in 1963 and started her career there as Joan of Arc in *The Wars of the Roses* (1962–64). The RSC gave her the opportunity to play many of the Shakespearean heroines, including Rosaline in *Love's Labour's Lost,* Portia in *The Merchant of Venice,* Ophelia in *Hamlet,* Kate in *The Taming of the Shrew,* Beatrice in *Much Ado About Nothing,* Celia and Rosalind in *As You Like It,* Lavinia in *Titus Andronicus* and *Cleopatra* in 1973.

"Text is character!" she continued adamantly:

You glean the nature of the character from what he or she says. The job in a rehearsal is to see whether you have a consistent and provable interpretation of a character, filtered through your own personality. The only certainty about Shakespeare is that we know the plays work; they have been often enough tested in performance to tell us they are alive with interest and bitingly accurate psychology. But most of all they celebrate the infinite complexity of human nature, and that is always contemporary.

Perhaps it is this extraordinary fusion of text and character that allows each generation to feel that Shakespeare is their contemporary and has something directly relevant to say about the world they live in. For all some directors and actors will attempt to tinker with Shakespeare it does seem that his real magic is that he is simply immune to the vagaries of time and taste. "Inevitably liberties are taken with his plays," admits Daniel Evans:

> We often edit the text, rearrange it, take some words from the folio, others from the quartos etc. So, whatever happens, we will inevitably end up with our own version of the play. There is no such thing as a definitive version.

But Daniel, who works as both an actor and a director, is the first to admit that he tends to be a bit more of a purist when things start to drift towards the extreme. "However, there are limits!" he clarifies. "I prefer the essence, the humour, to derive directly from the wit of the text rather than from an external concept."

I will leave the last word to Dame Janet who reflected on an observation made by Greg Doran who directed her in *Coriolanus* at Stratford in 2007. "Greg's view was that Shakespeare's plays, like iron filings to a magnet, tend to attract any crisis that is in the air. That is surely why they never lose their contemporary feel and why the richness of the language serves a deeper purpose than mere communication."

Now that is alchemy.

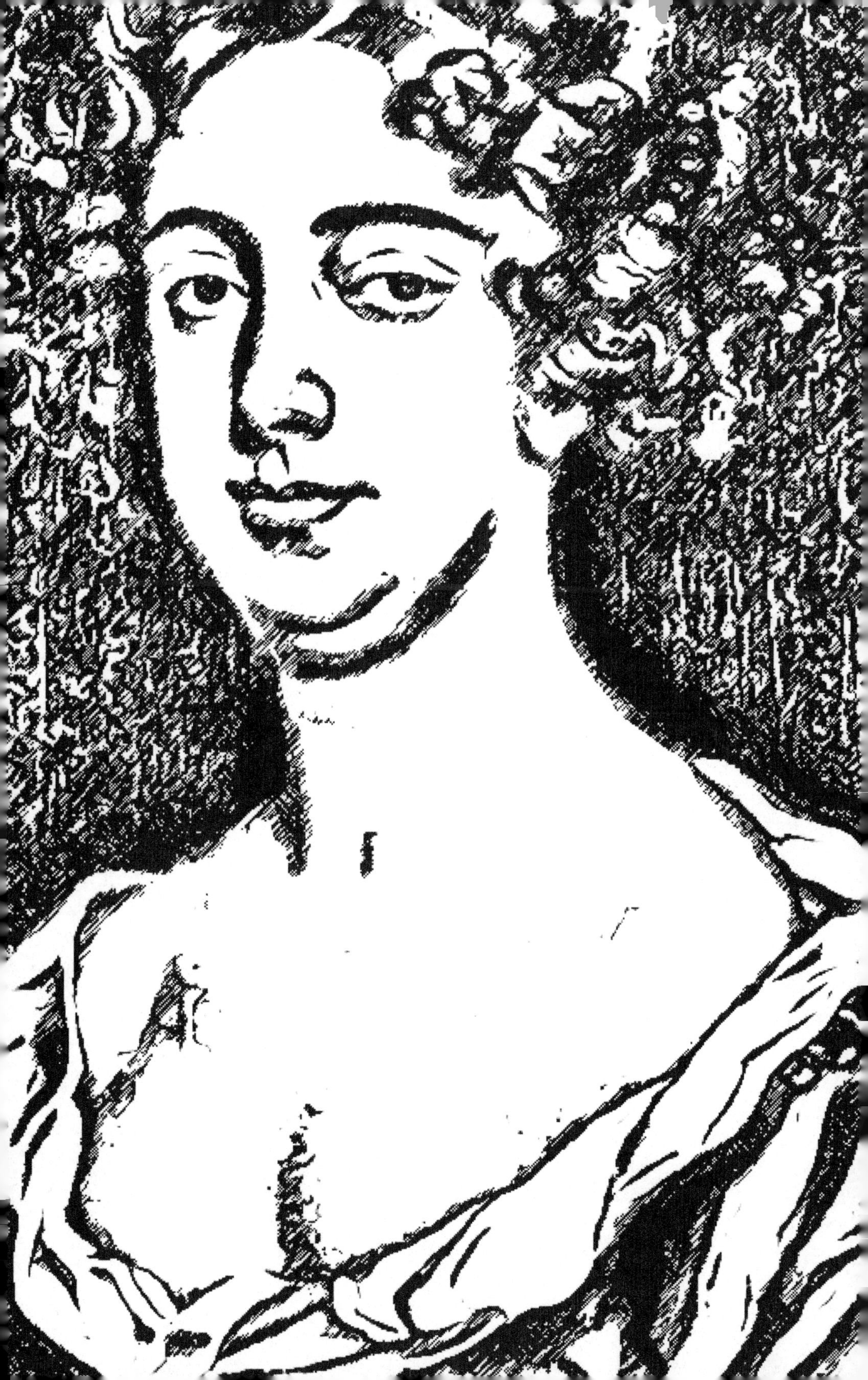

APHRA BEHN
Agent 160 - Punk Poetess

It is a quirk of history that the two most revolutionary kings that England ever had were never meant to be king. Henry VIII and Charles I were the younger brothers, the spares, and were only elevated to the Crown due to the untimely death of their siblings. Henry sparked off a reformation and Charles ignited a civil war.

Up until 1642, when the conflict between the king and his people began, the world of the theatre had been ticking along rather nicely. There were the open-air public theatres that Shakespeare knew so well, such as the Globe or the Fortune, there were the indoor private theatres, such as the Blackfriars and the Salisbury Court Playhouse and there were the very private indoor theatres belonging to the court at Whitehall and in the Banqueting House.

These latter theatres benefitted from considerably larger production budgets and access to some of the finest talent in the land. King James and his wife Queen Anne, as we have seen, had a particular liking for the extravagance of the masque and employed the genius of Ben Jonson and Inigo Jones to make them happen.

Like father like son - Charles I and his French wife Henrietta Maria also had a penchant for extravagance and spectacle and rapidly added

Shirley and Milton to the Jonson/Jones team. *The Triumph of Peace* performed on 3rd February 1635 cost £21,000. This is £2.5 million in modern money or 3,296 horses, 3,896 cows and 300,000 day's pay for a skilled tradesman. Like her mother-in-law, Henrietta Maria was a keen performer herself and on Shrove Tuesday in 1626 she was described as the 'principal actress'.

On 9th January 1633 she and her ladies-in-waiting appeared upon the stage at Somerset House in a masque called *The Shepherd's Paradise*. The production was again designed by Inigo Jones, had nine sets, took four months to rehearse and enjoyed a running time of eight hours.

Such extravaganzas were to end abruptly when the civil wars erupted, and all the theatres were closed by Act of the Puritan Parliament on 6th September 1642. They would not re-open for eighteen years by which time Charles I was long dead; his body being unceremoniously interred in an unremarkable vault beneath the choir of St George's Chapel in Windsor. Lying next to him, equally without monument, is the body of Henry VIII.

Charles' son, the future Charles II, had fled by 1646, living in France, the Dutch Republic and the Spanish Netherlands. Accompanying him was a court in exile made up of loyal cavaliers with their eyes and ears continuously keeping a close check on the mood music emanating from Oliver Cromwell's Commonwealth. Way before James Bond this was a time of the gentleman spy.

In 1658 Cromwell was succeeded upon his death by his son Richard thereby making England an hereditary republic. Such illogicality eventually allowed for the return of Charles, and he was duly restored to the English throne in 1660 arriving in London on 29th May.

After almost twenty years of turmoil England was clearly desperate for some sense of normality to be restored along with the King. In August 1660 the Act of Indemnity and Oblivion was passed. This was essentially an attempt to airbrush the civil wars and Oliver Cromwell out of history. It involved pardons for all (except the men who had signed Charles I's execution warrant) and legal amnesia of the entire Interregnum - in perpetuity.

Also in August of 1660 came the re-opening of the theatres, which shows an interesting sense of priorities. Charles II was keen to reward those supporters who remained loyal to him whilst he was in exile and a bounty of baubles and properties were doled out to these faithful cavaliers. Two of these baubles were patent letters granting monopoly rights to form theatre companies and present theatrical productions in London. One patent went to Thomas Killigrew, the other to William Davenant.

Thomas Killigrew was the son of a courtier of King James I, a Royalist, a Catholic, a playwright and a wit. He followed Charles into exile in 1646, living in Paris, Geneva, Madrid, Rome and Venice, and became a useful set of eyes and ears for the future king. After the Restoration Samuel Pepys recorded in his diary that:

> Tom Killigrew hath a fee out of the Wardrobe for caps and bells under the title of the King's Foole or jester; and may with privilege revile or jeere anybody, the greatest person, without offence, by the privilege of his place.

With his patent Killigrew founded the King's Company which set up shop in the old Gibbon's tennis court near Lincoln's Inn Fields. The French had led the way in converting indoor tennis courts into theatres (consider David's painting of *The Tennis Court Oath* during the French

Revolution) and no time was wasted in re-building the Gibbons as an end-on indoor theatre not unlike the structure Burbage had erected in the Blackfriars. It opened on 8th November 1660.

Sir William Davenant had an interesting pedigree for a future man of the theatre. His godfather was William Shakespeare. His parents, Jane and John, ran the Crown Tavern in Oxford where Shakespeare broke his journey on his regular commute from Stratford to London. He certainly knew the family well enough for them to name their son after him. William junior claimed throughout his life that his mother had pulled more than pints at The Crown and that he was in fact not just the godson but the illegitimate son of Shakespeare. Not a bad thing for one's career to have the great bard's blood coursing through one's veins.

Sir William succeeded Ben Jonson as Charles I's Poet Laureate in 1638, supported the King throughout the civil wars, was appointed Lieutenant Governor of Maryland by the exiled Charles II and spent all of 1651 as a prisoner in the Tower of London. He also had a tin nose. Syphilis, or the Grand Pox as it was known, was an occupational hazard in the seventeenth-century, but Davenant survived it after treating his nose with mercury for three years. Alive but disfigured, he was accepted by his friends but teased and ridiculed by his enemies. "His art was high, though his nose was low," mocked one cruel wit. Another, Thomas Warren of Braintree, lived to regret his bullying bon mots at Davenant's expense. Or rather he didn't. William stabbed him to death.

Such homicidal frenzy is not unique amongst Shakespeare's followers. Almost a hundred years later, possibly with her nerves worn to a frazzle by years of introducing generations of children to Shakespeare through her and her brother Charles' book *Tales of Shakespeare,* Mary

Lamb was to stab her over-demanding mother to death with a table knife. Not a story often told in the nursery.

With the second theatrical patent in his possession, Davenant founded the Duke of York's Players under the patronage of the King's brother, James. His first home was the old Salisbury Court Theatre but by 1661 the company had moved to Lisle's Tennis Court, also by Lincoln's Inn Fields. Here he set about making the theatre accessible to a war-weary public. He re-wrote Shakespeare's *Two Noble Kinsmen,* calling it *The Rivals,* and introduced two brand new acts written by his own hand. The audience clearly approved as it was still being played at court in 1667. He next cut and adapted *Hamlet* to suit contemporary tastes and in 1666 *Macbeth* was improved by cutting half the drunken porter's speech for being unseemly, expanding the part of Lady Macduff to make her more sympathetic and cutting the last witches' scene entirely. The production was also littered with special effects. Samuel Pepys thought it 'one of the best plays for a stage and variety of dancing and music that I ever saw'.

This 'all singing, all dancing' *Macbeth* ran for 200 performances and dominated the stage until Charles Macklin (1699-1797) calmed it down again with his 'restored' *Macbeth* in 1774.

Working with the great man of letters John Dryden, Davenant next launched himself at *The Tempest* in 1667. After re-naming it *The Enchanted Isle,* symmetry was everything. Miranda, who has never seen a man but her father, is balanced by Hippolito, a man who had never seen a woman. She also gains a sister, Dorinda, as does Caliban. Not to be left out, Ariel gets a girlfriend called Milcha - so all in all quite a busy island. No wonder Prospero wanted to get off. Shakespeare's play gets cut out of all recognition and the gaps are delightfully filled by duets and dancing, choruses, masques and drunken hornpipes. The real star of the show though was the wind-machine.

The legacy of this version was immense. The King himself loved it so much he personally financed five more performances over the next six months and as far into the future as the early nineteenth century it was still going strong. In the playbill for *The Enchanted Isle* at the New Theatre Royal on 8th January 1810, we are warned that:

> On account of the immense quantity of machinery, music etc in *The Tempest,* and to prevent young persons from being kept to a late hour …the doors will be opened at half-past five and the performance begin at half-past six.

This machinery created such audience delights as 'Prospero's Magic Grotto' (interior and exterior!) and 'the Seashore with trees torn at the roots and various effects after the storm'. This storm included 'waves advancing and retreating - never before attempted' and a visible shower of rain. There was 'lightning', there were 'moveable clouds and cloudlings' plus 'Planets' and a 'Brilliant Rainbow'. Producing Spiderman on Broadway would have been less stressful.

Davenant was not alone in taking free rein with Shakespeare. In 1679. Dryden was to take the sting out of *Troilus and Cressida* by making them faithful to each other throughout and in 1681 the 29-year-old son of a Puritan clergyman, Nahum Tate, began to hack away at *King Lear*. His mission? To make it more morally suitable for the poor, easily corrupted theatregoer. Where is the moral message in killing off Lear and Cordelia? Nowhere! So Tate resolved not to kill them. In his version the Fool is cut entirely, Lear lives happily ever after and Cordelia marries Edgar.

Shakespeare ended his play with Edgar's mournful plea:

The weight of this sad time we must obey;
Speak what we feel, not what we ought to say.
The oldest hath borne most; so we that are young
Shall never see so much nor live so long.

Nahum Tate's ending has a much more uplifting and virtuous finale:

Divine Cordelia, all that Gods can witness
How much thy love to Empire I prefer!
Thy bright Example shall convince the World
(Whatever Storms of Fortune are decreed)
That Truth and Vertue shall at last succeed.

And this was the only version of *King Lear* performed between 1681 and 1838.

The Restoration also led to another major revolution in the theatre: the introduction of women to the English stage. Since the time of the Greeks it had been a principle of moral rectitude that all female roles be acted by men or teenage boys - a woman on the public stage would have been a danger to public stability. Not so in seventeenth century France where Charles' court in exile had been able to enjoy the real thing - actresses.

On 8th December 1660 Killigrew's King's Men presented *Othello* with Desdemona played by either one Margaret Hughes or another young woman named Anne Marshall. The former boy-actor Thomas Jordan wrote the prologue for the production proudly proclaiming:

The woman plays today, mistake me not.
No man in gown, or page in petticoat.

It must have been a heady time for these ground-breaking women as they shattered the glass ceiling of the London theatre. In addition to

Margaret Hughes and Anne Marshall, Killigrew's company recruited Katherine Corey, Mrs Eastland, and Mrs Weaver. Over the road William Davenant (who had actually cast a woman, Mrs Coleman, in a private performance of an opera as early as 1657) introduced Hester Davenport, Mary Saunderson, Jane Long, Anne Gibbs, Mrs Jennings and Mrs Norris to a, no doubt, extremely appreciative male audience.

And herein lies the rub. There is no doubt that these first English actresses were objectified by the gentleman theatregoers of the day and often reduced to little more than theatrical bunny girls. Numerous scenes of rape start appearing in the dramas and there are multiple engravings showing the newly introduced topless scenes in tragedies such as *Othello, Anthony and Cleopatra* and *Cymbeline*.

The plots of Restoration comedy are usually based around sex, class and money and, just as Shakespeare got around the problem of boy actors playing women by creating plot devices in which they had to disguise themselves as men, so the Restoration playwrights created a genre called Breeches Parts. These involved creating circumstances in the storyline in which the actress had to disguise herself as a man and, through wearing breeches rather than the fashionable long dresses of the day, produced the delightful happenstance (for the gentlemen in the audience) of revealing the curve of the actresses' calves and buttocks. Of 375 plays produced on the London stage between 1660 and 1700, 89 included cross-dressing. Breeches roles became pretty much de rigueur and their descendant is the principal-boy in the modern pantomime.

Despite such bawdy trivialities, some women rose to extremely high positions in the London theatre world. Elizabeth Barry (an actress who had allegedly been prepared for the stage Pygmalion-style by the notorious roué, John Wilmot, Earl of Rochester) and Anne Bracegirdle were the leading female players of tragedy and comedy respectively. They also managed to become patent-holders of the theatre in Lincoln's Inn Fields making them the first women impresarios in English history. Another glass ceiling shattered.

Nell Gwyn is the best-known actress of the Restoration period. Low born in or around 1650 in the parish of St Martin's in the Fields, she famously sold oranges, and probably herself, throughout London's new theatreland. We should not forget that theatre attendance was more informal and relaxed than our experience today; more like visiting a private club or a jazz bar. Chatting, eating, flirting and fighting were the norm over which the actors would try and make themselves heard.

As early as 1665, Nell had become a notable performer on the London stage and on 3rd April of that year Pepys records seeing 'pretty, witty Nell' in a 'not good' Davenant production of *Mustapha* by Lord Orrery, brother of the scientist Robert Boyle. By this time she was often appearing in productions with the leading actor Charles Hart, who was also her real-life lover. Hart was probably responsible for Nell Gwyn's original introduction to the stage and together they created the extraordinarily popular team of 'the Gay Couple'. Like Doris Day and Rock Hudson in another era they transported the knock-about, screw-ball humour of *Much Ado's* Beatrice and Benedick to the world of the 1660s and audiences adored them.

By 1667 Nell had elevated herself by becoming mistress to a second Charles - Charles Sackville, Earl of Dorset. Through him she received her entreé to the court. In 1668 she duly became the lover of King Charles II who was thereafter daringly referred to by Nell as Charles III, for accounting reasons. In 1671, Nell Gwyn retired from the theatre and moved into a comfortable Crown-owned townhouse at 79 Pall Mall where she died of a stroke in 1687.

Of all these remarkable first generation women of the theatre by far the most remarkable was the innocuously born Aphra Behn, née Johnson. Born in Kent in 1640, Aphra was the daughter of a barber-surgeon called Bartholomew Johnson and a wet-nurse called Elizabeth Denham. Growing up against the backdrop of the Civil War and the Commonwealth she would develop an arch-royalist devotion to her Stuart kings and, whilst being a committed atheist, was also much attached to Catholic ritual.

One of the extraordinary things about Aphra Johnson is just how a working-class girl, I repeat – girl - from Kent became one of the most independent and literate thinkers of the seventeenth century. As she herself observed in verse later in life, education at this time was actively denied to women.

> And more the scanted custom of the nation
> Permitting not the female sex to tread
> The mighty paths of learned heroes dead.
> The Godlike Virgil and great Homer's muse
> Like divine mysteries are concealed from us,
> We are forbid all grateful themes,
> No ravishing thoughts approach our ear,
> The fulsome jingle of the times
> Is all we are allowed to understand or hear.

It seems that her escape route from her humble beginnings came through a young gentleman her mother had nursed as a baby. Thomas Colepeper was three years older than Aphra and it is reasonable to imagine that the two toddlers, despite coming from such different backgrounds, became childhood playmates. Young Thomas was the son of Sir Thomas Colepeper, the Lieutenant of Dover Castle and his mother had family links to the aristocratic families of the Earl of Leicester and the Viscount Strangford. Thomas' parents both died when he was just six years old and he was sent to live with the Strangford family and his half-brother Philip, the 2nd Viscount. Both were staunch royalists.

If one dares to presume that Thomas and Aphra remained in contact throughout their childhood and adolescence, then the door to a completely different world had been opened to her. She was clearly an exceptionally bright young woman with ambition and ability, so she perhaps made the very best of these opportunities to 'better' herself. Mixing in these elevated royalist circles would have also provided connections, after the Restoration, to men of influence and of letters. Men such as Thomas Killigrew.

We should remember that Killigrew had acted as an intelligence gatherer in the Low Countries for Charles II when he was in exile. We should also know that women were regularly employed in matters of espionage by the Stuart courts - partly due to the power their physical sex could have over men and partly because, when they were not being sexually alluring, nobody paid any attention to women.

We know that this pair knew each other in later life but if Aphra Johnson had fallen into Killigrew's orbit earlier it would have been perfectly logical for him to recruit this robust, smart woman into working for the security services.

In 1663 Aphra Johnson sailed from England to Virginia and then on to Suriname in South America which was then being cultivated by the British as a source of tobacco and sugar. It was also a territory being jealously watched over by the Dutch Republic who would eventually swap it for New York. Not a bad deal!

One of the young British colonists in Suriname out to make his fortune was named William Scott. His father was Thomas Scott who had run the secret intelligence services for Oliver Cromwell during the

Commonwealth and had put his name to Charles I's death warrant. Unsurprisingly Thomas had not found his name on the list of those pardoned in Charles II's Act of Oblivion. He was hanged, drawn and quartered as a Regicide on 17th October 1660.

Not exactly persona grata with the new regime William decamped to Suriname as Deputy Governor in 1663 but Charles II's government wanted to know what plots this son-of-a-regicide might be hatching with the Dutch. It was these potential plots that Aphra Johnson was sent to discover.

Life for a woman in the New World was obviously considerably different from life in Kent. Settlers were tougher and rougher folk and Aphra soon discovered that she could drink and smoke with the best of them. She was also fascinated by the exotic sights she saw, from ostrich feathers to native Indians. A whole universe of noble savages living in Arcadian innocence uncorrupted by civilisation entered into her imagination. And in this colony she had time not just to observe but to write. The pen name she chose was Astrea.

How successful her mission was we will never know - no documents exist which, in the secret world, is unsurprising. She returned to England in 1664 and was granted an audience with the King to deliver an oral report. Whether she chose to mention it to Charles II or not, she did have some dramatic news - she had married.

Johan Behn was a merchant she had met either in Suriname or on the boat home. His relevance to her life is limited since he promptly died in 1665 probably of the Great Plague of that year (Daniel Defoe later wrote about this pestilence in his early experiment in 'faction,' *The Journal of the Plague Year*). Behn's contribution to theatre history is simply that his wife now not only had a nom de plume but a new name for life - Aphra Behn.

The economic trade wars with the Dutch Republic were hotting up by this time and in 1666 Aphra Behn found herself in Antwerp, thereby deftly missing the Great Fire of London. Antwerp was the sugar and diamond capital of Europe; it has kept its dominant hold on the diamond trade to the present day. But as early as 1540, the city was the epicentre of commercial intelligence from where global trade between Venice, Holland, France, Switzerland and England was covertly monitored. Then, as now, economic intelligence mattered just as much as military intelligence.

Aphra Behn arrived in Antwerp, via Bruges, in August 1666. Her mission was to re-connect with a man she had met in Suriname - William Scott. He had fled the sugar plantations of South America to avoid his creditors and was clearly, in the minds of the English security service, ripe for the picking. Behn's mission was to 'turn' Scott; to get the son of a regicide to inform on his anti-royal contacts across the continent. The promise of a pardon, financial support and the sexual lure of an independent woman, with whom he had very likely had an affair in Suriname (a honey trap?) might just be enough to sway him. The mission was supervised by an old royalist spook, Major James Halsall who had once plotted to assassinate Oliver Cromwell, and he allocated code names to the principal players. Scott was 159 and Behn was 160. Overseeing the whole project, Agent 160's ultimate Control, was Thomas Killigrew.

Whether Scott succumbed we will never know for the whole endeavour descended into farce. Aphra had been given a grant of £50 to cover the mission but with travel expenses, a poor exchange rate and the general financial incompetence of both Behn and Killigrew (and the callous, dare I say 'cavalier' refusal of Charles II to pay his dues to loyal servants) she went bust. On returning to London, this time she was not rewarded by an audience with the King but by a spell in debtor's prison.

On her release it was essential that, as a widow, she generated an income in order to survive. One of her unique selling points was her literacy which, combined with her theatre contacts, would change her life. Perhaps by way of an apology Killigrew introduced her to William Davenant who needed someone to copy out parts of plays for actors; scribing was cheaper than printing.

At this time Davenant's company was specialising in new writing and Mrs Behn found herself spending her days reading and copying out scripts for the newly re-opened theatres. Clearly it crossed her agile mind at some point that she could do better. And so, she did.

The Forc'd Marriage or *The Jealous Bridegroom* was staged by the Duke's Company on 20th September 1670. It starred the lead actor of the day Thomas Betterton and featured all the standard Restoration tropes of sex, power and politics. *The Forc'd Marriage* also introduced themes that Aphra Behn would explore for the rest of her life. These included the penchant for elderly men to marry younger brides (and the misery and duplicity that thereby ensues), sexual jealousy and hypocrisy and the fundamental question as to whether a woman can be truly free.

Drawing on her experiences in Suriname, she also began to ponder an Arcadian golden age before men had invented marriage to subjugate women. Having mixed with cavaliers and colonials, Aphra Behn was completely familiar with the idea of the man as libertine. Her question was could such social, moral and sexual freedoms apply to women as well?

On 24th February 1671, the curtain rose on her second play, *The Amorous Prince,* revealing two post-coital lovers on the stage in a state of undress and discussing the fact that each is married to someone else. So far so good as far as the audience was concerned. Bald references to homosexuality and paedophilia rub nicely alongside a standard plot filled with eavesdropping, asides and mistaken identities. For an extra frisson, Behn makes her first use of the cross-dressing Breeches Role when the naive Cloris disguises herself as a pert-buttocked boy only to discover that certain gentlemen find her equally enticing.

Many playwrights never found their way into print but it was a sign of Aphra Behn's popularity and success that almost all of her works were published in her lifetime. Whilst she was never paid as much as male contemporaries like Dryden, she nevertheless started to make a comfortable living out of her wit and her pen.

Well able to cut it with the boys she had also joined one of the rowdier literary circles of the age and at this stage in her career I rather like to think of her as a seventeenth century version of Dorothy Parker in The Algonquin Club. Behn had joined The Merry Gang which thrived between 1665 and 1680. The club's leading light was John Wilmot the Earl of Rochester, a debauched poet and aristocrat who we have already met through his playing the role of Henry Higgins to Elizabeth Barry's Eliza. On top of training Barry (who was also his mistress) he drank, fought duels and died of syphilis at the age of thirty two.

Other members included Charles, Earl of Dorset, the former lover of Nell Gwyn and the playwrights and poets William Wycherley, George Etherege and George Villiers, Duke of Buckingham. This was exalted company for the girl from Kent. Pepys captures the flavour of the gang's antics in his report of a dissolute evening held on 16th February 1669:

The King dining yesterday at the Dutch ambassador's, after dinner they drank and were pretty merry; and among the rest of the King's company there was that worthy fellow my Lord of Rochester, and Tom Killigrew, whose mirth and raillery offended the former so much that he did give Tom Killigrew a box on the ear in the King's presence, which do give much offence to the people here at Court.

Rochester was briefly banned from court!

The man in this libertine circle who most transfixed Aphra Behn was a devilishly handsome young lawyer called John Hoyle. Unusually, considering the company he kept, Hoyle was a republican and had a reputation for extreme violence. In 1663 he was arrested for the murder of a watchmaker but, despite multiple witnesses, got off through the legal loophole of Ignoramus - essentially a verdict of 'bloody dodgy but not proven'. Ignoramus came to Hoyle's aid again in 1667 when he was let off for the repeated male rape of a young boy called Benjamin Bourne in his chambers at The Temple.

Batting for both sides was a bit of a Restoration cliche; Aphra herself was not opposed to the occasional sapphic embrace. However Hoyle had a much darker side, and this atmosphere of sexual danger is clearly what made him such an attractive prospect to men and women alike. He was stabbed to death in a tavern brawl in 1692.

Hoyle was undoubtedly the love of Aphra's life however rotten their love might have been. Straight out of Tennessee Williams theirs was a sultry, steamy relationship based on obsessive passion rather than romantic fidelity and it became the talk of the town. Intimate letters between them were published and they were a tabloid sensation for several years - much to the delight of the public. This was probably much to their own delight as well since celebrity can be addictive and it is always better to be talked about than not talked about, however ghastly the private agony might be. Like so many artists, they found the heady combination of sex, danger, passion and publicity irresistible.

Hoyle and Rochester were eventually conflated in Aphra Behn's imagination and became the central character of her 1677 success *The Rover*. The play was initially based on an earlier work by Thomas Killigrew called *Thomasso* written in 1654 in Madrid and based upon his time flitting around Europe whilst the King was in exile. In Behn's version the central character is a charming, alpha-male, roguish cavalier in exile called Willmore (rather than Wilmot). It is set in Naples during the time of Carnival and is a boisterous romp about the loves and intrigues of a bunch of Englishmen a long way from home. In its own time it was Aphra Behn's most popular work and it is the one that remains in the repertoire to the present day. Sex, sun, and songs - what's not to like?

The production was such a triumph that Aphra Behn produced a sequel in 1681 - so no flies on her. A novel followed in 1688 which places her amongst the alumni of the earliest English novelists. It is also one of the first novels set in the New World and certainly, I suspect, the first anti-slave novel. Partly autobiographical (unless you subscribe to the view that Behn never left Kent and made the entirety of her life up - which in itself would be remarkable and would have preceded modernists such as Fernando Pessoa by some 250 years) she draws on her experiences in Virginia and Suriname to tell the tale of an honourable African Prince - *Oroonoko*.

In all its melodrama *Oroonoko* is a tale of fidelity and infidelity within both white and black communities. Lovers will be parted and re-united - but only on the most tragic of terms. The young Prince will finally disembowel himself rather than be hanged, drawn, and quartered by his English oppressors and the narrator will flit in and out of reality telling the tale of a 'great man, worthy of a better fate'. It is part Behn's autobiography and part *Arabian Nights* - probably rather how she liked to see herself.

Her last play was also set in the British American colonies - again a complete first. *The Widow Ranter* saw the light of day in 1689 and its heroine is a Calamity Jane figure who can drink and jest and smoke with the best of the men - nothing autobiographical here then! Left a widow but wooed by a beau how can she know if the wooing is for love or for dough? To resolve these conundrums a lot of cross-dressing ensues and not a few battles. The play was not a triumph (and is rarely revived) but this bothered Behn little. By the time it opened at Drury Lane she was dead.

Her time was up. Her parsimonious hero and king, Charles II, had died in 1685, the love of his people entirely burned out through the decadent heat of his attempts to be a Sun King. His brother James did his Catholic runner to the continent in 1688 and the great summer of love that had run for twenty-eight years finally fizzled out forever. A Dutch protestant monarch, King William III, usurped the English throne and there was nothing glorious about it at all. Its modern parallel is when the joy, decadence and chaos that entered the world in 1968 was snuffed out when the grown-ups took back control in 1979/80 in the form of Thatcher and Reagan.

Aphra Behn would have enjoyed the 1960s and 1970s I feel. She was a genuinely unique spirit out of time who refused *not* to live freely and thrive within her own time. Controversial then, and for the next quarter of a millennia (a woman writing comedies about sex?!) Behn died five days after the coronation of King William and Queen Mary. The very epitome of ambiguity in both her life and in her plays, she was described within her lifetime as being 'punk and poetess'. This was not a compliment. In many ways she was the true revolutionary of her times. She believed that men and women could be equal in vim and vigour - and in love. She was buried in Westminster Abbey which indicates the status she held with her own peers. The epitaph on her simple black marble stone reads:

> Here lies a proof that wit can never be
> Defence enough against mortality.
> It was written by John Hoyle.

Over two hundred years later Virginia Woolf would grace Aphra Behn with a second epitaph:

> All women together ought to let flowers fall upon the
> Tomb of Aphra Behn,
> For it was she who earned them the right to speak
> Their minds.

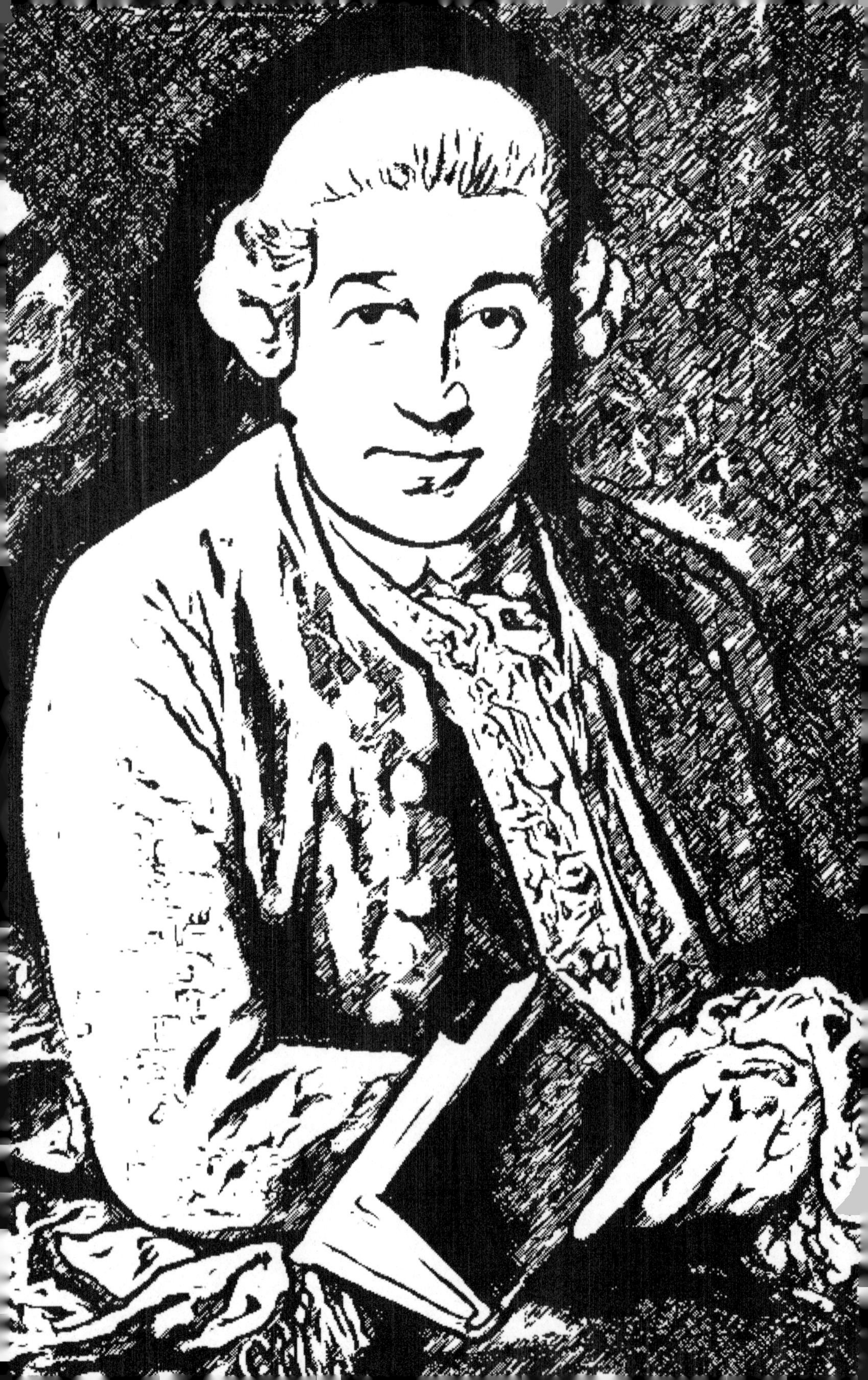

DAVID GARRICK
Actor and Impresario

Once upon a time there was a young man with a weight problem, bad skin and mental health issues. Naturally, he became a teacher. In 1735 at the age of twenty-six he had managed to establish his own small school, Edial Hall, which had a bounteous roll-call of three pupils, one of whom would transform the theatrical world in England forever.

The boy's name was David Garrick, and the other two pupils were his younger brother, George, and a lad named Lawrence Offley who was the nephew of a Whig MP, went to Cambridge and died in 1749. The school closed in 1736.

The de la Garrique family had originally fled to England from Southern France in the 1680s as part of a Huguenot exodus. By 1695 they had taken British citizenship, anglicised their name to Garrick and settled in Hereford. Young David was born in 1717 and soon after the family moved to Lichfield in Staffordshire where he attended the local grammar school and staged a production of Farquhar's *The Recruiting Officer* taking the role of Sergeant Kite. Whether he moved on to Edial

Hall after school because he was particularly bright or particularly stupid is unclear but once it closed other plans had to be made. London beckoned.

Theatre in the capital had changed beyond recognition since the days when Killigrew and Davenant dominated the scene. From his Lincoln's Inn Fields base, Killigrew had expanded his empire up to Covent Garden where in 1663 he opened a 700-seat theatre alternately known as the King's Playhouse or the Theatre Royal which was entered via an alleyway called Bridges Street. It was a wooden structure with the pit open to the air for light, albeit covered by a large glass dome which, according to Pepys, leaked when it rained. Pepys also complained about the poor acoustics in the building.

The ever-developing technology that had made it possible for the masques in the royal palaces to become so extravagant under the watchful eye of Inigo Jones was now imported into the public theatres. There was an arms race afoot between Killigrew's and Davenant's companies as to which of them could provide the most spectacular visual effects. Monorails allowed for elaborate flying scenes whilst revolving prisms and flats on wheels made rapid set changes possible, all in front of ever more sophisticated lighting employing oiled paper, coloured lenses and spinning globes. When the Bridges Street Theatre burned down nine years later (no doubt due to the sophisticated lighting) it was rapidly redesigned and reopened in 1674 as the Theatre Royal, Drury Lane.

William Davenant had not been idle in these years either, having kept a firm finger of control in both the old Cockpit Theatre and the Salisbury Court, as well as transforming his theatre in Lincoln's Inn Fields into what would reopen in 1671 as the Dorset Gardens. Here

Henry Purcell's *The Fairy Queen* would premier in 1692. However, Davenant was to die in 1668 and his sons Charles, and later Alexander, were doomed to take over the business. Lacking all the charm and talent of their father, the Davenant boys began to run the theatre project into the ground just at a time when Killigrew's company was also in trouble.

The rebuild at Drury Lane had virtually bankrupted the King's Men and in 1682 the company merged with the Duke's Men. Thomas Killigrew died in 1683 and, as with Davenant, his sons Thomas and Charles were little more than crooks. Theatre in London was in artistic and financial chaos which, combined with the political unrest leading up to the Glorious Revolution of 1688, meant that little of artistic substance could be achieved. For a while a joint company was run by the lead actor of the day, Thomas Betterton, but he was forced out in his turn by an unholy alliance between Charles Killigrew and Alexander Davenant. By 1693 the latter was fleeing to the sunshine of the Canary Islands to avoid charges of embezzlement finally leaving the company in the hands of its lawyer, Christopher Rich.

Rich bought out Killigrew Jnr and ran the company for the next sixteen years but whilst he kept control of the finances he did so at the expense of the actors. Fed up with his autocratic, salary slashing approach Thomas Betterton led a walk out of actors (including stars Elizabeth Barry and Anne Bracegirdle) to set up a co-operative company of their own. The decimated Patent company limped on until the by now despised Christopher Rich was forced out in 1709 - stripping the theatre buildings of all their fixtures and fittings as he left.

Determined not to be thwarted, Rich took the lease of the now deserted old theatre building in Lincoln's Inn Fields and built a brand-new theatre on Portugal Street, which opened on 18th December 1714. However, Rich did not attend the opening as he died on 4th November.

The man who did in fact open the theatre was Rich's son John. John Rich was likeable, talented and a true man of the theatre. Quite how the genes had jumped this way is anyone's guess but suddenly London's theatreland found itself in safe hands.

Primarily a dancer, having a weak stage voice, John Rich was much taken by the Italian performances of the Commedia dell'arte - a form of improvised comedy based around stock characters such as the miser Pantalone, the beautiful young girl Columbine and the irreverent servant Harlequin.

John Rich created his own silent version of Harlequin whom he named Lun (short for lunatic) and this madcap dancing clown would dominate the London stage for decades. Much attracted by spectacle and illusion Rich created a charming world of fantasy and magic, acrobatics and special effects. These Harlequinades, as they became known, would in time transform themselves into what we know as the modern pantomime.

Having nothing to do with the silent form of mime the great British Pantomime is a cacophony of noise. The origins of the word stem from the Greek *'pan'* meaning *'all'* and *'mimos'* which translates as *'to imitate'*. Originally it was a form of dance drama that grew out of the dithyramb in which one or several speechless actors played all the parts of a story by means of hand and body movements, accompanied with singing or music. If you think of Japanese Noh drama, you are barking up the right tree.

It is a long journey from ancient Athens to the Hackney Empire in east London but there is a through line that leads from one to the other. If I had to name a founder of the genre, I would have to choose the god Dionysus/Bacchus who, as the god of fertility and the overseer of the harvest, was essential to human survival. As we have seen, he was also the god of the vine that allowed us to produce wine which in turn allowed us to drink ourselves into a frenzy. The human need to occasionally let it all out is a fundamental one and it is sometimes through the transformative power of chaos that we can fully appreciate the benefits of order.

The Bacchanalia of the Greeks in time developed into the Roman Saturnalia which just happened to be in December. If you add in the bubble-pricking element of the satyr plays that followed the great Greek tragedies and further consider the exuberance of present-day Carnival and Mardi Gras then you are starting to get a sense of a festival that acts as a pressure valve for the human spirit. I related earlier how by the medieval period in England all this happy chaos took the form of the Feast of Fools which was a form of state-sponsored, time-limited anarchy with our friends the Boy Bishops and the cross-dressing Lords of Misrule. The latter can be viewed as the great, great, great grandfather/mother of the pantomime dame. The influence of the Commedia dell'arte with its central character of Harlequin also cannot be underestimated any more than can the influence of the medieval Mummers with their traditions of disguising, dancing and the exchanging of gifts.

We can be ridiculously precise about the origins of the modern British pantomime. On 2nd March 1717 a man called James Weaver staged a dance drama at Drury Lane called *The Loves of Mars and Venus* which was billed as 'a dramatic entertainment of dancing attempted in imitation of the pantomimes of the ancient Greeks and Romans'. This became a riotous success and was picked up by the ever-entrepreneurial John Rich who, in his Harlequinades, applied the full technology of the day with trap-doors, star-traps and other scenic devices, allowing Lun to appear and disappear much to the delight of the crowds.

There are two other major figures who stand out in the further development of the pantomime. The first was the great clown Joey Grimaldi (1778-1837) who, through his comic genius, began to squeeze out the figure of Harlequin and push his own creation of 'Clown' centre stage. Clowns to the present day are known as Joeys in honour of Joey Grimaldi and it was Grimaldi in the early 1800s who introduced a recognisable precursor of the pantomime dame in his performances of Mother Goose and Dick Whittington's mother. It was a popular comic innovation but let us not forget that the Nurse in Romeo and Juliet was originally played by a bloke in a frock.

If you want a pithy definition of pantomime just remember - a man, dressed as a woman, has a son who is a girl dressed as a boy who falls in love with a girl (who really is a girl) and they are all helped by two other human beings dressed as an animal. All clear?

The second key figure was Augustus Harris (1852-1896) who drew all the most popular elements of Harlequinades and Pantomimes together and created the format that has survived to the present day. He had great commercial success with shows such as *Puss in Boots*, *Sleeping Beauty* and *Cinderella* all of which are still very much in the repertoire. The shared experience of children, parents and grand-parents watching the staging of these tales which they have all known since the cradle must be one of the central reasons behind their continued popularity.

A third figure who I should mention here is George Wild Galvin (1860-1904) who, under the stage name of Dan Leno, set the gold standard for all subsequent pantomime dames. That standard is that the Dame should be recognisably a man in a dress with the hem of his trousers virtually showing under his frock and his stubble showing through his make-up. If any children in the audience think that the Dame is a real woman then the magic of the role has been shattered. As we have already seen the pantomime convention of the Principal Boy, in which the leading male role is played by a woman, harks back to the Breeches Parts played by the first actresses of the Restoration stage.

Good pantomime always acknowledges its origins and some of the great set-pieces such as the mirror routine or the cooking routine with the chucking of custard pies date back over 150 years. Some other conventions date back even earlier, such as the practice of the villain entering stage left (sinister) and the good fairy entering stage right (dexter) which harks back to the medieval Mystery plays when the entrances to heaven and hell were placed on these sides.

I have known American theatres attempt pantomime but it rarely works. I am not being rude to Americans here but, as audiences, Americans are simply far too polite and fail to throw themselves into the show with enough raucous gusto. The same could be said of pantomimes in some genteel English towns where the audiences are sometimes just a little too reverential and polite - even at Christmas. For my money, the best shows can be found in venues like the Theatre Royal, Stratford East, and the Hackney Empire where all ages, classes, races and creeds cram together and completely let themselves go. We must remember that the origin of pantomime was 'frenzy', and it is this spirit of letting go of all inhibition, both on stage and in the audience, which appeals so directly to children - 'did Grandma really shout that?'. And, since for most of us going to a pantomime as a child was our very first experience of live theatre, it makes sense why many of us as adults choose, once a year, to throw caution to the wind and take ourselves back to our childhoods and allow ourselves a couple of hours of delightful misrule. Or as the eighteenth-century critic Leigh Hunt put it:

> "Not to like pantomime is not to like love, not to like a holiday, not to remember that we have been children ourselves."

Anyway, back to John Rich, who was a shrewd producer as well as an entertainer. In 1728, he commissioned the satirist John Gay to write a topical popular musical entertainment. It was called *The Beggar's Opera*. Not really an opera at all, Gay's work lampooned the pomposity of this grand Italian art form and dragged it cheerfully down to the level of the people. Inspired by an idea of Jonathan Swift's to create a 'Newgate pastoral among the thieves and whores there' Gay created a world of melodious low-life and populist characters such as the feisty Polly Peachum and the charismatic criminal Macheath.

Mocking politicians in general and the prime minister Robert Walpole in particular *The Beggar's Opera* was an immediate hit with the public, and it ran for sixty-two consecutive performances which famously made John Rich gay and John Gay rich.

On the back of this triumph, John Rich invested his profits into a new theatre building just round the corner from Killigrew's old Drury Lane venue. The Theatre Royal, Covent Garden opened on 7th December 1732 and Rich entered his new 1,400 seat venue as part of a triumphant procession through London complete with banners proclaiming 'Rich Forever!'.

In Covent Garden, Rich continued to dance his fantastical Harlequinades as well as staging elaborate visual feasts for the ever-gawping public. He also presented a smattering of Shakespeare's plays. He died in 1761 and, after a series of refurbishments necessitated usually by fire, Rich's theatre (built on the proceeds of an anti-opera) still stands today as the Royal Opera House.

A few hundred yards away the Theatre Royal, Drury Lane was being run by the very man who had forced John Rich's father Christopher out of business - the actor-manager, poet, playwright and all-round mountebank, Colley Cibber. This building also faced several rebuilds over time - most notably in 1794 and again in 1812. It too still stands and there is something deeply pleasing that both these stalwart London landmarks trace their origins back to the original patents of Killigrew and Davenant granted in 1660.

This was the London that the young David Garrick entered in early March 1737. The theatres had survived civil war, commonwealth and chaos and were now enjoying a period of magnificent consolidation. But Garrick's eyes were firmly set on a career in the law.

Following the failure of Edial Hall, arrangements were made for him to prepare for admittance to the Temple so on 2nd March 1737 he left for London. Accompanying him was his erstwhile teacher. At twenty-eight, this teacher was eight years Garrick's senior but also now his friend. Nothing sinister here - just two young men setting off together to make their fortunes in the world. The scrofulous schoolmaster's name was Samuel Johnson.

That same month David's father died leaving him just enough money to risk a detour in life. He and his elder brother Peter pooled their resources, drew on their French heritage and set themselves up in the wine trade just off the Strand.

This middle-class Midlands' mafia of the Garrick brothers and Johnson had good connections in London - not least in the theatre. Johnson was at this point touting around his truly dreadful play *Irene* (a pure Christian woman is tediously corrupted by a wicked Turkish sultan) and one of his victims had been Charles Fleetwood who was Colley Cibber's business partner at Drury Lane.

To promote his work, Johnson organised a reading of his blank-verse monstrosity in the autumn of 1737 at the Fountain Tavern, just round the corner from the Garrick's wine business. What a riotous evening that must have been!

However, 1737 was a momentous year for the theatre in other ways as well. In that year Robert Walpole, tired of the satirical attacks on him by Whig playwrights such as John Gay and the prolific Henry Fielding, introduced the Theatre Licensing Act. All plays now came under strict censorship by the government. The thought police, under the new office of Examiner of Plays, now read and red-penned, every new script as well as regularly inspected theatre buildings to ensure their 'safety and comfort'. Not for the first time was health and safety used as an excuse to curtail joy.

The unexpected consequence of the Theatre Licensing Act was that satirical playwrights such as Fielding gave up on the theatre and turned instead to writing the uncensored novel. In many respects we have Walpole to thank for *Tristram Shandy*, *The Vicar of Wakefield* and *Tom Jones*. Less pleasingly the 1737 Act stayed, to all intents and purposes, in effect until 1968.

By April 1740, the presumptive wine-merchant David Garrick had written his own, politically uncontroversial play, *Lethe*, and had it staged at Drury Lane starring one of the leading actor-managers of the period, Henry Giffard, who was also an investor in Garrick's wine business. In July 1741 the Examiners of Plays churlishly closed the London theatres so Giffard took his company on tour to the Tankard Theatre in Ipswich with a stage adaptation of Aphra Behn's novel *Oroonoko*. In the acting company was David Garrick appearing under the stage-name of Lyddall.

On 19th October 1741 Garrick was back in the capital playing the title role of Richard III at Giffard's East End theatre, the Goodman's Fields. The playbill describes him as 'a gentleman who never appeared on any stage' which was, of course, a big fat fib but great marketing. The house was full and the reception rapturous. Garrick was the overnight talk of London due to his rejection of the declamatory style of acting popular with most actors, choosing instead a more naturalistic style of characterisation.

The bombastic acting style with actors directly addressing the audience had dominated the English stage since the medieval period. Lines were learned and vomited over the audience accompanied by elegant and imposing gestures. Rehearsals were optional. The man who changed all this was that great Methuselah of the stage, Charles Macklin, who was somewhere between 97 and 107 when he died. An Ulsterman by birth, he arrived in London around 1725 and played a famous Shylock in 1744. In between he had set up a small school for elocution and oratory in Covent Garden where he trained aspirant actors in how to speak in the theatre as if they were in the real world.

Encouraging them to consider character development, to vary tone and to take time to show transitions of thought and emotion, Macklin promoted the dramatic value of the 'pause' over two hundred years before Harold Pinter. Macklin is one of the unsung heroes of English theatre and one of his pupils was David Garrick.

By 1742 Garrick was a fully-fledged man of the theatre with several roles at Drury Lane under his belt (including King Lear) and an actress, the beautiful Peg Woffington who had played Cordelia, as his mistress. The wine-business on the Strand stood empty.

James Quin, one of the stalwart declamatory actors of the age, observed about Garrick's new naturalism that 'if this young fellow is right, then I and the rest of the players must have been all wrong'. The translator and historian Nicolas Tindal commented 'the deaf hear him in his action and the blind see him in his voice'.

By 1747, Garrick bestrode theatreland like a colossus having taken over the lease of Drury Lane - a theatre he would run for the next twenty-nine years. He further consolidated his position by jettisoning poor Peg Woffington and settling down to a blissfully happy married life with a German dancer named Eva Marie Veigel.

Garrick's first great love was for Shakespeare and he was deeply sceptical about the superficial spectacles and Harlequinades that John Rich was staging at Covent Garden. Sceptical that is until he discovered how much money Rich was making from such low-brow fare. Garrick's first 'show' was *Harlequin's Invasion* which was presented in 1756 and included a rousing musical number with words written by Garrick himself. *Hearts of Oak* remains in the public consciousness to the present day as the official anthem of the Royal Navy.

However, it was his naturalistic interpretations of Macbeth, Romeo and Hamlet for which he was best known. In playing the latter, Garrick created a contraption attached to his wig that allowed him to pull a string and make his hair literally stand on end. So, when Hamlet saw his father's ghost for the first time, the audience shivered in delight.

In 1767 the worthy city burghers of a Warwickshire backwater called Stratford-upon-Avon had a bright idea. Francis Wheler and the soon to be town clerk, William Hunt, hatched a plan to lure the celebrity actor and famous admirer of Shakespeare to their hometown and open the new town hall. Initially enticing him to Stratford by electing him as an Honorary Burgess and presenting him with a box made out of Shakespeare's mulberry tree the plan eventually grew like Topsy.

By 11th May 1769 the London Chronicle carried its first report that David Garrick was planning to produce a major jubilee at Stratford to celebrate the anniversary of the birth of its most famous son. The fact that Shakespeare had been born in 1564 and they were all five years late does not seem to have worried the celebrity or the fawning councillors one jot. Why let mere dates get in the way of a good bit of PR?

By June 1769 Garrick was up in Stratford making plans and by July 100 trees were cut down to clear a site for the festivities. There would be a rotunda built to seat a thousand people and an Ode to Shakespeare would be composed and delivered by Garrick himself. Great dinners would be hosted, a statue of the bard would be unveiled and a lavishly costumed pageant incorporating all of Shakespeare's best-loved characters would be staged. It never seems to have crossed anyone's mind to actually stage a play by the great man.

The London papers were full of the story and all the great and good of stage, society and court began to make their plans to decamp to Stratford for the celebrations. They duly arrived in early September and on 6th September the carnival began. Cannons were fired, church bells were rung and an oratorio by Dr Thomas Arne (composer of *Rule Britannia*) was performed in the parish church. Over lunch Garrick sang his own truly shaming composition - *The Ballard of Shakespeare's Mulberry-Tree*:

> Behold this fair goblet, 'twas carved from the tree,
> Which, O my sweet Shakespeare, was planted by thee;
> As a relic I kiss it, and bow at the shrine,
> What comes from thy hand must be ever divine!
> All shall yield to the Mulberry-tree,
> Bend to thee,
> Blest Mulberry,
> Matchless was he
> Who planted thee,
> And thou like him immortal be!

Garrick was clearly not the first, and certainly not the last, celebrity to let publicity send a rush of blood to his head. The wine flowed, lunch concluded and the evening's ball commenced an hour late at 10pm. It lasted until after 3am and Mrs. Garrick danced an exquisite minuet.

The next morning began with heavy rain and sore heads all round. During late morning ablutions Garrick's barber managed to carve a slice out of his face 'from the corner of his mouth to his chin'. As the Avon began to break its banks Garrick appeared at the rotunda, bandaged but undaunted, and delivered his Ode to the 'blest genius of the isle' and unveiled the new statue of Shakespeare. And still it rained.

By the evening the rotunda had begun to flood, the masquerade ball had descended into chaos and the much-anticipated firework display was aborted. Friday saw the cancellation of the great costumed pageant and the gradual exodus from Stratford of the great and the good through streets that had now turned into swamps. James Boswell, who had been in attendance with Samuel Johnson, quipped 'after the joys of the Jubilee came the uneasy reflection that I was in a little village in wet weather and knew not how to get away'.

Egg spread firmly all over his face, Garrick returned from the debacle to London to face the delighted wrath of the newspapers and the spiteful sniping of society. Everyone loves a flop. Behind a rictus grin of self-deprecation, however, Garrick's mind was clearly whirring away on how to redeem the situation. The jubilee might have been a wash-out but the pageant had never been staged and all the costumes were ready and waiting for use. On 14th October at Drury Lane, he presented *The Jubilee*. It ran for a record ninety-two performances and made Garrick a small fortune.

In 1768, the architect Robert Adam and his brothers began work on a block of luxury, neoclassical town houses between the Strand and the river Thames. The Adelphi, as it was called, opened in 1772 and the Garricks moved into it in March. Dividing his time between this smart London pad and his large country house in Hampton David continued to run Drury Lane and add new roles to his acting repertoire until he retired in 1776. He died peacefully at home in the Adelphi on 20th January 1779. His last words were 'Oh dear!'.

David Garrick was buried with full ceremony in Westminster Abbey and the procession stretched from Poet's Corner right back to his home at the Adelphi. The site of this Adam building off the Strand was Durham Yard. The exact spot where he and his brother Peter had set up their wine business forty-two years earlier.

But David Garrick's importance to the theatre was not just the innovations he brought to acting. As the manager of Drury Lane he also introduced major reforms to the building and, more controversially, to the behaviour of the audience.

The generation before Garrick had seen considerable changes in the way they went to the theatre. In the 1690s performances still began in the late afternoon to catch the last of the day's light through the leaking glass dome of Drury Lane. By the 1720s a more mercantile class who wanted to complete a day's commerce before relaxing had shifted the start time to the early evening - around six o' clock.

Once in the theatre audiences could expect to be entertained firstly by a Prologue. This might take the form of a stand-up comedian, a warm-up act, perhaps even mocking some of the celebrity actors who were about to appear on the stage. Then a five-act play would commence, interspersed with musical interludes so that the stagehands could winch down the great chandeliers above the stage and change the candles. The music that played in these intervals would have been the contemporary songs of the day. It was as if you went to see *King Lear* now and they played the Spice Girls in the breaks.

This marathon was followed by a series of specialty acts - the precursor of the music hall - including animal acts, dancing and acrobatics. Finally, the evening ended with an Afterpiece such as a great procession (in the eighteenth-century people loved processions), a re-staging of the coronation of the King or even the Shakespeare Jubilee.

Eating and drinking during the show was de rigueur and gentlemen might even set up a dining table on the stage for the actors to navigate around. Those sitting in the side boxes had access to a corridor that provided convenient access to the actresses' dressing rooms (how many cues were missed?) and in between the five-act play and the specialty acts the theatre doors were re-opened and the great unwashed were allowed in to enjoy the remainder of the evening at half-price. No hallowed silence in awe of the actors here. The modern actor who suffers apoplexy at every squark of a mobile phone would have received little sympathy from the thespians of the eighteenth century.

It was Garrick who swept (or attempted to sweep) all this Hogarthian bawdy out of the theatre. He banished the gentlemen from the stage, closed the convenient corridors and provoked riots by stopping the half-price, half-time entry. He put the audience in its place. Despite provoking several riots at the time the generation after Garrick accepted all these controversial reforms as the new norm.

Actors were also knocked into shape with the abolition of 'roles for life'. No longer could they play Romeo or Juliet until the day before their retirement. Ian McKellen's 2021 Hamlet at the age of eighty-one would never have been allowed on Garrick's stage. Rehearsals were now obligatory not optional and Garrick fined actors who failed to attend.

In writing his epitaph Dr Johnson observed of his friend 'his profession made him rich, and he made his profession respectable'.

As a man of Gallic descent, Garrick holidayed in France and often attended the theatre. There he saw the technological advances they had made, particularly regarding lighting, and he transplanted them to the London stage. Revolve lighting (which was a series of bookshelves filled with lights and set on spindles so that they could be swiftly spun around to illuminate or darken the stage) was introduced thus creating side-lighting which allowed for the whole depth of the stage to be used. No longer did the lead actor have to stand front and centre to be seen whilst he struck a pose and declaimed his lines.

Garrick also brought the leading lighting designer of the day to Drury Lane. Phillipe James de Loutherbourg was born in Strasbourg in 1740 and over many years travelling throughout Europe had perfected the alchemy of lenses and lighting and their effect upon pigments in paint. By the time he settled in London in 1771 his scenic illusions could transform a green forest on the stage into one of autumn russet and then take the seasons further on into an icy winter. All before the audience's very eyes.

By 1781, de Loutherbourg had also invented the eidophusikon which was a magic box of delights combining every permutation of miniature winches, pulleys, lenses, stained glass and candles. It also included the newly-invented Argand lamp that burned ten times brighter than any previous lamp. Through this extraordinary application of technology and science de Loutherbourg effectively invented Moving Pictures.

Panoramas and rolling dioramas were spectacularly popular with the London audiences as were the regularly churned out effects of spectres appearing and disappearing, waterfalls tumbling and fully staged naval battles. Spectacle was all in the eighteenth-century theatre, wherein lies its fundamental flaw. The plays of the period were eminently forgettable. As Goethe would later observe: "English plays, Atrocious in content, Absurd in form, Objectionable in action, Execrable English Theatre!".

The perfect storm of Robert Walpole's Licensing Act and the commercial taste for sentiment and spectacle had driven the playwright from the stage. The gain to the English novel was the English theatre's loss and it is not until the end of the eighteenth century that we start to see the re-emergence of playwrights who in any way deserve to be included in the repertoire today.

Garrick himself rejected Oliver Goldsmith's masterpiece *She Stoops to Conquer* possibly because he, like many others, found the author to be a deeply annoying man. It was however reluctantly staged at Covent Garden on 15th March 1773 when this new 'laughing comedy' was, to everyone's surprise, an immediate overnight hit. Goldsmith's 'laughing comedy' was in direct response to the 'sentimental comedy' that had dominated the stage for over fifty years.

The moral majority crave correction not laughter. If you consider the 'virtue signalling' and 'wokeness' of current times then you will get a feel for some of the humourless cant that pervaded England and the English stage in the eighteenth century. Not all charitable giving by the great and the good (such as at Coram's Foundling Hospital) was meant to go publicly unnoticed and not all publicly 'correct' attitudes were comprehensively believed in private. It was socially dysfunctional Oliver Goldsmith who dared to observe that the chasm between the moral high-ground and human reality was more amusing in the theatre than attempts at moral reform.

Human hypocrisy and mistaken identity have always been a ripe source for comedy from the Roman writer Plautus to Moliere to John Cleese's *Fawlty Towers*. *She Stoops to Conquer* is no exception. This comedy of manners, with its relentless nailing of the neuroses and hypocrisies of the English middle classes, through jokes rather than moral messages, delighted even George III at the time and has continued to delight audiences ever since.

Another author who redeemed the reputation of English playwrighting was Richard Brinsley Sheridan. He was born into a literary family in Dublin, where his actor father ran the Smock Alley Theatre, and he was educated at Harrow School in London. By his early twenties Sheridan had fought two duels, eloped with a singer and was living a life of glamorous pleasure way beyond his means.

He began writing plays in the hope that theatre would be his way to easy money. In 1775 his first play, *The Rivals* (those duels had not gone to waste), was presented at Covent Garden. In 1776 he had bought out Garrick's patent and in 1777 he presented *The School for Scandal* at what was now his own theatre, Drury Lane. By 1780 he had also been elected to Parliament - a position he held for the next thirty-two years; the only Englishman ever to have distinguished careers in both theatre and politics.

Although they were politically scurrilous in their day, time has now rendered Sheridan's plays politically irrelevant. They remain to us simply as splendidly superficial firework displays of wit and bold characterisation, and they are none the weaker for that. *The Rivals* gift to humanity was the broadly drawn, but easily recognisable, Mrs Malaprop who, whilst no fool, is just foolish enough to want to appear more learned than she is. Grasping around for language to impress she ends up instead desperately clutching the poor relations of the words she aspired to. Impatience tripping up intellect. "He is the very pineapple of politeness," she squawks.

Mrs Malaprop's delusional but ruthless social aspirations re-emerged in later centuries in the form of Oscar Wilde's Lady Bracknell in *The Importance of Being Earnest* and the BBC's Hyacinth Bucket in *Keeping Up Appearances*. It is no accident that the son of the latter is called Sheridan.

The pinnacle (or pineapple) of Sheridan's theatrical success was *The School for Scandal*. Harking back to the Restoration sex comedies of Aphra Behn (indeed Sheridan's 1779 play *The Critic* was a re-writing of George Villier's 1671 *The Rehearsal*) *Scandal* retreads the fertile comic ground of the older man marrying a younger wife. Attacking the hypocrisy of 'men of sentiment' this good-natured, stylishly written and perfectly plotted romp reveals us to ourselves in all our ridiculous horror - and we laugh.

All flames burn out and Sheridan was no exception. In 1809 whilst in the Palace of Westminster he received news that his great investment, Drury Lane, was burning down. Shortly after he was spotted viewing the conflagration from a nearby cafe with a drink in his hand. "A man may surely be allowed to take a glass of wine by his own fireside," was his only comment.

He lost his parliamentary seat in 1812 and, having always spent more than he earned, his creditors swooped down and pecked away at him for the last three years of his life. Always a heavy drinker 'Old Sherry' as he was known ended his days in complete and squalid penury. This great old rogue of the theatre died in a Soho garret at noon on 17th July 1816 and an age stretching back to Killigrew and Davenant died with him.

A DIGRESSION ON VICTORIANS
Shakespeare and Elephants

Contrary to popular myth, Queen Victoria loved to be amused. In the year of her coronation in 1838 she attended the public theatre and opera thirty-six times and that was on top of the private performances she enjoyed at Windsor Castle. Charles Kean, whose revolutionary, 'authentic' productions of Shakespeare we shall touch on later, was a regular performer at Windsor and Victoria so appreciated his production of *Macbeth* in February 1853 that she went to see it several more times afterwards in London.

For your less aristocratic theatregoer there was also plenty of uplifting entertainment to be found. For elegant, graceful productions of Shakespeare's plays you could see John Philip Kemble acting alongside his sister, Sarah Siddons. A protege of David Garrick, Siddons would play most of Shakespeare's leading ladies over a forty-year career as well as famously portraying Hamlet multiple times. Maintaining the Georgian tradition of 'a role for life' Kemble and Siddons played Macbeth and Lady Macbeth from 1785 up until Siddons' retirement in 1812. At this farewell performance on 29th June 1812, the Covent Garden audience were so overcome that, once she had left the stage following the sleep-walking scene, they gave her such an ovation it was impossible for the play to continue. Eventually the curtain re-opened and Sarah Siddons was revealed sitting on the stage in her own clothes and proceeded to deliver an emotional farewell to her devoted fans. Presumably, Macbeth and Macduff had sensibly gone to the pub.

At the more feral end of the spectrum was the 'mad, bad and dangerous to know' Edmund Kean (father of Charles) who had begun his career by playing Hamlet at the age of fourteen in York. After a triumphant and sensitive portrayal of Shylock at Drury Lane in 1814 Kean's reputation was assured and he was to become a major celebrity on both sides of the Atlantic, making tours to New York in 1820 and 1825. Early in his career Jane Austen wrote to her sister stating 'places are secured at Drury Lane for Saturday, but so great is the rage for seeing Kean that only a third and fourth row could be got'. Coleridge reported that 'seeing him act was like reading Shakespeare by flashes of lightning'.

One of the more significant developments in the theatre of the early Victorian period was an increased interest in introducing faux-historical realism to the stage. Previously actors had portrayed characters from Hamlet to Juliet wearing their own contemporary dress; whatever made them look good. An engraving of Kean's 1814 Macbeth shows him instead wearing a rather revealing kilt in an unlikely plaid. Such triumph of romance over realism can be blamed on Sir Walter Scott; the influence his romantic historical novels had on society was massive. The playbill of Kean's *Macbeth* also lists fifteen Principal Singing Witches and a chorus of about fifty witches and spirits. The music was advertised as being by Matthew Locke (who had died in 1677) and the sets the audience were about to see are described in loving detail from Macbeth's banqueting hall to Hecate's cave. This production was clearly the same 'Macbeth the Musical' that Samuel Pepys had enjoyed under the direction of William Davenant in 1663. Ben Jonson's prophecy in

Shakespeare's epitaph that 'he was not of an age but for all time' had patently not been fulfilled.

Another Victorian phenomenon was child actors playing adult roles - Shirley Temple plays Cleopatra. The chief proponent of this was William Henry West Betty, more popularly known as Master Betty. Born in 1791, by the age of eleven he had taken Belfast and Dublin and by 1804 armed guards had to be stationed outside Covent Garden for Master Betty's debut as *Hamlet* in case the crowds lost all rational control of themselves. Betty's star was so much in the ascendant that King George III personally introduced him to the Queen, and the Prime Minister, William Pitt the Younger, adjourned parliament so that members could make it to the theatre on time. Dubbed 'the Young Roscius' (after a famous Roman actor) Betty, having fermented an early Victorian version of Beatlemania, quit the stage in 1808 to take a degree at Christ's College, Cambridge. After his few attempts to be taken seriously as an adult actor failed, as did his suicide attempt at around the same time, Master Betty formally retired in 1824 and dedicated the rest of his life to working for theatrical charities. He died aged eighty-three in 1874.

Outside Shakespeare, the Victorian entertainment scene was a cornucopia of shiny delights. Harlequinades were transforming themselves into pantomimes, Gilbert and Sullivan operettas were on the rise and music hall acts were abundant. These included everything from dancing elephants and juggling monkeys at Sadler's Wells, to George Ware (who wrote *The Boy I Love is Up in the Gallery*), Arthur Lloyd and George 'Champagne Charlie' Leybourne keeping the crowds happy at Wilton's Music Hall in London's East End. Performing dogs had their own fan base as they barked their way through the role of Poor Dog

Tray (who was a sort of proto-Lassie forever saving damsels in distress) and from America came the extraordinarily popular Minstrel Shows.

On top of all this national freak-shows paraded everything from dubious mermaids to bearded ladies to Joseph Merrick, the Elephant Man. Towards the end of his life the latter was befriended by the Princess of Wales, Princess Alexandra, who sent him a Christmas card every year and around 1887 his surgeon, Sir Frederick Treves, smuggled him into a private box at Drury Lane to watch one of Augustus Harris's extravagantly produced pantomimes - probably *Puss in Boots*. Treves recalled that Merrick watched the production with pure delight as if every element of the fantasy were in fact true:

> the palace was the home of kings, the princess was of royal blood, the fairies were as undoubted as the children in the street, while the dishes at the banquet were of unquestionable gold. He did not like to discuss it as a play, but rather as a vision of some actual world.

Once, before his death in 1890, Joseph Merrick commented to Treves: "I wonder what the prince did after we left."

With his sense of childlike absorption Merrick was in very good Victorian company. Like children in a sweetshop the audiences of the nineteenth century gathered in these gilded palaces of delight and relished the spectacular feasts that were presented to them. As an up-and-coming playwright of the late nineteenth century observed: "I regard the theatre as the greatest of all art forms, the most immediate way in which a human being can share with another the sense of what it is to be a human being." That playwright's name was Oscar Wilde.

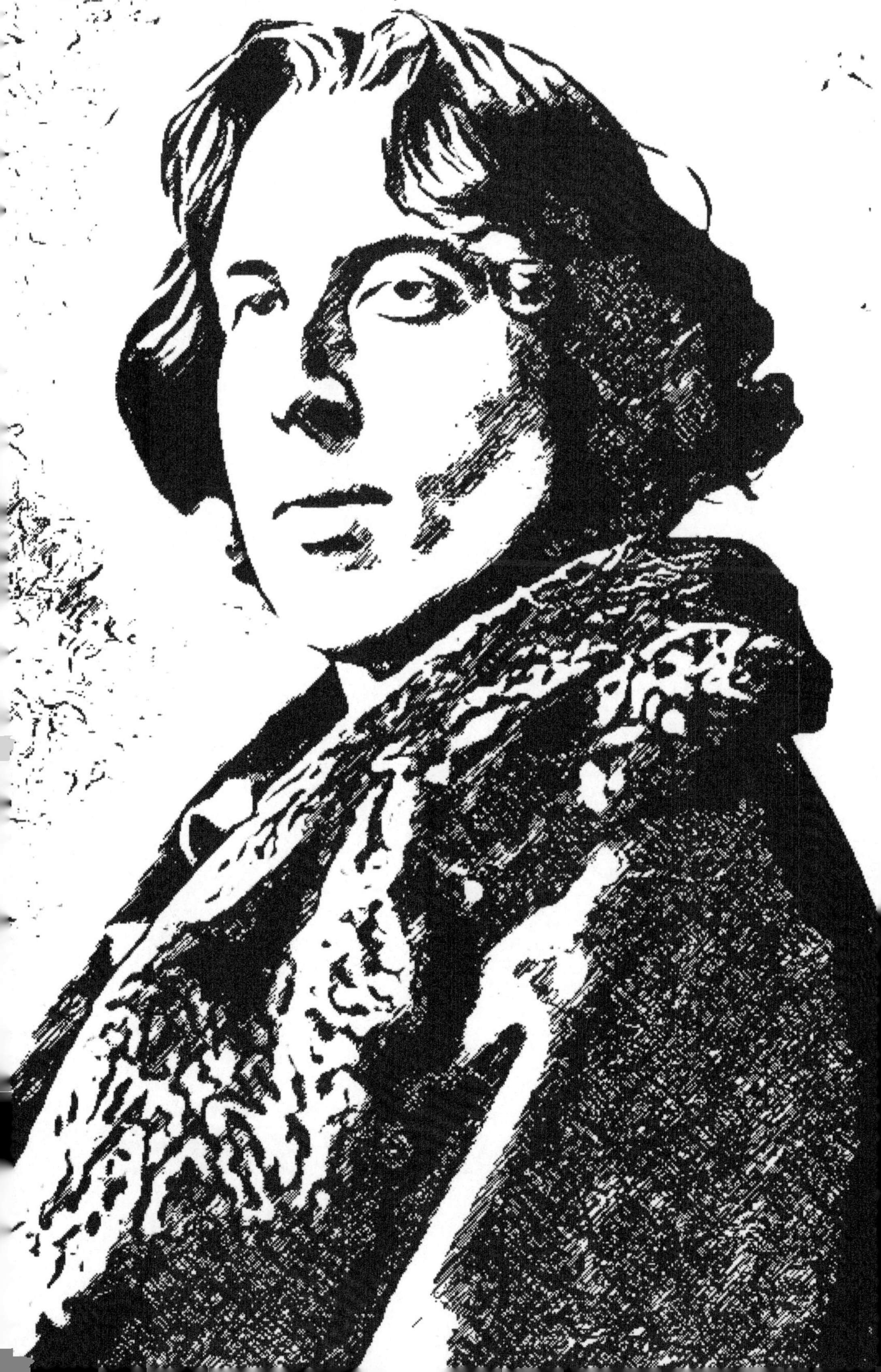

OSCAR WILDE
A Well-Polished Paradox

For seven days in December in the second half of the nineteenth century Dublin was transfixed by a scandalous court case. The legal matter was libel, the subject matter was sex and the defendant was called Wilde.

But it wasn't Oscar. It was his mother.

The Wilde family were exotic fruit. Oscar's father William was a medical man specialising in diseases of the eye and ear and was appointed oculist to Queen Victoria. For this service he was awarded a knighthood in 1864 despite never having had to actually treat her. Like any true Victorian gentleman he was also a dabbler in everything from travel writing to biography and took a keen interest in Irish history, folklore and politics. He also bred children. Willie, Oscar and Isola were legitimate whilst Henry, Emily and Mary hailed from the other side of the blanket. All six were well aware of each other as they grew up in this strangely extended family so when Emily and Mary tragically burned to death at a Halloween party in 1871, having stood too close to the fire causing their crinolines to ignite, the tragedy was shared by all.

Sir William's wife, Jane Francesca Agnes Elgee, was the daughter of a Wexford solicitor who claimed direct descent from Dante (a patent fabrication). A keen Irish nationalist and a passionate supporter of the arts she hosted regular salons for all the great and the good of Dublin and wrote nationalist verse under the pen-name of Speranza - Italian for hope. Whenever I consider Lady Wilde I can't help but think of an exuberant, exhausting and exasperating hybrid of Florence Foster Jenkins and Bianca Castafiore from the Tintin books.

Her first two children, Willie and Oscar, were born in a very comfortable but unremarkable Georgian terraced house at 21 Westmorland Row. Willie emerged there in 1852 and would go on to become a brilliant journalist and disreputable drunk whilst Oscar made his debut in 1854. By the time Isola was born in 1857 the family had moved up in the world to the far grander address of 1 Merrion Square. Accompanied by six live-in servants, Lady Wilde was now perfectly placed to play lady bountiful to Irish society. But life would never go entirely smoothly for the Wildes and Isola would sadly die of a fever aged nine. When Oscar Wilde's possessions were filleted after his death, amongst them was a lock of his poor little sister's hair; another tragedy shared.

Merrion Square was also the location of William Wilde's surgery and it was there in 1862 that a young woman called Mary Travers claimed to have been rendered unconscious and sexually assaulted by the great man. William had without doubt clearly taken a close interest in Mary since the early 1860s but this relationship, whatever form it took, had patently soured. Following the alleged assault Mary Travers launched a sustained campaign of character assassination against William publishing pamphlets, threatening suicide to anyone who would listen and, rather bizarrely, placing garlic in the soap-trays of the Merrion Square surgery.

Understandably less than entirely delighted by this increasingly public misbehaviour Lady Wilde wrote to Mary's father complaining about his daughter's disreputable and disgraceful behaviour. Mary read the letter and, clearly viewing herself as neither disreputable nor disgraceful, sued Lady Wilde for libel. Thus the whole demented crew found themselves appearing in the Court of Common Pleas on 17th December 1864. The media of the day could not have been more delighted.

Willie and Oscar Wilde were moderately disconnected from the scandal by being happily locked away at their boarding school, The Portora Royal School in Enniskillen, some 100 miles north of Dublin; a school that also later educated Samuel Becket. Back in the city the jury eventually found in favour of Mary Travers but awarded her a farthing for her reputation. The Wilde's had to pay costs. It was clearly a verdict of a plague on both your houses.

So, by the age of seventeen, young Oscar had suffered family humiliation in a very public scandal, the death of his blood sister and the immolation of his half-sisters. Perhaps it was with some sense of relief that he left the family home and took up a scholarship to read Classics at Trinity College, Dublin in 1871. Whilst there he fell under the influence of two great Trinity polymaths: Robert Yelverton Tyrrell and John Pentland Mahaffy. They helped Wilde turn his already brilliant brain into a finely-tuned intellectual machine. Wilde was never anyone's fool - apart from when other people were listening. Mahaffy once quipped that one should 'never tell a story because it is true; tell it because it is a good story' - advice Oscar clearly took to heart.

At Trinity, Oscar was also influenced from further afield by poets such as Charles Baudelaire whose book *Les Fleurs du Mal* (1857) explored the place of beauty in the modern industrial world together with themes of decadence and the erotic. Algernon Charles Swinburne was another writer whose subject matter including homosexuality, cannibalism, pagan sensuality, time and death clearly also pricked Wilde's youthful interest.

In 1866, Swinburne published the following lines in his *Poems and Ballads*:

> Could you hurt me, sweet lips, though I hurt you?
> Men touch them, and change in a trice
> The lilies and languors of virtue
> For the raptures and roses of vice.

Such an alluring dilemma presented as a struggle between beauty and decay, between virtue and vice, was one that would transfix and inform Oscar Wilde in both his work and his life.

In 1874, Wilde arrived at Oxford and found the aesthetic life of the university dominated by two other great men of letters: John Ruskin and Walter Pater. Ruskin argued that Art had a social purpose and he focussed on the ethical, moral, social and economic benefits that could be derived from artistic endeavour. This, in more general terms, would be manifested in the work of William Morris and his mantra that one should 'have nothing in your houses that you do not know to be useful or believe to be beautiful'. Ruskin ran a ditch-digging club in Oxford so that hearty young undergraduates could display their worthiness and, unlikely as it sounds, Wilde was a member.

The renaissance scholar Pater, on the other hand, believed that we 'should burn always with this hard gem like flame, to maintain this ecstasy is success in life'. No horny-handed sons of toil for him (at least not in academic terms); instead, the purpose of Art was to transform the individual, to generate intense life-changing epiphanies that would speed on the aesthetic evolution of the self. Art for art's sake.

These two camps, as it were, should not be viewed as being mutually exclusive. Ruskin was not above a little bit of individualistic intensity himself having once being spotted crossing an Oxford bridge with his eyes squeezed tightly shut. When asked why he was risking life and limb in this way he explained he was trying to hold the image of a beautiful sunset in his mind's eye for as long as possible.

These two artistic belief-systems created a kaleidoscope of ideas that entranced Wilde just as he would juggle with the conflicts and contradictions of atheism, Anglicanism and Catholicism until, literally, the day he died.

All undergraduates have a duty to reinvent themselves and Oscar was no exception. Having discovered the liberating delights of financial credit, Wilde spent the next four years setting himself up (as his mother had done in Dublin) as the doyen of student salon society. With striking clothes, hair and height (Wilde was significantly over six feet tall) he was certainly not going to go unnoticed. At one Sunday Salon held in his beautifully decorated rooms he quipped: "I find it harder and harder every day to live up to my blue china." Such flippancies may well have delighted those present but Wilde's words could already offend those of a more sober nature. To those who believed that it was the duty of a young man to live up to his Lord and Saviour rather than his blue china, such jokes were no laughing matter. A sermon was preached at the university church condemning such irreverence as heathen behaviour that people of sterner sensibilities should 'crush out'. The moral majority were upset; Wilde was already making enemies.

But he was also making friends. It was at Oxford that Wilde met Frank Miles, who was the son of a well-heeled and well-connected Nottinghamshire cleric. Miles was carving out a significant career for himself as a London society portrait artist at the time. It is possible that they met through Ruskin. Clearly entranced by his metropolitan glamour Wilde allowed a firm friendship to develop which assisted his entry into London Society. There he began mingling with Miles' social circle and subjects including such glitterati as Lillie Langtry and Sarah Bernhardt.

In 1877 Miles secured Oscar an invitation to the opening of the new Grosvenor Gallery in Bond Street. This was the major social event of the season. The Grosvenor was dedicated to promoting the work of avant-garde artists from the pre-Raphaelite brotherhood as well as their associates from the Aesthetic Movement, such as Edward Burne-Jones, William Morris and James McNeil Whistler. Knowing that all the great and good of the city including the Prince of Wales would be in attendance Wilde was, as ever, determined to stand out. He had his tailor run up a frock-coat cut in the shape of a cello. It is so much easier to become known if one is noticed! Perhaps at this stage in his career we should think of Wilde as the grand-daddy of more recent image-shaking artists such as David Bowie or Boy George who equally understood that the cut of your cloth can make your name.

Wilde graduated with a double first in 1878 and moved his blue china to London where he took rooms off the Strand at 13 Salisbury Court. Frank Miles lived in the rooms above. Here their salon life bloomed and Wilde was often seen walking down Piccadilly with his arms filled with lilies for his celebrity friend Lillie Langtry. London was a much smaller city at that time so little eccentricities such as these were bound to be noticed, just as Oscar intended.

When Frank Miles moved to the newly fashionable artist quarter of Chelsea and took residence at Number 1 Tite Street, Wilde moved with him. However, wonderful as his life currently was, a rather ugly problem was rearing its head and staring Oscar firmly in the face. For all his flamboyance, minor fame and celebrity friends, Oscar had not actually *done* anything and people were starting to notice.

He attempted to set this right in 1881 by self-publishing a book of poems which, whilst receiving some positive reviews, was pilloried in the satirical magazine *Punch*. Caricaturing Wilde as a wilting sunflower the caption read:

Aesthete of Aesthetes!
What's in a name?
The poet is Wilde,
But his poetry's tame.

Wilde was already a favourite target of *Punch* having become firmly associated with the aesthetically ridiculous character of Jellaby Postlethwaite created by the cartoonist Gerald du Maurier (grandfather of Daphne). Postlethwaite was the epitome of the fey young aesthetes of the beau monde, mincing his way through the art-world, and simpering at sunsets and sunflowers. Over time the cartoons increasingly resembled Oscar just as Oscar (who was never one to miss free publicity) increasingly resembled the cartoons. Life could indeed imitate Art.

This strange association served Oscar well after Gilbert and Sullivan created their satire on the vanity and superficiality of the aesthetic movement, *Patience*. If Jellaby and Oscar were twins, the central character of *Patience*, Reginald Bunthorne, made them triplets. Bunthorne stormed the London stage with the hairstyle and monocle of Whistler, costumed in the velvet jacket of Swinburne and the knee breeches of Wilde. Whilst Bunthorne was not a direct parody of Oscar but rather a figure mocking all aesthetes, *Patience* nevertheless strengthened the connection between the Aesthetic Movement and Wilde.

Consequently, when the shrewd impresario Richard D'Oyle Carte was planning to tour *Patience* around north America, who better to send out as an advance advertisement for the show but Oscar Wilde? A lecture tour was arranged.

Clutching a contract from D'Oyle Carte that insisted he wear silk stockings and breeches, a velvet jacket, a floppy hat and a cape at all appearances, Wilde set sail on the SS Arizona and arrived in New York on 2nd January 1882. It was here whilst passing through customs that he famously stated: "I have nothing to declare but my genius." Such studied flamboyance once again delighted some with its wit and revolted others with its arrogance. But the tour was a substantial success and what had been planned to last four months in fact stretched out for almost a year. He met with all the American great and good from General Ulysses S Grant to Walt Whitman and the press cheerfully raved about this eccentric, effete Irishman as he toured from Philadelphia to San Francisco.

Gradually, however, the media mood turned and comments began to appear that Oscar Wilde was not so much aesthete as attention-seeker. A cartoon appeared with Oscar admiring a sunflower that was filled with dollar signs. The counsel from friends and family back in London and Dublin was that he should cut his losses and return home but, not for the last time in his life, Oscar was to ignore sound advice. Acting on his own observation that 'there is only one thing in the world worse that being talked about, and that is not being talked about' he continued the tour until January 1883.

Before his return, he convinced a young star of the American theatre, Marie Prescott, to appear in his first play *Vera*. This deservedly forgotten tragedy about Russian nihilists was not quite the success that

Wilde had hoped for. It was eventually staged at the Union Square Theatre in New York in August but received dismal reviews and closed early. Another cartoon of the day depicted Oscar Wilde skulking out of America clutching a swag bag and dressed in rags. Under his arm is the script of *Vera* and the caption reads: "A thing of beauty, not a joy forever. Rise and fall of a 'vera' Wilde aesthete."

Once back in London, an undeterred Wilde continued giving lectures on the subject of giving lectures in America and on *The House Beautiful*. We should perhaps think of him at this point in his career as a moderately well-known host of a daytime TV show. He also began work on a second melodrama *The Duchess of Padua* which he was convinced would bring him the long overdue reputation as a serious writer that he so craved. Filled with self-belief he decamped to Paris between February and May 1883 where, with characteristic generosity, he picked up the restaurant bills for all and sundry claiming 'we are dining on the Duchess tonight!'.

Paris was the city of his early hero Charles Baudelaire, and of Verlaine and Rimbaud, and Wilde clearly felt very much at home in the freer, more progressive and unashamed atmosphere of the French capital. It was a refreshing change from stony-faced England. Here, in cafes such as Le Chat Noir, he mixed with writers and painters of the decadent school discussing art, drinking absinthe and exploring the beauty of decay to the full. In a captivating painting by Toulouse-Lautrec, *La Danse Mauresque*, Oscar Wilde can clearly be seen in a seedy cabaret bar in the Moulin Rouge sporting a top hat (and significant jowls) and surrounded by Parisian low-life as he peers at the notorious and exotic can-can dancer La Goulue.

In 1884 Wilde returned to Dublin to lecture at the Gaiety Theatre where he was reintroduced to a young lady he had first met in 1881.

Her name was Constance Lloyd and something clearly clicked for the two were married in May of the same year. They set up home in Oscar's old stamping ground of Chelsea renting 16 Tite Street and this is where two sons were born - Cyril in 1885 and Vyvyan in 1886. From this happy house Oscar commuted into town to his work as an editor - first of a monthly review called *The Nineteenth Century* and subsequently of a new magazine named by Oscar himself, *Woman's World*. Domestic bliss. Except it wasn't.

After the birth of their sons Oscar Wilde turned against Constance gynaecologically speaking. Separate bedrooms became de rigueur. Something about menstruation, pregnancy and childbirth did not sit well with Oscar's sexual aesthetic and if he had ever been deluding himself in the past he was clearly coming to the unhappy conclusion (for a nineteenth century male celebrity) that he, as Stephen Fry's character in the 1992 movie *Peter's Friends* pithily put it, 'was not in the vagina business'.

The business he was in was revealed to him by a rather knowing seventeen-year-old Canadian boy called Robert Baldwin Ross. Ross had come out of the closet with the velocity of a 303 bullet and, utterly unashamed of his sexuality, was studying in London for the entrance exams to King's College Cambridge when he met Oscar Wilde in 1886. It is indisputable that seventeen-year-old Robbie seduced thirty-two-year-old Oscar and not the other way round but, having been introduced to the 'crimen sodomitae', Oscar was clearly determined to make up for lost time. By 1889, he was in a clandestine relationship with the handsome John Gray.

It was during this same transformative period in his life that Wilde's literary output took a turn for the better. Coincidence? In 1888 he published a selection of stories he had invented to entertain his much-adored sons, *The Happy Prince and Other Tales*. In 1890, he was invited, along with a young Arthur Conan Doyle, to submit an original work to the American publication *Lippincott's Magazine*. Doyle presented the world with the second Sherlock Holmes saga *The Sign of the Four* and Wilde produced *The Picture of Dorian Gray*.

Today even those who have never read this novella are probably familiar with the gist of the tale. The handsome young man (the surname Gray is clearly no accident) who makes a Faustian pact and sells his soul for eternal youth whilst his portrait ages inexorably and horribly in the attic. The favoured theme of vice beneath beauty had clearly not been abandoned. Critics and the moral majority immediately criticised the story for its decadent and homo-erotic sub-text but many bright young things were titillated and intrigued by its daring. A twenty-three-year-old Lord Alfred Douglas, then an undergraduate at Oxford and an aspirant poet, read Dorian Gray over a dozen times and was so enamoured of the tale that he managed to contrive an introduction to meet the author.

Douglas had a friend and lover, Lionel Johnson, who had met Wilde at Oxford earlier in the year when the latter had been visiting Walter Pater. Arrangements were made and the two young undergraduate fans duly turned up at the celebrity's Tite Street door at the end of June 1891. Homage was paid and Wilde was utterly smitten by Lord Alfred Douglas, the fair-haired youngest son of the Marquess of Queensbury, who would come to ruin his life.

Oscar returned to Paris in October 1891 where he managed to dash off, in French, a biblical piece of exotica called *Salome* about the temptress who would only execute the Dance of the Seven Veils in return for the head of John the Baptist. Sarah Bernhardt agreed to play the role in London but the project fell foul of the Lord Chamberlain's office who denied it a licence due to its depiction of biblical characters. The play was never staged in England in Wilde's lifetime, the ban only being removed in 1932.

However, the New Year of 1892 saw preparations well underway for the production at the St James' Theatre of Oscar Wilde's first attempt at a social comedy, *Lady Windermere's Fan*. The play opened on 20th February 1892 and Wilde packed the audience with friends and familiars ranging from his wife Constance to his latest conquest, a sales-assistant from his publishers Bodley Head, the neurotic Edward Shelley. For his inner male circle Wilde asked each of them to wear a dyed-green carnation. When asked what this symbol meant Wilde replied: "Nothing whatever! But that is what nobody will guess."

"I want a good many men to wear them tomorrow," Wilde continued. "It will annoy the public." And annoy them he did. Whilst the opening night was generally considered a success, the curtain speech that Wilde chose to deliver at the end of the performance was not. Standing in front of the curtain puffing away at a cigarette Wilde teased:

> Ladies and gentlemen: I have enjoyed this evening immensely. The actors have given us a charming rendering of a delightful play and your appreciation has been most intelligent. I congratulate you on the great success of your performance, which persuades me that you think almost as highly of the play as I do myself.

Witty enough perhaps, but to some it reeked of arrogance. The moral majority were starting to tut at Wilde again - and you do not smoke in front of the ladies in the audience.

In almost every aspect of his life Oscar was now tempting fate. Dazzled by his own fame and his recent literary triumphs he had become, in his mind, untouchable. He was utterly intoxicated by his own brilliance and cunning. Of course he could get away with anything! Lord Alfred Douglas had presented a particularly delicious temptation when he introduced Oscar to the gay sub-culture that thrived in London at the time. 'Feasting with panthers' is how Wilde would later describe his visits to the low-life haunts of the male brothels that Douglas frequented.

Blind eyes had always been turned to the private habits of certain gentlemen but in 1870 a member of parliament, Lord Arthur Clinton (who was also the godson of Prime Minister William Gladstone), brought unwelcome attention to such discreet hobbies. Clinton had been happily living 'as husband' with an Ernest Boulton who was a publicity seeking cross-dresser who went by the name of Stella. With his friend Frederick Park (who went by the name of Fanny) the two gentlemen would dress as ladies and parade in their crinolines throughout London's West End.

Favourite venues were the Burlington Arcade, the Royal Alhambra Theatre in Leicester Square and the Strand Theatre. It was in a box at the latter, when attending a burlesque of *St George and the Dragon* following a particularly long liquid lunch, that Fanny and Stella screeched their way into the public's attention. Something about these shrieking, hirsute ladies attracted the attention of a particularly perceptive policeman who promptly arrested them. They ended their night in the cells, subsequently being charged with 'conspiring and inciting persons to commit an unnatural offence'.

The howls of moral outrage that erupted in an otherwise titillated England, prompted Henry Labouchere MP in 1885 to enact an amendment which criminalised all male homosexual activity for the first time in British history. It was under this amendment that Oscar Wilde was prosecuted ten years later. A further scandal broke in 1889 when it was revealed that the telegraph boys of the Cleveland Street Exchange were delivering more than telegrams and some of their high-class clients included peers of the realm and members of the royal family. The country was clearly going to the dogs and the British public were in no mood to be lenient when it came to homosexual indiscretions.

Before this tide turned however Wilde was riding everything, including the crest of the wave. In 1893 *A Woman of No Importance* opened at the Theatre Royal, Haymarket and the same theatre premiered *An Ideal Husband* in 1895. These society melodramas, which coyly lifted the hem of Victorian hypocrisy, owed a lot to Ibsen but the naturalistic content was entirely and deliberately eclipsed by the epigrammatic wit of Wilde's writing. Whether this is a good thing or a bad thing comes down almost entirely to the taste or mood of the observer - or to the quality of the production. However, this paradoxical juxtaposition of truth and artifice, of the tragic and the trite, is at the very essence of what we call 'Wildean'.

On 14th February 1895 Wilde's triumphs continued unabated as his second West End show of the year was about to open at the St James Theatre. Billed as a 'trivial comedy for serious people' this 'delicate bubble of fancy' (as Wilde put it) was 'written by a butterfly for butterflies'. It was called *The Importance of Being Earnest*.

There is no reality in *Earnest*; Wilde had grown out of such dull cares. All the characters are witty and elegant and even when they are being vile remain utterly, utterly charming. Babies are casually lost, people lie through their teeth but all is well in this cucumber-sandwich world. But all was not to be well in Oscar's world. He had made a major enemy.

The Marquess of Queensbury (of the boxing rules) was in every possible way, to use a technical term, a nutter. Madness ran through his family in general and anger coursed through his veins in particular. His atheism meant that he was banned from taking up his seat in the House of Lords and his violent bullying and adultery meant that his wife was none too keen on him either. She won a divorce in 1887 and he would die of syphilis in 1900 aged just fifty-five. Once he became aware of his youngest son's homosexual relationship with an older celebrity, Queensbury was inflamed. When he realised that his eldest son and heir, the Viscount Drumlanrig, was also in a homosexual relationship with the Foreign Secretary, soon to be Prime Minister, Lord Rosebery, he was incandescent. When Drumlanrig committed suicide in a staged shooting accident in October 1894, Queensberry was almost certainly rendered insane.

The 1895 Valentine's Day opening of *The Importance of Being Earnest* could have ended very differently. The Marquess had hired paid ruffians to invade the theatre and pelt Oscar Wilde with rotten vegetables. However word got out and Wilde and the theatre's management hired police to prevent the protest. Thwarted and furious, four days later Queensbury stormed over to Oscar Wilde's club on Albemarle Street (incidentally the only London gentlemen's club at the time to admit women) and left a message scrawled on his visiting card. Virtually illegible it read something along the lines of: 'for Oscar Wilde. Posing sodomite'.

Once the club porter had delivered this missive to Wilde, all his sensible friends suggested he simply throw it on the fire, since only the porter had seen it. But Lord Alfred Douglas was not a sensible friend; he was a narcissistic, vengeful pederast who saw instead the perfect opportunity to be finally avenged against his bullying father. If Oscar sued his father for libel, then the wicked old man would be thrown into prison and all would be well with the world. Thus went the reasoning of twenty-four-year-old Alfred and thus the fuse that exploded the life of Oscar Wilde was lit.

The trial began on 26th April and it was the Marquess who sat in the dock. It was also the Marquess who had the money to hire one of the best upcoming barristers to represent him, one Edward Carson. The Marquess also had the money to employ droves of private detectives to interview every male prostitute in London as well as the chambermaids of hotels like the Savoy who had had to change the sheets after a night of Oscar-Alfred excess. Once this motley crew had given their testimony in public it was palpably clear that no libel had been committed. The Marquess was swiftly released and Oscar Wilde was arrested under a charge of gross indecency according to the Labouchere amendment of 1885.

The press, of course, loved it. The second trial, but the first with Oscar in the dock, ran throughout April but was thrown out after a hung jury had been swayed by Wilde's eloquence (and some magnificent playing to the gallery) in his justification that 'the love that dares not speak its name' (a line from one of Douglas's better sonnets) was as ancient as that of David and Jonathan, Michaelangelo, Shakespeare et al. Quite whether these giants of history appreciated being outed by Wilde played little on the conscience of the second jury who at the retrial in May 1895 found Wilde very much guilty as charged.

Middle-aged celebrity sleeps with teenage boys. Found guilty. It is hardly new.

What is interesting though is that the original defender of the Marquess of Queensbury, Edward Carson (who had known Oscar as a boy back in Dublin days), approached the prosecutor to ask him to drop the trial entirely arguing that Wilde's reputation was shot and that he had suffered enough public humiliation. The prosecutor by this stage had been appointed by the government and was no less an establishment figure than Sir Frank Lockwood, the Solicitor General. His reply to Carson was: "I would. But we cannot. We dare not." So, who is the 'we'?

It seems likely that the 'we' was the Liberal government of the day who had been indirectly bullied by the Marquess of Queensbury to see Wilde into hell or otherwise face the public revelations of how their Prime Minister had been using his son as a catamite. That against the background of the memory of Gladstone's godson Sir Arthur Clinton being 'married' to Stella was enough to close the deal on the greatest playwright of the age. Not for the first time, Wilde was going down.

Wilde was sentenced to two years hard labour and the judge would have given more if the law had allowed. Clearly though Wilde still had a few loyal fans left from his American lecture tour. The *St. Louis Post* of Missouri ran a headline stating:

Moral Lepers of London
English Public Opinion Cries
'Unclean Unclean!'
WILDE WILL BE PUNISHED
It seems certain he is to be made a
Scapegoat for the sins of others
Equally guilty.

Which sums up the whole sordid mess rather neatly.

Oscar had his head shaved and was initially sent to Newgate prison, then on to Pentonville and then on to Wandsworth Prison. In each of these hells he walked the treadmill and tore his nails out picking oakum - which is separating the salvageable fibres from old navy ropes. At

Wandsworth he collapsed through exhaustion and damaged his right eardrum in the fall. Infection set in and the rotting mastoid would develop into a major contributory factor to his death.

On 23rd November 1895 Oscar was transferred to Reading Gaol via Clapham Junction Railway Station and was made to stand on the central platform for an hour in his prison uniform and manacles. The passing crowds inevitably spotted the former celebrity and began spitting and jeering at him with a fervour that only the English at their most sanctimonious can truly muster. The butterfly was being mercilessly broken on the wheel.

Incarcerated in the third cell on the third level of C ward, at Reading Wilde was simply known as C33. It was here in February of the next year the news arrived that the mother, to whom he had brought the extremes of both pride and shame, had died. At the time of her death she was living with her eldest son Willie in London but his alcoholism had reduced their circumstances to the extent that the family could not afford a tombstone. Speranza was laid in an unmarked grave.

Wilde's life was unremittingly bleak but due to the campaigning of his few remaining friends he was finally allowed access to books and to writing materials at Reading. Whilst he was certainly not allowed to write plays or poetry, he was allowed to write letters and it was between January and March of 1897 in the pits of despair he began writing a long letter of agony and of love to Lord Alfred Douglas.

In *De Profundis* or *From the Depths* Wilde picks through his relationship with Douglas with the same painful precision he had used to pick oakum. Sometimes he allocates blame, sometimes he expresses affection, sometimes anger, sometimes shame. This 50,000-word dramatic monologue also explores aspects of theology, philosophy and art and their relationship to the development of the individual. Each day

Oscar had to hand in the pages he had written but on his release from prison on 19th May 1897 the Governor returned the entire work to its author. Wilde in turn entrusted it to his loyal friend Robbie Ross who had it partially published in 1905. It took until 1962 for the unexpurgated work to enter the public domain.

Fully comprehending that he was now a complete pariah in England, on his release Oscar Wilde moved to a hotel in the seaside village of Berneval-le-Grand in Northern France. He also changed his name to Sebastian Melmoth. The name Sebastian was in homage to the martyred (and more than mildly homoerotic) Saint Sebastian and Melmoth was after a character in a gothic novel written by his great-uncle. Melmoth had been condemned to wander the earth in hope of redemption from a misguided pact with the devil.

Here, by the sea, Wilde began writing again, producing his last work of note, *The Ballad of Reading Gaol*. A beautiful poem about brutality it was published in 1898 under the pen-name of C33. Small royalties began trickling in. On the economic front his estranged wife Constance (now living in Switzerland with their sons under the assumed name of Holland) also generously agreed to provide Oscar with an allowance on the proviso that he had no further contact with Lord Alfred Douglas. Needless to say this proved a stipulation too far for Oscar and by August 1897 he and Douglas were reunited in Rouen and spent the rest of the year dilly-dallying around Naples and Capri eating and drinking and flirting with waiters and soldiers. This fiasco of a relationship fizzled out in December when Douglas departed for Rome leaving Wilde to ricochet around southern Italy until, emotionally and financially burned out, he returned to his beloved Paris in February 1898.

Alas, the heady Parisian days when 'dinner was on the Duchess' were over and in April 1898 came the terrible news that Constance had died of blood-poisoning following a back operation in Genoa. One of her last comments on Oscar had been a typically generous observation 'my poor misguided husband, who is weak rather than wicked'.

Cutting an increasingly sad figure in the heatwave that blasted Paris that summer, Wilde's anaesthetic of choice was now absinthe; but champagne, beer and brandy were also convivial chums. The Australian opera singer Dame Nellie Melba, who had known Oscar at his peak, later recalled bumping into a shabby man in Paris who had said to her: "Madame Melba – you don't know who I am? I'm Oscar Wilde. I am going to do a terrible thing. I'm going to ask you for money." She emptied her purse, he snatched the money and was gone.

Following a death-bed conversion to Catholicism, Oscar Wilde died of meningitis at 1.58pm on 30th November 1900. At his bedside was the ever-loyal Robbie Ross. Always Oscar's 'fixer', Ross subsequently scoured Europe re-purchasing the rights to his literary estate, as his literary executor, which he then passed on to Oscar's orphaned boys so that they would have an income for life. It was Ross who continued to take an active interest in the arts by mentoring two young poets - Siegfried Sassoon and Wilfred Owen. It was Ross who had Oscar's body moved from the suburban cemetery of Bagneux and had it reinterred in 1909 at Pere Lachaise and then organised for the Epstein memorial to be erected over it in 1914. And it was Ross who, thirty-two years after his own death in 1918, had his ashes placed in a niche in the memorial thereby lying forever with his beloved, flawed friend.

As for Douglas? In 1902 he married an openly bi-sexual heiress called Olive Custance with whom he had a son, Raymond, who became estranged from his father and died in a mental asylum in 1964. In 1911 Douglas converted to Catholicism and began a lifelong campaign against homosexuals, particularly against Robbie Ross. In 1920 he founded a right-wing, Catholic, anti-Semitic magazine called *Plain English* and began a second career as a professional claimant for libel. No slight was left unpursued, and he became a regular figure in the law courts. In 1923 he was, in his turn, sued by Winston Churchill for his libel that Churchill had been a profiteer during the First World War. After being found guilty, he served six months in Wormwood Scrubs prison. He died aged seventy-four in 1945. In Hove.

His funeral on 23rd March was sparsely attended but one of the few who turned up to bid farewell to the sleazy sonneteer was a young actor from the Brighton Little Theatre. His name was Donald Sinden.

Opposite the house in Dublin's Merrion Square, where young Oscar was first encouraged to converse wittily with the great and the good at his mother's salons, stands a memorial to Wilde. Designed by Danny Osborne it shows Wilde reclining on a large quartz boulder wearing a green jacket of jade with pink thulite lapels. He gazes out lovingly towards two plinths on the other side of a path. On one plinth stands a bronze sculpture of a beautiful, naked, pregnant Constance. On the other stands the nude torso of a beautiful young man - Dionysus. The delightful thing is that you can't quite tell which one Oscar is looking at.

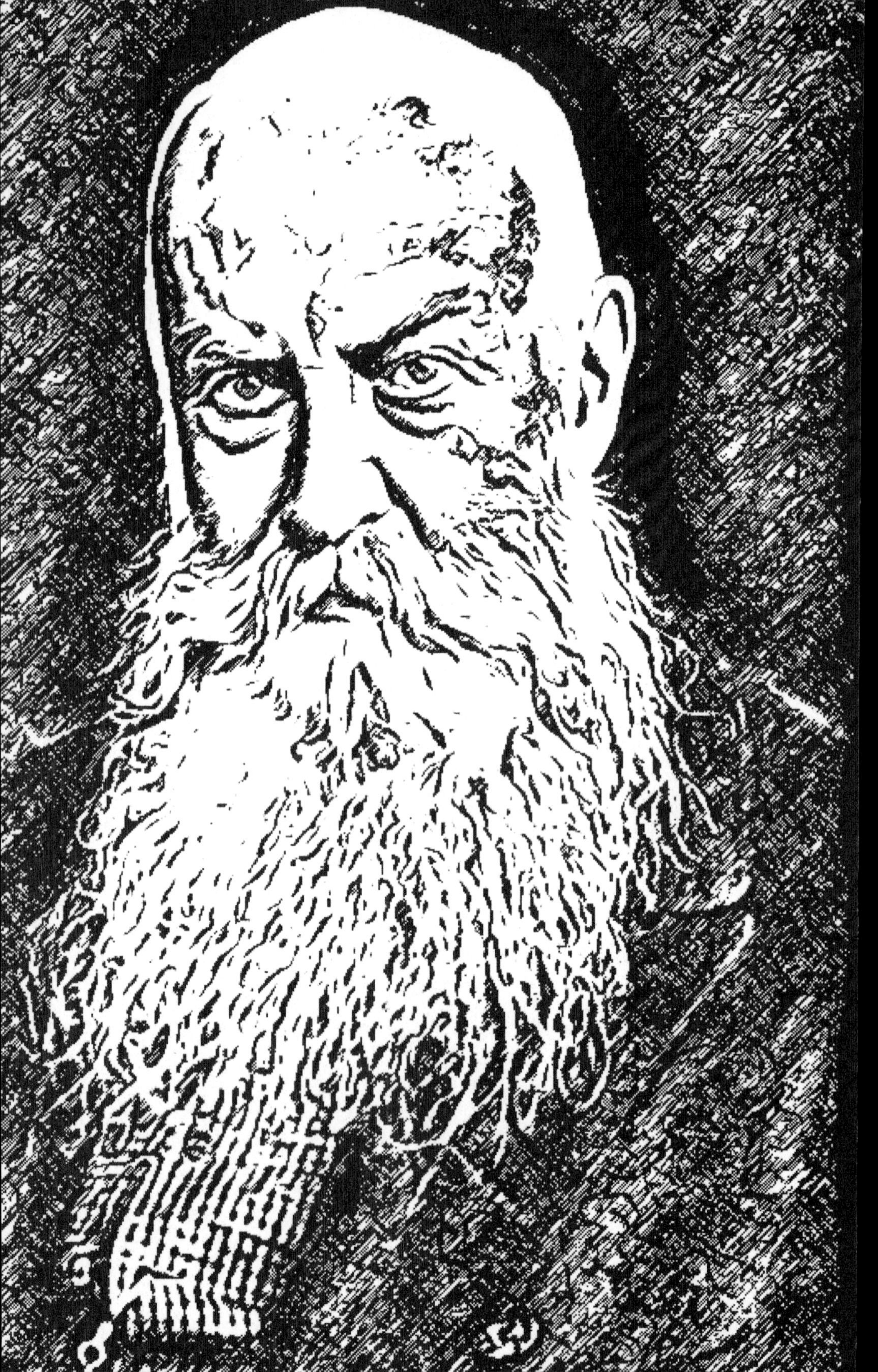

GEORG II, DUKE OF SAXE-MEININGEN
The Maker of Modern Theatre

L et us begin with Darwin. When he published *The Origin of Species*, in 1859, his radical ideas were readily accepted by the chattering classes of the day. The educated bourgeoisie were clearly happy to dispense with the idea that the world and his wife had all sprung fully formed from some divine forehead at one fixed point in time. The idea that rocks and stones and apes and men had developed gradually and that every aspect of the world had a back-story clearly had some appeal. Nothing comes from nothing. And if one could excavate the layers of the natural world and thereby gain new insights might this not be equally true of characters within novels and plays?

Alongside Darwin was Marx and Engels' *Communist Manifesto* of 1872, Nietzsche's post mortems on God in the 1880s and 1890s and, by the end of the century, Freud's invention of psychoanalysis. To add to these changing times there were eight Impressionist exhibitions in Paris between 1874 and 1886 while Wagner, Puccini and Verdi had become the dominant forces in opera. Brahms, Mahler, and Tchaikovsky bestrode the world of classical music and Zola, Tolstoy, Conrad and James led the field in the realm of the realistic novel. The chattering classes had a lot to chat about.

Captivated by all of this was a young man with a pedigree, an inheritance and a stork's nest of a beard - Duke Georg II of Saxe-Meiningen. Born in 1826, Georg was an aristocrat with far more than a passing interest in the arts. In his late teens and early twenties he travelled widely around Europe like a young Scott Fitzgerald and, as a young prince, had easy access to all the very finest of galleries, theatres, concert halls and people. Whilst extremely well-versed in the renaissance masters, he was also much attracted to the new, modern, more realistic work of painters such as Adolph Menzel or Eugene Delacroix and their unseemly depictions of unmade beds - 170 years ahead of Tracey Emin.

Georg II was not much taken with German theatre productions. In the mid-1850s there were still too many actors merely delivering stock-character performances derived from the Commedia dell' arte - young soldier, old miser, ingenue, crone. These type-cast thespians took their positions on the stage and flew solo - there was no pretence at listening or reacting to what other characters said. On the nineteenth century stage all men were islands. The sets were equally dismal, relying continuously on perspective-driven painted canvasses hung at the back of the stage thereby making it impossible for actors to move away from the front in case they ended up towering over the supposedly illusory trees and houses behind them.

After he returned home he looked at his own court theatre, the Meiningen Theatre, in a new light. It had been founded in 1776 and re-housed in 1831 and was a professional if overly traditional entity that served both the court and the community. Its associate court orchestra had been founded in 1690 and over the years it had attracted musicians of the calibre of Brahms, Liszt and Richard Strauss. However, when Georg ascended to the Dukedom in 1866 it was time for a change.

Opera and music productions were scaled down, not because he disliked them but simply because he had the good sense to realise that if his changes were to be successful then his resources must not be spread too thinly. Also, theatre had become his primary passion. During his stay in London in the 1850s he, like Queen Victoria, had been much impressed by Charles Kean's epic and historically realistic productions of Shakespeare. Georg had also absorbed the productions of another Londoner, Samuel Phelps, when they were to tour Berlin in 1859. As an actor-manager it was Phelps who, at Sadler's Wells, had begun to present Shakespeare's plays in their original form, dispensing with all the happy endings of William Davenant, Nahum Tate and David Garrick that had persisted since the 1660s. Throughout his creative life Georg saw it as his sacred duty to serve the playwright and remain true to the text.

Georg II was revolted by a theatre in which nothing was connected. Like his friend Richard Wagner who had dreamt of 'a unified work of art' Georg wanted all the disparate elements of a theatrical production - actor, dancer, musician, designer, poet and playwright - to be integrated into a satisfying whole under the direction of one man. That man, of course, was Georg.

A skilled graphic artist himself, his primary contribution to the new theatre was in the field of design. From the multitude of beautifully executed sketches for sets and costumes that still exist today, we can see the duke's beady set eye firmly on both the micro and the macro effects that could be achieved on the stage. From goblets to togas, to swords, to buttresses, to trees and to towers no aspect of what was to appear on the stage was left unconsidered. Uniquely, Georg also populated his sketches with people. He was creating a movie-style story-board, playing the entire production out, in advance, in his mind's eye.

Not for Georg the tired old painted backdrops; his theatre was going to be three-dimensional. "Don't paint me any furniture on walls!" he barked at his set builder Max Bruckner (who with his younger brother Gotthold ran the most important scenic design company in Germany. Their work included all the sets for Wagner's operas at Bayreuth). Georg cheerfully ransacked his own castles and museums for real chairs, tables, chests and wall hangings. He also understood the importance of using, to best advantage, the technology of lighting. Like Philip de Loutherbourg (Garrick's set and lighting designer) before him, Georg was way ahead of his time, using focussed electric lamps as early as 1872. One Austrian critic raved about the transition from midnight to dawn in the Meiningen production of *Julius Caesar* as being 'an optical masterpiece - never have we seen anything like this in Vienna'. These visual effects were further enhanced by the radical practice introduced by Georg of darkening the lighting in the auditorium. All eyes were now on the stage. Another innovation was the 'quick curtain' which was dropped at the end of the scene just as the last bit of action was taking place. This created a sort of snap black-out that helped maintain a sense of momentum and energy in the production.

Sound was not forgotten either. The company became famous for the attention paid to the creation of everything from thunder and lightning to gunfire and church bells. As for the actors, they were rehearsed within an inch of their lives (rehearsals were known to go on until two o'clock in the morning) and they were instructed not to act out to the audience but to engage entirely with each other on the stage. Rather than shutting the public out, this practice further lured them in. There were also no unthinking supernumeraries in these presentations - every role was played by an experienced actor who had prepared an entire back-story that motivated his character's actions. In *Julius Caesar* presented in the first season of 1866 (alongside *Hamlet* and the *Oedipus Trilogy*) the crowds listening to the oratory of Brutus and Mark Antony reacted not as a uniform mass but as true individuals responding to a political debate that might shape their lives. And there were no stars in the Meiningen company. You might be Caesar in one production and a spear-carrier in the next. The ensemble was what mattered; the whole.

In time audiences would be bowled over by what the Meiningen Players offered them. The kaleidoscope of action and effects in no way distracted the audiences but instead forced them to consider every aspect of the story the playwright was telling them because that, to Georg, was the entire purpose of the theatre.

Georg was not working alone. He was ably supported by his third wife (the previous two had both tragically died young) the former leading actress Ellen Franz and by another former actor (who had played Guildenstern in the 1866 production of *Hamlet*) Ludwig Chronegk. Georg provided the overall vision and the designs, Ellen, who was well-versed in literature and criticism, provided the literary research and Ludwig managed the intense rehearsals of the productions.

It was also Ludwig Chronegk who, in time, managed the international touring of the company. In the second half of the nineteenth century it was not seemly for a Duke to physically tour with his troupe of actors however magnificent they were. Instead, this task fell on the shoulders of Chronegk who, through a combination of circumstances, skill and industry, was to fundamentally influence the future direction of Western theatre.

In the late 1800s the Meiningen Players presented their radical productions in Berlin, Vienna, Budapest, Cologne, Frankfurt, Dresden,

Hamburg, Prague, Amsterdam, London, St Petersburg, Moscow, Warsaw, Antwerp, Brussels, Copenhagen, Stockholm, Kiev and Odessa. Throughout Europe young audience members, who had dreams of one day working in the theatre themselves, were inspired by this startlingly new way of presenting plays.

In Russia, Constantin Stanislavsky and Vladimir Nemirovich-Danchenko saw the 1885 production of *Julius Caesar* and were directly inspired to establish the Moscow Arts Theatre which was to create all the original productions of the plays of Anton Chekhov.

In Paris, Andre Antoine, who worked as a clerk for the city's gasboard, established the Theatre Libre to present a dramatisation of the novel *Therese Raquin* by Emile Zola. In 1888, he had travelled to Brussels where Chronegk & Co were presenting twenty-nine performances. Antoine was so captivated, he sat through twelve of them. On his return to Paris the developments in naturalistic acting and staging that Antoine introduced to his theatre transformed French drama forever. Like a massive stone thrown in a still lake the ripples caused by Georg II were spreading.

And it was not just realistic revivals of the classics that were included in the Meiningen repertoire. In 1886 Georg was in communication with a radical playwright from Norway called Henrik Ibsen. A production of his shocking 1881 drama, *Ghosts,* was scheduled for performance that December.

Ibsen was born in 1828 to a wealthy merchant family who lived in Skien but whose fortunes had waned by the mid 1830s. After leaving school at fifteen, young Henrik initially trained as a pharmacist but instead got distracted by dreams of becoming a playwright and the realities of fathering an illegitimate son. Although he financed the boy until he was fourteen he never met him, but instead decanted himself to the city of Christiania, now called Oslo. After failing to enter the university, he continued writing and based his plays largely on Norwegian folk-tales. These were far from triumphs but in 1851 he was appointed as writer in residence and stage-director of the newly established National Theatre in Bergen. Once there he was involved in the production of over 140 plays as either writer, producer, or director. Not a bad apprenticeship.

It was in Bergen that he also met his future wife Suzannah Thoreson. She was to become the quiet but determined force that steered his career on track whilst also being the inspiration for some of his major female characters. The couple moved to Christiania in 1858 where Ibsen took up the post of Director of the Theatre and soon after fathered a legitimate son. Sigurd Ibsen (who was destined in 1903 to become Prime Minister of Norway) later observed of his parents: "He was the genius. She was the character. She was his will and well he knew it."

However, in 1862 the theatre had gone bankrupt and by 1864 Ibsen, utterly disillusioned by life in Norway, took his family travelling around Italy and Germany. He would barely return to Norway for the next twenty-seven years.

Something was evidently released in exile because by 1865 he had written his first truly memorable play *Brand* and by 1867 his poetic epic *Peer Gynt*. The former, having begun as a 50,000 word poem, analyses the purpose of a human life and the essential human need to realise one's mission whatever the cost; the latter is the antithesis of *Brand*, as the happy-go-lucky Peer roams the world (both real and fairy-tale) living life to the full rather than searching for existential meaning. Both are verse-dramas, a style that Ibsen was soon to abandon once he realised that on this earth we live our lives in prose. "We are no longer living in the age of Shakespeare …. What I desired to depict were human beings, and therefore I would not let them talk in 'the language of the gods," he wrote to his English translator Edmund Gosse.

Three of the realistic human beings that Ibsen depicted were women and they became some of the most enduring characters ever created for the stage - Nora in *A Doll's House* 1879, Mrs Alving in *Ghosts* 1881 and Hedda in *Hedda Gabler* 1890.

When *Ghosts* premiered in London in April 1891 the critics were hysterical. The Daily Telegraph called the play:

> an open drain; a loathsome sore unbandaged; a dirty act done publicly; a lazar (leper) house with all its doors and windows open…Candid foulness…Offensive cynicism… Ibsen's melancholy and malodorous world…absolutely loathsome and fetid.

You get the drift.

What Ibsen had in fact done was show society to itself, warts, and all. When the curtain was raised on his central naturalistic dramas the audience were shown a drawing room that looked remarkably like their own drawing room. A woman might come on stage looking remarkably like your wife. A man entered who could easily be your husband. A lawyer visited and he was just like your lawyer. A doctor ministered and he was just like your doctor. It was a cosy, recognisable world. And then, in a play like *Ghosts* Ibsen peeled back the layers of the onion to expose the dark rot within.

Mrs Alving, the central character in *Ghosts*, is a widow and is maintaining the public memory of her husband, who was an honourable man, by building an orphanage in his name. When her son Oswald returns home from Paris and begins an affair with the serving maid old secrets and hypocrisies are revealed since she is in fact his half-sister being the illegitimate daughter of his father who was not quite so honourable after all. Despite being aware of the facts Mrs Alving had always been persuaded to 'do the right thing' and maintain the fiction of her happy family. At times she possibly even chose to believe it. This syndrome has often been referred to as 'Ibsen's saving lies' - the untruths we allow ourselves to believe because they make life bearable. A self-delusional coping mechanism.

As the play develops it becomes clear that Oswald is terminally ill with hereditary syphilis; the sins of the father have been visited on the son. Mrs Alving is faced with the impossible and unavoidable reality that, come the time, she will have to euthanise her own beloved son.

None of these were viewed at the time as being in any way proper subjects for public discussion as the *Daily Telegraph's* review made patently clear. *Lloyds Weekly* went further describing it as a 'morbid, unhealthy, unwholesome and disgusting story…a piece to bring the stage into disrepute and dishonour with every right-thinking man and woman'. Needless to say, young people loved the play.

Mrs Alving had submitted to life, she had 'fitted in' and she had not been rewarded for her compromises; anything but. In many ways she is an alternative-universe version of Ibsen's other major characters, Nora, from *A Doll's House* and the eponymous Hedda Gabler. Hedda, in seeking distraction from boredom, achieves only destruction. Her way of escaping from her social confines is suicide; a strong-willed woman choosing death before dishonour. This play, written in 1890, has been shrewdly described as 'Portrait of the artist as a young woman'. Against all kindness or wisdom in 1889, at the age of sixty-one, Ibsen developed a reciprocated but (probably) unconsummated passion for a twenty-nine year old fan named Emily Bardach. The impotent frustrations experienced by Ibsen through this entirely inappropriate liaison are clearly paralleled in the claustrophobic agonies of Hedda.

In *A Doll's House* of 1879 the central character of Nora eventually refuses to accept the confines of social convention at all and at the end of this startling play decides to leave not only her husband but her children as well. Not since Lady Macbeth, not since Medea had a woman behaved in such an inhuman, unfeminine and un-maternal manner; and in 1879! But Nora, in the course of the play, had learned something fundamental about human freedom. As she prepares to march out of their apartment into an uncertain future she tells her husband: "I cannot be a good wife or mother until I know who I am." Then she slams the door.

Ibsen made it extremely clear throughout his writing life that he was never engaged in an exploration of womens' liberation. At a time of political and economic revolution across the western world Ibsen was convinced that the real revolution, for men and for women, must come from within not without. Nora's husband Torvald is just as much a victim of society's conventions and expectations as Nora; he behaves in exactly the way expected of a man of his age and his standing. He has been programmed and his tragedy is that he cannot see this.

Another aspect of human existence that Ibsen instinctively understood, a generation before Freud or Jung, was that we are not always in control of our own destinies. For all our rational attempts to take charge of our lives there are other elemental pressures out there. From deep, dark fjords to ancient trolls to long lingering ghosts, these almost chthonic forces will always come back and bite us.

Towards the end of his career Ibsen became increasingly reflective and introspective, examining the consequences of actions rather than the actions themselves. In *John Gabriel Borkman,* an 1896 play about a disgraced financier (imagine Bernie Madoff is hiding in the attic), pretty much all the truly dramatic action has taken place decades before the first scene of the play. It is the aftermath of life that now interested the ageing Ibsen. It has been observed that if Ibsen had written *Romeo and Juliet* he would have begun at Act Six with the Montagues and Capulets standing before the statue of the now dead lovers bemoaning how such tragic events had ever come to be.

After his death in 1906 an inscription in the grand old man of letters own hand was found in the flyleaf of one of his books. It read: "To live is to war with trolls in heart and soul. To write is to sit in judgement on one's self."

If Ibsen ruffled a few of society's feathers, equally shocking for the late nineteenth century were the demonic outpourings of August Strindberg. Born in 1849 in Stockholm, Sweden, Strindberg's father was an unsuccessful shipping agent with an aristocratic heritage, while his mother was a serving maid with no heritage whatsoever. The observed tensions between the sexes, within and without marriage, were to become one of Strindberg's abiding themes. His most performed play is *Miss Julie* in which an upper-class woman seduces her servant. It is a conundrum as to which was the more shocking in 1888 - sex between the classes or a woman actually having and enjoying a libido. Either way it does not end well. Like Hedda Gabler before her, Miss Julie will decide that death is preferable to the degradation of the self - yet somewhere in her nihilism lurks decency. That is perhaps because, as French actress Juliette Binoche stated when she played the role in 2012, there is something noble in 'searching for the impossible idea of loving'.

If Ibsen wrote from the head, then it might be fair to say that Strindberg wrote from the gut. His plays are passionate, turbulent and extreme as he explores the unending war, as he saw it, between men and women. On the night of his honeymoon with his second wife she woke to find Strindberg with his hands around her throat. On being questioned as to why he replied: "I was dreaming of my first wife."

Strindberg was a whirlwind of contradictions. An obsessive, violent misogynist who married three times; a man who railed against the theatre (and Ibsen whom he loathed) yet made it his life. Words one associates with him are maniacal, violent, passionate, extreme, destructive, paranoid, elemental. None of them are words one would associate with Ibsen. There was something raw about Strindberg. In some ways he swapped 'slice of life' naturalism with 'slice of death' and the motto on Christopher Marlowe's portrait comes to mind - 'what feeds me will destroy me'.

Miss Julie premiered in Copenhagen in 1889 at a theatre founded by Strindberg himself; a theatre dedicated solely to the works of one playwright - August Strindberg. The Scandinavian Experimental Theatre was directly inspired by Andre Antoine's experiments in extreme naturalism at the Theatre Libre in Paris (Antoine staged *Miss Julie* there in 1893). The individual theatre practitioners who had been mobilised by the example of the Meiningen Players were now becoming an interconnected movement.

In London, a Dutch émigré known as J. T. Grein staged *Ghosts* in 1891 at the Independent Theatre Society, an organisation he had founded that same year. This was a subscription-only private members club (thereby getting around the censorship of the Lord Chamberlain's office) dedicated to 'special performances of plays which have a literary and artistic rather than a commercial value'.

Again, inspired by Antoine's Theatre Libre, Grein would *'borrow'* theatres that were dark on a Sunday and between 1891 and 1897 staged works by Ibsen, Zola, Maeterlinck and a young Bernard Shaw. In this way he introduced a challenging, naturalistic style of theatre to a whole new generation including Thomas Hardy, Arthur Wing Pinero, Henry James and the leading actor of the day, Sir Henry Irving. Irving had been much taken by the performances given by the Meiningen company when they had enjoyed a two-month residency at the Theatre Royal Drury Lane in 1881, as had the impresario William Poel.

In 1895 Poel founded the English Stage Company which was dedicated to presenting Shakespeare on an open stage with very little scenery or spectacle and using Georg II's style of unified, ensemble acting. Poel's work at the Old Vic would later lead to the great Shakespeare seasons with John Gielgud and Lawrence Olivier under Lilian Baylis in the 1920s. In time the Independent Theatre Society would be replaced by the Incorporated Stage Society which was created in 1897 in order to mount 'new and experimental plays'. The Meininger legacy was deepening like a coastal shelf.

The Incorporated Stage Society would, in its turn, be one of the catalysts for the Abbey Theatre in Dublin in 1904 and the English Stage Company at the Royal Court which would stage John Osborne's *Look Back in Anger* in 1956. Georg II casts a long shadow.

Ever since they had been transfixed in Moscow by the Meininger production of *Julius Caesar* in 1885 the actor/director Constantin Stanislavsky and the critic and literary scholar Vladimir Nemirovich-Danchenko had been determined to bring truth to the stage of Russian theatres.

"I value the good which the Meininger brought us, that is, their director's methods for showing the spiritual content of the drama. For this they deserve great thanks. My gratitude to them is unbounded and will always live in my soul," recorded Stanislavsky in his memoirs. In 1898 he and Danchenko founded the Moscow Arts Theatre and began presenting the work of Tolstoy, Shakespeare and Ibsen in a naturalistic manner. However it was the production that opened on 29th December 1898 which would make their names.

The Seagull by Anton Chekhov premiered in St Petersburg in 1896 as part of a gala evening to celebrate the career of a celebrity actress. Since the audience had come to see a star not a seagull they were puzzled, confused and bored by this seemingly incompetent play. They booed it off the stage. It was the 1898 Moscow revival that saved the play, and its author, from oblivion and a seagull remains the emblem of the Moscow Arts Theatre to the present day.

Chekhov was born in 1860 in the maritime town of Tagenrog in the south of Russia. His father had been a serf who, unusually for the time, had managed to buy his freedom and become a grocer. He was also a religious tyrant who regularly beat his six children. When Chekhov was fifteen his father became bankrupt and the entire family moved to Moscow - all except Anton who was left alone in Tagenrog to finish his schooling and mind what was left of the shop. Only joining them three years later, the young Chekhov trained as a doctor and supported himself and his family by writing comic sketches and unorthodox short stories for the weekly periodicals.

His understanding of human nature was deep and his capacity to express it on the page remarkable. People have complained that in Chekhov's plays people just sit around, drink tea and nothing happens. But what Chekhov understood and revealed in his plays is that characters on a stage should be 'just as complex and as simple as life itself. People have dinner, that's all they do, they dine; yet during this time their happiness is established or their lives fall apart'.

Reaching far further than the stage verisimilitude of even other practitioners such as Georg II or Antoine, Chekhov truly moved the drama behind the eyes as he searched for the inner psychological truth of a character; for the emotional sub-text. In a production of *Uncle Vanya* that Chekhov saw on tour in 1900 he reprimanded Stanislavsky for having directed the actress playing Sonya to collapse to her knees and kiss the professor's hands on the line 'Father, you must try and understand'.

"You mustn't do that. After all, it's not a drama," Chekhov advised. "The whole meaning and the whole drama in a person's life are located inside, not in externals."

Creative tensions dominated the working relationship between Chekhov and Stanislavsky. The former thought he had been writing comedies whilst the latter was determined to direct them as tragedies. Also, Chekhov was moving beyond pure realism and beginning to introduce moments of abstract symbolism to his plays such as the rupturing cable sound in *The Cherry Orchard*. In contrast Stanislavsky was determined to pull out all the bells and whistles of set design, lighting and sound to create a natural world on stage. Exasperated, Chekhov once told a friend:

> I shall write a new play and it will begin with a character saying 'How wonderfully quiet it is! There are no birds to be heard, no dogs, no cuckoos, no owls, no nightingales, no clocks, no harness bells and not a single cricket'.

As Chekhov wrote elsewhere, "Don't tell me the moon is shining, show me the glint of light on broken glass."

This elliptical world view is where Chekhov's true strength lay. His is a world where a man can feel melancholy but also feel hope, feel misanthropy but also recognise the nobility of man. A world where life can be empty whilst pregnant with potential, a world where we can live badly whilst we can also live well. Chekhov engages with all of the big questions about life and death, but he does it with an incredible lightness of touch. He always denied that he had any agenda but claimed that he was simply interested in human beings and how they interact and was trying to represent them on the stage as they really were. Perhaps that is why Russians refer to Tolstoy and Dostoyevsky as great writers, great geniuses, but to Chekhov as a friend. Chekhov observes but he does not judge.

The world Chekhov captured was a dying world. Since the emancipation of the serfs in 1861 the golden age of country houses and country families had been built on sand. His plays chart the slow decline of the Russian lower gentry as they are inexorably ousted from their estates, their homes and their previously comfortable way of living. Viktor Simov, who was the principal scenographer for the Moscow Arts Theatre, commented that in his naturalistic designs he was trying to express a provincial existence 'where colours fade, thoughts become debased, energy gets smothered in a dressing gown, ardour is stifled by a house coat, talent dries up like a plant without water'.

From Uncle Vanya in the play of the same name, thwarted in academe and in love, to Olga, Masha and Irina in The Three Sisters pining for the city of Moscow to where, deep down, they know they will never return, Chekhov's characters are always ruefully aware that real life is just out of reach. And so they sit and drink tea and nothing happens.

At the very end of his last play *The Cherry Orchard* of 1904 Chekhov hands the stage to a minor character - Firs, the ancient family retainer.

Having talked throughout the play about how much they loved him the family have in fact forgotten him and accidentally locked him in the now abandoned house. He takes centre stage and, fifty years before Samuel Beckett, addresses the audience directly. "My life's gone by, and it's just as if I'd never lived at all," he ponders before he lies down on the floor and quietly dies. Chekhov ends the drama with some simple stage directions:

A sound is heard in the distance, as if from the sky - the sound of a breaking string, dying away, sad.

Silence descends, and the only thing that can be heard, far away in the orchard, is the thudding of the axe.

And thus the world of old Russia leaves the stage. Chekhov, the writer of the heart, died of tuberculosis at the age of just forty-four on 2nd July 1904 immediately after finishing a glass of champagne. That same year saw the sinking of the entire Russian fleet in the Russo-Japanese war and by 1905 what was left of old Russia was being torn apart by its first revolution.

Ludwig Chronegk died in July 1891 and by the early 1900s Georg II was becoming profoundly deaf. By 1909 he no longer attended performances although he continued to design for them. However, in 1912, at the age of eighty-six, the Duke of Saxe-Meiningen rallied and with the aid of his beloved wife, Ellen, directed Bernard Shaw's *Caesar and Cleopatra*. He died on 25th June 1914.

The great theatre duke's funeral was held in the public cemetery of Meiningen on 28th June 1914. At 10.45 that same morning, the Grand Duke Franz Ferdinand of Austria was assassinated in Sarajevo.

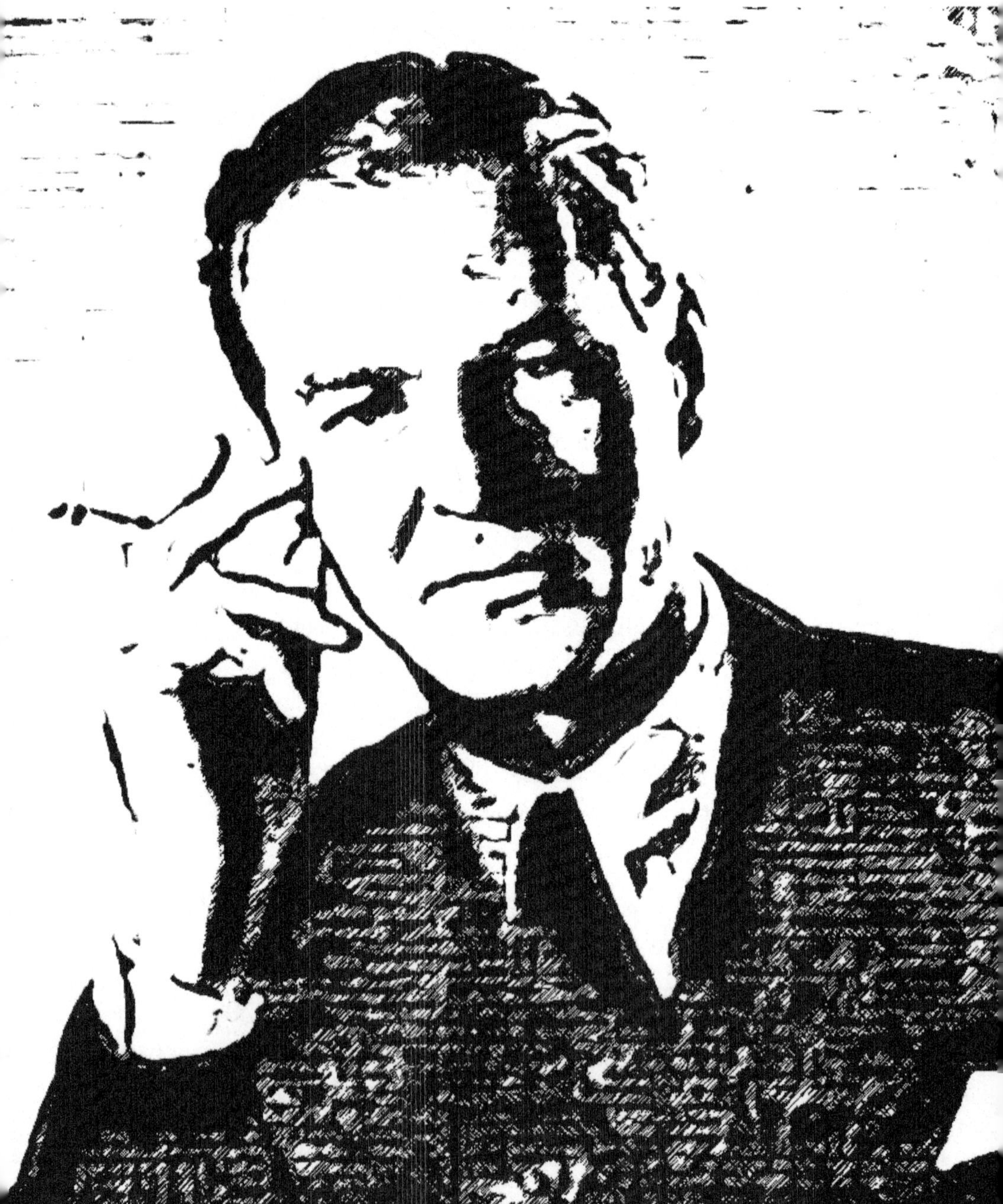

TERENCE RATTIGAN
Part One - Passion Restrained

To be educated and elegant in England has always been frowned upon. After the Second World War it became virtually illegal. In his lifetime Terence Rattigan was found guilty on both counts and suitably punished by his fellow countrymen. But now, almost fifty years after his death, it seems he has been quietly awarded a posthumous pardon and allowed to take his proper place in that rare pantheon of British playwrights; those who actually matter.

The twentieth century was an age of extremes - two world wars and the Holocaust stand in brutal contrast with the moon-shot and other life-changing innovations for good, such as penicillin and Waitrose. However, the century began with a death. Queen Victoria died in 1901 and her funeral was the last time the great and not-so-good, crowned heads of Europe gathered in their martial boots and ostrich plumes. The Great War then tore their world apart.

Born in 1911 in South Kensington, Rattigan came of age in the aftermath of this first mechanised war when the London theatre was dedicated primarily to the art of escapism. The comforting world of the Whodunnit, where obstacles are overcome and crises resolved, dominated the West End. Productions ranged from adaptations of mysteries by Edgar Wallace or Agatha Christie to the immensely successful dramas of Patrick Hamilton such as *Gaslight* and *Rope*. By 1924, Noel Coward had also stamped his mark on early twentieth-century theatre with his controversial work *The Vortex* that dared to refer to recreational drug abuse at a time when alcoholism was not even mentioned on the stage.

Little Noel had slipped in as a Christmas baby and a late Victorian on 16th December 1899. His father, Arthur, was a failed piano-tuner turned piano salesman and his mother, Violet, ran boarding houses. One of these was in in Pimlico where a young Edith Evans lived next door. Coward's mother was keenly ambitious for her son to develop the artistic talents he displayed from an early age and he was soon sent off to a dance school. By 1911 he had gained his first professional engagement as Prince Mussel in a children's play *The Goldfish,* where he was spotted by the actor-manager Charles Hawtrey. By the end of 1912 he had performed at the Garrick Theatre, the Savoy and the Coliseum - all in London's West End. The stage *was* Coward's schooling, and he learned his lessons well. His first play, a psychological drama called *The Rat Trap* was performed at the Everyman Theatre in Hampstead in 1918 which he followed up with the light comedy *I'll Leave it to You* in 1920. By 1921, the ever precocious Coward had taken himself to New York and by 1924 *The Vortex* was playing in the West End.

Fallen Angels was viewed as equally scandalous in 1925, with the spectacle of two ladies getting riotously drunk whilst waiting for their shared lover to join them. *Hayfever* also opened in 1925 by which point Coward had bought himself his first Rolls-Royce. *Bitter Sweet* opened in 1929 and *Private Lives* in 1930 by which point the Cowardian style was set. He once observed that 'the secret of comedy is to play things swiftly', an insight he masterfully applied to his writing. *Hayfever* was completed in five days, *Present Laughter* in four, *Blithe Spirit* in six and *Private Lives* in four - from his sick-bed, in Shanghai.

It is all too easy to compartmentalise Coward as the master of well-crafted light comedies who had left the shock-tactics of *The Vortex* a long way behind him. However, he was always more provocative than that. Consider, when Amanda and Elliot make their initial appearance on their respective balconies at the start of *Private Lives* it is immediately apparent that they are divorcees. This was not at all seemly to an audience in 1930, most of whom had probably been born in the 1870s.

In these inter-war years escapism was everything and Noel Coward was not the only playwright to realise that the elegant world of country-house living and Mayfair apartments sold. Night after night the curtains in theatreland opened on splendid drawing rooms replete with elegant cocktail cabinets rattling with martini glasses as dinner-suited gentlemen peered out through French-windows over perfectly manicured lawns that rolled down to the ha-ha and then on to the ubiquitous tennis court. It was one of the conventions of theatre companies at this time (and up to the 1950s) that actors, male or female, would only be provided with historical costumes. They were expected to provide all contemporary dress themselves. For gentlemen this meant tennis whites for Act One and black or white tie dinner dress for Act Three.

This was the elegant world of the self-invented éminence grise of the commercial West End theatre, Binkie Beaumont. Born Hughes Griffiths Morgan in Cardiff, Wales in 1908 the name Binkie came from a nickname bestowed upon him as a baby by ironical neighbours. 'Binkie' in the local vernacular meant blackened or dirty and when people saw the blond-haired, well-scrubbed, pink-faced baby 'Binkie' was obviously the witty Welsh response. I suppose you had to be there. Anyway, the name stuck. The name Beaumont derived from his step-father with whom his mother had eloped in 1910. He was to die in 1920 and Mrs Beaumont soon took in a lodger who was promptly promoted to the rank of 'close companion'. He was a former Army Entertainments and Welfare Officer named Major Harry Woodcock and he had just been appointed as the manager of the Cardiff Playhouse. Thus the door to Binkie's career was opened. Additionally, across the road, lived an older boy also destined for a life in the theatre - Ivor Novello.

At the age of fifteen, Binkie left school and took up a post in the box office at the Playhouse. A year later he was promoted to the rank of assistant manager at the Prince of Wales Theatre, also in Cardiff, where he was to learn the essential skills of managing a budget, staff and the press and deftly handling the extraordinary and sometimes irrational demands of touring actors. He also had a habit, which was unusual for a theatre manager, of watching the play every single night from start to finish thereby learning instinctively the alchemy of what truly worked on the stage.

By 1925 the seventeen-year-old Beaumont had moved himself to London to help run a venue in Barnes which, during his tenure, transferred five productions to the West End. He acted as business manager on each of these productions.

It was during this period that he came to the attention of Harry Tennent who was the senior manager of the largest chain of theatres and music halls in the UK, Moss Empires. The two men started working together in 1929, eventually creating in 1936 the company H.M. Tennent Limited. When Tennent died in 1941, Binkie Beaumont took sole control of the company; a position from where he dominated the London theatre world until his own death in 1973.

Binkie never sat in the audience, even on opening nights, choosing instead to stand at the back of the stalls, blending in unnoticed, quite unknown to the public. In the office he treated his staff with immense respect and courtesy (even the office boy who was called Cameron Mackintosh) and Hugh, as they called him, not only ordered lunchtime sandwiches for himself from Scott's of Mayfair but also for the staff, however lowly. Yet his eye was always on the game. One of his former secretaries, Wendy Lister, recalled his conviction that 'theatres should remain dark for as short a time as possible - always a new play en-route and in quickly'. He also never lost his attention to detail and his recognition of rank. "All letters at H. M. Tennent had to have the correct address at the top - a standard printed heading for usual letters; raised-type, die-stamped for the more important actors and directors," Wendy remembered. Beaumont would regularly run his finger over the header to make sure the correct one was being posted out.

His portfolio in the early days ranged from Edith Evans' *The Importance of Being Earnest* to Gielgud's *Hamlet*. Later he worked with writers such as Tennessee Williams and Robert Bolt whilst also having immense successes with such minor shows as *West Side Story* and *My Fair Lady* (although he did carelessly reject *Oliver* which went to Charles Albery's New Theatre instead). Contrary to lazy myth Beaumont was not solely addicted to the commercial West End. He became a founder member of the board of the state-subsidised National Theatre and championed new writers of the period such as Peter Shaffer.

Binkie Beaumont died in his bed on 22nd March 1973. Earlier that same day he had received John Gielgud and Ingrid Bergman (who were both working in his last show *The Constant Wife* by Somerset Maugham) as guests in his Georgian house by Westminster Abbey. He then attended a party where he donned a top hat and impersonated

Marlene Dietrich singing *Falling in Love Again*. Then he returned home and went to sleep.

It was Binkie's elegant world that Terence Rattigan was destined to conquer. His father Frank was a diplomat, a womaniser and a gentleman roué and his mother Vera was what is known in the trade as a long-suffering woman. However, the family trundled along elegantly enough and young Terence was sent to prep school in Surrey and then to Harrow on a scholarship in 1925. His father had been forced into early retirement after falling out with the Foreign Secretary, and whilst the family were certainly not poor, their circumstances were significantly reduced. The house in Kensington was swapped for an apartment and Terence became the boy who was allowed to visit his school-friends at their homes but not to invite them back to his. Perhaps this, alongside the realisation that his early homosexual fumblings were going to be more than a passing phase, led him towards the outsider status he maintained for the rest of his life.

In 1930 Rattigan went up to Trinity College, Oxford where he joined the Oxford University Dramatic Society and in 1932, he played (very badly by his own account) the role of 'First Musician' in *Romeo and Juliet*. He was clearly not destined for a career as an actor but this experience enabled him to observe those with greater talent at close range. A fellow undergraduate named George Devine (who would a quarter of a century later produce *Look Back in Anger* at the Royal Court) had managed to persuade an up-and-coming actor named John Gielgud to direct the show. Gielgud had, in his turn, brought up Edith Evans to play the Nurse and Peggy Ashcroft to play Juliet. Connections were made and the flame of theatrical ambition had been fanned.

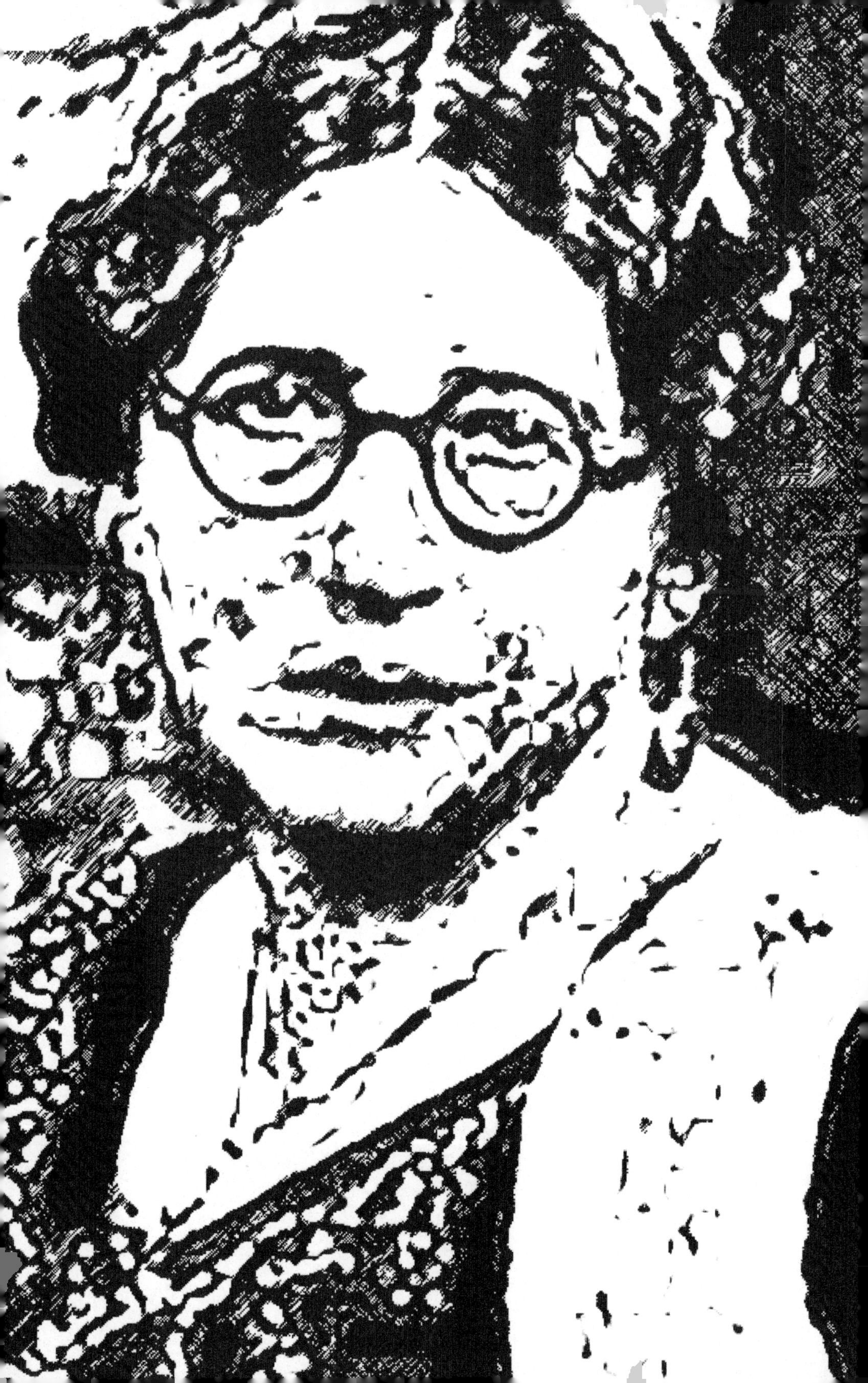

LILIAN BAYLIS
Acting for God - Praying for Lust

In a parallel universe on the wrong side (south) of London's River Thames, a year after Devine's glamorous production of *Romeo and Juliet*, a quirky, misshapen woman called Lilian Baylis was planning a casting coup for a long-planned production of Shakespeare's last play *Henry VIII*. In 1933 Charles Laughton had become a household name after starring in Alexander Korda's blockbuster movie *The Private Life of Henry VIII*. Which actor could be better casting (and publicity) for the culmination of Baylis's twenty-year project - the staging of the full cannon of Shakespeare's plays?

The project began in 1912, the year after Rattigan's birth. Lilian Baylis had an aunt on her mother's side called Emma Cons who was a philanthropist of the old school. Born in 1838 Cons trained as an artist (she restored manuscripts for John Ruskin) and, through the Ladies Art Guild, became connected with Octavia Hill the founder of the National Trust. The pair became life-long friends and it was through Hill that Cons began to address matters of social housing in south London. She became the first woman Alderman on the London County Council and social-housing and accessible arts became her life's mission. For her it was 'a crusade against ugliness'. A force to be reckoned with, Emma

Cons was noted for her extremely loud voice and her ability to occasionally wade into groups of unruly men and break up brawls. It might be fair to surmise that she erred on the butcher side of Sapphism.

By the late 1870s her alert eye had fallen on the run-down Princess Victoria Theatre by Waterloo Station. Built as the Coburg in 1816 it had changed its name in 1833 but, due to its unfashionable location, was never destined to be a venue for the higher arts. Essentially a music hall the Old Vic, as it was known locally, was the home for popular entertainers such as Grimaldi, Edmund Kean and Paginini.

After clearing out decades of shrimps' heads, periwinkle and nut shells and sack-loads of dried orange peel from the pit (nineteenth century audiences clearly being as keen on snacking during shows as their Elizabethan predecessors) the theatre re-opened on Boxing Day 1880 as a temperance meeting house for the working men and women of south London. A place of solace and self-improvement. Shakespeare was high on Emma Cons' list of what the working people of Lambeth needed alongside the more conventional and commercially viable entertainments of acrobatics, performing animals and minstrel dancing - all carefully vetted for potential impropriety.

No director herself, Cons had the good sense in 1881 to appoint the actor-manager William Poel as artistic director of the Vic where he remained until 1883. Greatly impressed by the Meiningen productions of *Julius Caesar, The Winter's Tale* and *Twelfth Night* at Drury Lane, Poel was revolted by the lavish end-on proscenium productions of Shakespeare presented in the West End with their distracting obsession with spectacle and epic crowd scenes. At the Old Vic Poel began to develop his lifelong practice of 'open-stage' Shakespeare. This minimalist style with its strict loyalty to the text became the Vic's house style and eventually the dominant style of presenting Shakespeare's work throughout the twentieth-century. Showing slightly less good sense Cons twice turned down the young Charlie Chaplin's applications to perform at the Vic because he had omitted to enclose a stamped addressed envelope.

The Cons' family money came from Manchester mills but the family obsession was music and philanthropy. Lilian Baylis' mother Elizabeth was a professional contralto singer and pianist who married a professional baritone, Newton Baylis, in 1873. Lilian was born one year later in Marylebone and from a very early age received musical tuition, particularly in the violin. She was taught by the superlatively named John Tiplady Carrodus who was the principal violin at Covent Garden. Also encouraged to play the banjo and sing young Lilian was clearly being groomed to participate in the family business.

From 1889 her parents ran an up-market and fashionable band known as the Gypsy Revellers who, in full Neapolitan Romany costume complete with guitars, cellos, lutes, tambourines, violins and banjos, performed to the great and good throughout London's larger private houses. In June 1890, for example, they played in Piccadilly at a party given by the Duke of Devonshire and attended by the Prince of Wales, the future Edward VII. However, in 1891 the entire family decamped to South Africa to fulfil a touring contract and Lilian remained there until 1897 when she contracted a kidney infection. Too ill to tour she returned to England to convalesce at the home of her aunt Emma Cons.

After 1900 Lilian took the burden of running the theatre project from her aunt's shoulders and this was the work that Baylis was fated to continue when Cons died in July 1912. Lilian immediately decided to follow her true passion for opera and applied to amend the Music Hall licence so that full operas could be staged two or three times a week. Crucially, they needed to be accessible to the local Londoners by being cheap and by being performed in English.

The character of this local audience was captured in 1911 in an adulatory description of the Old Vic which appeared in the journal *Musical Opinion*.

> The people in the stalls and balcony are mostly of the small shop-keeping and superior working classes; but it is the gallery that interests one most. One's first feeling is astonishment at finding these people present, as they mostly look like people to whom a serious work of art would not appeal. They are obviously poor, and very good-tempered tonight, taking in an excellent part the discomforts incident to a crowded house…The bulk of the people come from the neighbourhood. They are thoroughly happy; and, in the matter of quiet attention, setting an example to some West End audiences that I have known. I have never seen a more attractive or appreciative lot of people.

The Shakespeare productions continued to run on Mondays, Wednesdays and Fridays, with operas being presented on Thursdays and Saturdays. Saturday matinees alternated between the two. Ever a deeply religious woman, Baylis always claimed the Vic Shakespeare Company had been founded on the direct orders of God himself. According to her version of events she had been crying herself to sleep with stress one night when a 'strong, manly voice came out of the darkness' and told her to 'choose a company of players' and run the plays 'as you do the operas'.

Less divinely, Baylis allowed the Shakespeare productions to continue for several very practical reasons. Firstly, there were no royalties to be paid. Secondly, William Poel's legacy of experimental 'open-stage' production style kept costs very low and became 'bare-boards' Shakespeare. A disciple of Poel, Robert Atkins, became artistic director in 1921 and continued the tradition of Shakespeare on-a-shoe-string as well as building a thrust stage over the orchestra to recreate the ambience of an Elizabethan playhouse.

The third case for Shakespeare was that he was on the school syllabus which guaranteed student audiences - however unruly. In one week in 1915 an astonishing 4,000 children from the London suburbs sat through a production of *As You Like It*.

The final reason was that decent productions of Shakespeare's works were becoming a rarity on the commercial London stage. Consequently, if any serious actor wanted to broaden their repertoire and stretch themselves by playing the classics, there was only one place to go - the Old Vic.

Sybil Thorndike was one of the earliest 'names' who began to be associated with the Vic and at the start of the First World War she got to play many of Shakespeare's male leads as well as the female ones due to the increasing unavailability of men as they were called up to the front. As a way of boosting the audience's morale Baylis had two lines from *King John* hung above the stage:

This England never did, nor never shall
Lie at the proud foot of a conqueror.

Whilst historically untrue they hung there for the duration of the war.

Thorndike had been invited to join the company in the early part of the First World War by its then artistic director, Sir Philip Greet. He wrote to her saying: "There's a strange woman running a theatre on the Waterloo Road, you'd find her exciting, Syb, because you're as mad as she is … you'll like Lilian Baylis, she's got ideals."

By 1921 a young John Gielgud was playing non-speaking roles at the theatre (he returned as their star actor between 1929 and 1930) and between 1925 and 1926 Edith Evans starred in fourteen Shakespearean productions. Tyrone Guthrie, Lilian Baylis' last artistic director, continued the drive for celebrity casting (including Charles Laughton) much against Baylis' better judgement - until she saw the increase in paying audience.

All of these productions were done on the smallest of budgets in keeping with the parsimonious philosophy of the whole enterprise. The theatre critic William Archer recalled looking down during one performance to see a rat gnawing at his shoe. The stage curtain itself dated back to 1835. Made up of sixty-three mirrors the 'looking glass curtain' reflected the audience back at themselves, weighed five tons and was only replaced when it began to risk pulling the whole roof down. Ever frugal, Lilian Baylis had the curtain cut up and the mirrors placed in the dressing rooms.

She kept a small office just off to the side of the stage and during performances she would continue her work in one of the boxes. Water for the entire theatre came from a single supply on the prompter's side of the stage and the only way to heat it was on a gas ring that Baylis also used to fry up bacon and eggs for the company.

Baylis was also the mistress of cutting actors down to size. Constantly referring to God for advice on how to run the theatre, her response to actors requesting pay rises was simple. She went off into her office to pray, invariably returning with the answer 'God says no!'. She was once watching a particularly passionless rehearsal of one of the Isabella and Angelo scenes in *Measure for Measure* when she was heard to quip from the box 'well, dear - all we can do now is get on our knees and pray for lust'.

Ramshackled as the whole enterprise was, Lilian Baylis was a shrewd fundraiser and from 1923 onwards she allowed the BBC to record performances so long as they were broadcast live from the Old Vic thereby generating considerable free publicity across the nation. In interviews she would describe the Vic as being the nearest thing Britain had to a national theatre, which was to turn out to be a self-fulfilling prophecy.

In 1925 she started a campaign to re-open a derelict theatre in north London called Sadler's Wells and succeeded in doing so by 1931. The original spring waters had been bricked up during the Reformation but were rediscovered by a Mr Sadler in 1683 who built a music house with entertainments and a spa on the site. Stars such as Edmund Kean and Joey Grimaldi were regular performers there and in the 1840s it had been run by Samuel Phelps as the venue for his restored Shakespeare productions which had so inspired the young Georg II of Saxe-Meiningen when they toured to Berlin. In the 1920s the demographic of this part of town was predominantly working class and this community bore many similarities to the 'great family with a collective soul' that Baylis was familiar with from the vicinity of the Vic.

In 1926 she appointed a young dancer, Ninette de Valois, to teach drama students at the Vic 'how to move'. By 1937 The Vic/Wells company had twenty women dancers, ten men, two resident choreographers, a resident conductor, and a ballet school of forty students.

That same year, on 25th November, Lilian Baylis died of a heart attack following the shock of hearing that one of her beloved, but famously nippy, lap-dogs had been run over. She was an incongruous and often graceless impresario (she was five foot five inches tall, weighed fourteen and a half stone, diabetic and the right side of her face had been paralysed since she was a girl) but by the time of her death an astonishing array of artists had passed through her hands. The famous names who worked for her included Laurence Olivier, John Gielgud, Peggy Ashcroft, Sybil Thorndike, Edith Evans, Alec Guinness, Michael Redgrave, Ralph Richardson, Tyrone Guthrie, Charles Laughton, Vivian Leigh, Ninette de Valois, Margot Fonteyn, Robert Helpman and Frederick Ashton.

Lilian Baylis strongly believed that 'as a vehicle for broadening people's minds, as a means of teaching, the theatre is still what the medieval church recognised it to be - the greatest weapon they possessed'. Completely ignoring the purely commercial aspects of the business, her promotion of serious art for art's sake can be seen in the 1920s and 1930s as a tsunami a long way offshore - and it was coming in whether Noel Coward or Binkie Beaumont liked it or not.

Out of Baylis' theatre work the National Theatre was created in 1963. Her work with dance at Sadler's Wells led to the formation of the Royal Ballet in 1956 and her promotion of opera sung in English led to the foundation of the English National Opera in 1974. Not a bad legacy for a jobbing banjo player from Marylebone. As Lilian Baylis might have said herself 'very nice dear'.

TERENCE RATTIGAN
Part Two - Passion Released

Back in the city of dreaming spires, rather than reading history books Rattigan had begun writing plays. In 1933 he co-wrote a play with a friend, Peter Heimann, about the bright young things of Oxford. It was called *Embryo*. By the autumn of the same year Rattigan invested part of a legacy from his grandmother in producing the play, now renamed *First Episode*, at the Q Theatre near Kew Bridge where it was spotted and by January 1934 had been transferred to the Comedy Theatre (now the Harold Pinter) in Canton Street just off Leicester Square. Rattigan was just twenty-three and he had cracked the West End.

One problem loomed. Frank Rattigan had always planned for his son to follow him into the Diplomatic Corps which was something that the newly successful young playwright had absolutely no intention of doing. By choosing to leave Oxford without sitting his finals Terence managed to thwart his father's scheme and he returned to London without a degree. Rather surprisingly, after an initial explosion, Frank, gave his son an allowance of £200 a year for two years and a room with a desk at the back of the flat in Kensington. Terence Rattigan had twenty four months to produce another hit.

Six plays were written in that time and sent out to agents and actors alike, but the inevitable rejection slips began to come back by return. By the autumn of 1936 the clock was starting to tick particularly loudly when Rattigan had a remarkable stroke of luck. A play at the Criterion Theatre on Piccadilly Circus flopped and its producer, Bronson Albery, desperately needed a cheap and cheerful replacement. It came in the form of a previously rejected script set in a French language crammer based on Rattigan's own experiences of similar establishments in France and Germany where his father had sent him in preparation for the dreamed of entry into the foreign service. Called *Gone Away* it was eventually re-named *French Without Tears* and scheduled by Albery to open on 6th November 1936 with a cast that included Kay Hammond, Trevor Howard and Rex Harrison. Harrison's rather superior attitude once manifested in his refusal to sign a fan's programme as he left the theatre. The upset fan duly slapped Harrison which provoked the observation that 'this was the first time the fan had hit the shit'.

Despite a dreadful dress-rehearsal and Rattigan's natural first night nerves, the opening was a success. The show ran for 1,049 performances and within a year was being performed in Paris and New York. Rattigan had more than hit his mark and rewarded himself with a Rolls Royce. In later life he would be chauffeur-driven around London whilst he sat in the back reading *The Socialist Worker.*

During an extended stay at New York's Waldorf Astoria in 1937, Rattigan began work on the play that he hoped would elevate him from the level of 'popular playwright' to the rank of 'critically acclaimed serious dramatist'. *After the Dance* follows a group of Mayfair-living, hard-drinking, bright young things of the 1920s who, by the late 1930s, were no longer quite so bright or young. The cocktail-fuelled banter between husband and wife David and Joan Scott-Fowler might appear to be Cowardian filigree-work but, beneath the lifelong veneer of superficiality, Joan had always loved her husband very deeply. When his affections are drawn towards a younger, more serious woman, Joan's centre cannot hold and she kills herself.

This idea of hidden emotions and love between two people being out of kilter are themes that will emerge more than once in Rattigan's work. W. H. Auden's 1957 poem *The More Loving One* conveys the latter dilemma well:

If equal affection cannot be,
Let the more loving one be me.

However sensitive *After the Dance* might have been the 1939 audiences were simply not in the mood for plays about suicide and the production closed after just sixty performances. One month later Britain was at war with Germany. Rattigan hit writer's block and began seeing an Austrian-born psychiatrist in Oxford who advised him that the best way to break out of his malaise was to join the RAF and see some military action. (Note to self: avoid Oxford-based Austrian psychiatrists).

Flare Path - a Comedy of the RAF was the patriotic result of Rattigan's time in bomber command and by 1945 it was adapted for the screen as the morale-boosting movie *The Way to the Stars*.

By 1946 Rattigan had completed *The Winslow Boy*. Ostensibly a well-made play about a petty theft committed by a young naval cadet and his father's fight against the establishment to clear his name it in fact plumbs deeper depths. At a time when, through necessity, individuals across the world had been sacrificed for the greater needs of the state *The Winslow Boy* is a subtle cry for human rights and justice. The New York theatre critic John Mason Brown observed of the play that 'a small boy and the Magna Carta suddenly and somehow found themselves fused'. Revealing a macrocosm from a microcosm was becoming one of Rattigan's greatest skills.

This theatrical trope cannot be displayed better than in Rattigan's finest play *The Browning Version,* which opened at the Phoenix Theatre in 1948. Running at only 55 minutes this jewel-box of a play focuses upon the desiccated and largely wasted life of an English public school master Andrew Crocker-Harris. Crocker-Harris is a classicist who has never been able to convey his genuine love of Latin and Greek to his pupils but who has instead hidden behind the shield of stern discipline throughout his career. As a result he is known as 'the Himmler of the lower-fifth'. He endures an equally arid relationship with his unfaithful and bitchy wife Millie whilst also suffering from poor health which has resulted in his being forced into early retirement by the school's headmaster.

Rattigan, whilst popularly known as the creator of well-made plays of ideas and sparkling comedies, deep down saw himself as an English Chekhov. If you consider how many of Chekhov's characters chatter about life ('Moscow, Moscow') but often fail to actually live it then you can start to understand Rattigan's self-comparison. From *The Seagull* to *The Cherry Orchard* Chekhov observes people who can see all they need to be happy right in front of them but utterly fail to reach out and seize the moment. Thus, life passes them by whilst they simply get on with living.

This is the world of Crocker-Harris until a young boy shows him a moment of kindness by gifting him a copy of Aeschylus' *Agamemnon* in a translation by Robert Browning. From this microcosm a universal moment of redemption is ignited, a genuine catharsis. Oedipus-like

Crocker-Harris weeps and, in the smallest way, is re-born ready to fight on both fronts - the school and his wife.

Love out of kilter, passion restrained and quiet moments of redemption are the key themes in Rattigan's best works. He knew each of these emotional states intimately through his own life as a discreet homosexual at a time when such a hobby was definitely not for public consumption. It was perfectly fine for Terry, Binkie and Noel to know in detail what each of the other was up to but the audience must never, ever know the truth. On 20th October 1953 John Gielgud was almost ruined when he was caught importuning men for immoral purposes in a Chelsea public lavatory. Gielgud's sexual learning curve was clearly not particularly steep since, in the July of the same year, he had got himself into a similar pickle in Bulawayo in Zimbabwe - then Rhodesia - whilst touring a production of *Richard II*. Considering the times, Gielgud got off lightly for his Chelsea escapade receiving a £10 fine. Fortunately for him, he had already received his knighthood from the Queen the previous June. Also, as it turned out, his audiences were remarkably generous and forgiving but that was not the general assumption or experience of the theatre fraternity at the time.

Rattigan's relationships ranged from the Member of Parliament Sir Henry 'Chips' Channon to a young actor named Kenny Morgan. Morgan, who was kept secret and compartmentalised from Rattigan's public life, became increasingly neurotic about their affair and then left him for a new boyfriend, Alec Ross, before committing suicide by gas on 1st March 1949. Statistically, for those of you who care about such things, gas was the suicide method of choice for men in that era. News was brought to Rattigan the next afternoon at his hotel in Liverpool where he was touring a show. Shell-shocked but functioning, by the evening he was heard to say 'the new play will open with the body discovered dead in front of the gas fire'.

It is at this juncture we should perhaps acknowledge the astounding fact that great artists aren't always normal. Rattigan was genuinely grief and guilt-stricken but this did not prevent him from multi-tasking and seeing the first scene of a play through his tears.

The play that emerged from this tragedy was *The Deep Blue Sea*. Contrary to theatrical gossip there never was a 'gay' version of this play. Instead, Rattigan translated the pain of the homosexual ménage into a heterosexual environment in order to smuggle his emotional message out to the stalls in a palatable manner that a 1950s audience would be able to accept. In many ways it is this very constraint on his writing that provides its strength. Through indirection Rattigan enables the emotionally inarticulate English to find their own direction out.

The Deep Blue Sea opens with Hester Collyer, the self-estranged wife of a High Court judge, lying unconscious in a down-at-heel boarding house by the gas fire having just tried to end her life. Having scandalously followed her obsessive passion for a feckless, alcoholic but handsome airman called Freddie Page, Hester had found herself marooned by him and forced to face the world alone; something she did not have the strength to do. After accidentally surviving her suicide attempt (there weren't enough coins in the gas meter) Hester finally finds the motivation to live 'beyond hope'. This is achieved through the redemptive intervention of a kindly fellow lodger - a struck-off doctor who has also known disgrace.

The same tactic of moving from microcosm to macrocosm that gave *The Browning Version* and *The Deep Blue Sea* their strength also creates the emotional motor behind Rattigan's 1954 *Separate Tables*.

Consisting of two one-act plays the themes of loneliness and humiliation arise again as a disgraced Labour politician and a disgraced army major try to find a modicum of victory in life through the rediscovery of self-respect. Chekhov understood the human heart and Rattigan understood that, contrary to popular misconception, the English middle classes also have feelings.

However, the times they were a-changin'. Long before Bob Dylan put pen to paper the Second World War, the Holocaust and the atom bomb had knocked the stuffing out of the status quo. In Britain the returning soldiers voted Winston Churchill out of office just two months after VE Day. Their fathers had returned from the trenches of World War One and been promised homes for heroes but little really changed. These young men were not going to make the same mistake and slowly, but inexorably, social deference was going to wither whilst social mobility was going to flourish.

Everything in Britain from the new Welfare State to the founding of the Edinburgh Festival in 1947 reeked of optimism and change. With the accession of a new young monarch in 1952 many in Britain were looking forward not backwards and for theatre audiences the 1950s were going to be a very exciting time indeed.

Not every member of an audience is there just to be entertained nor even just to be stimulated and challenged. Some are theatre Wannabes. They are the ones who want to become involved in the game, play their part and become the next generation of actors, directors, designers and writers. These Wannabees were there at the first performance of Marlowe's *Tamburlaine*, they were there for Garrick's debut as *Richard III* and they were there for the premiere of Ibsen's *Ghosts*. And when the curtain fell on each of these ground-breaking debuts the Wannabees sat up in their seats and knew exactly which direction they wished to go - ever forward.

If you were a young theatre Wannabe on the 3rd August 1955 you might well have made your way to Great Newport Street in London's Covent Garden and taken your seat in the gods of the tiny Arts Theatre. On that night English theatre history changed with the première of Samuel Beckett's *Waiting For Godot* directed by a young and ambitious Peter Hall. This is the play in which, famously, nothing happens – twice. Initially the critics detested the production and the great character actor Robert Morley observed: "I have been brooding in my bath for the last hour and have come to the conclusion that the success of Waiting for Godot means the end of the theatre as we know it."

The Sunday critics - Kenneth Tynan and Howard Hobson - thought differently. By September 1955, the production had transferred to the Criterion Theatre on Piccadilly Circus (where *French Without Tears* had opened) and ran until March of the next year. In one fell swoop Peter 'Very Sanderson' Hall had made his name and Beckett was in the English repertoire whether some members of the audiences liked the fact or not.

Beckett's plays are based not on plot but on place - even if the nature of that place is never clearly defined. His characters roam these wilderness-worlds, usually without hope of escape, confined within the limits of their own memories. Time is compressed to an eternal present and individuals are yoked to their neighbours by need, laziness or even by a rope. In *Godot* the four central characters, with their Russian, Italian, French and English names, form a composite Everyman with whom we either do or do not connect as they search for meaning in a seemingly meaningless universe.

Alternatively, in a parallel universe, Samuel Beckett is one of the most consummate old frauds the theatrical world has ever known. Devoid of plots, the canny Irishman's oeuvre consists entirely of half-thought-out sketches which, in the longer plays (knowing he has shamelessly omitted to provide a punchline) Beckett painfully extends and repeats in a loquaciously cyclical manner in order to distract the audience from the basic fact that within the work there is a staggering lack of content. Some people say that this is what life is really like. Bad luck them.

Many actors love Beckett. Partly because, without the distraction of having to drive the plot, they have the whole evening on the stage to themselves to display lots of lovely technique. Also, because in those grainy black and white photographs taken in enigmatic exile in Paris, our Samuel's face is far too romantically craggy not to be wise. There must be depth in those lines. Essentially, in Beckett's world, people bicker and nobody moves either because they are standing in dustbins, buried in earth or simply because there is nowhere for them to go. However, there is usually some wit in fraud and the plays can be extremely funny, even if it is the humour of the gallows.

"That passed the time" says Vladimir to Estragon, who replies, "it would have passed in any case."

It is not surprising that *Godot* has always gone down well in prisons (where the audience, like Beckett's characters, are forbidden to depart) including, in 1957, to an audience of 1,400 inmates of San Quentin State Prison in California.

Anyway, you can make up your own mind.

Rattigan's response to Beckett was clear. Two years before *Godot* opened in London he had created a controversial caricature of an archetypal theatregoer in the preface to his collected plays. He had called her Aunt Edna.

> Let us invent a character, a nice respectable, middle-class, middle-aged, maiden lady, with time on her hands and the money to help her pass it. She enjoys pictures, books, music and the theatre and though to none of these arts (or rather, for consistency's sake, to none of these three arts and the one craft) does she bring much knowledge or discernment, at least, as she is apt to tell her cronies, she 'does know what she likes'. Let us call her Aunt Edna.

There were several problems with this creation. Firstly, it made the creator seem smug, superior and out of touch whilst, secondly, it offended Rattigan's female fan base who did not much appreciate being depicted as 'middle-brow'.

It was in the voice of Aunt Edna that Rattigan responded to the production of *Godot* at the Arts Theatre. "How could I like the play," Edna opines, "seeing that Mr Beckett plainly hates me so much that he refused point blank to give me a play at all." With such condescension Rattigan missed the point that the tectonic plates of theatre were shifting beneath his feet and he was wearing the wrong shoes. That is the problem with revolutions in the arts - they make what came before suddenly look stale.

In 1956 the Berliner Ensemble arrived in London for the first time and introduced the radically innovative propaganda plays of Bertolt Brecht to all those eager young theatre Wannabes. Rattigan dismissed him as 'a cracking, pedantic, didactic, ill-translated old Marxist bore'.

But the Wannabes ventured to disagree - as they were to do again that same year over a production at the Royal Court Theatre.

George Devine, who we last met in Oxford producing *Romeo and Juliet*, escaped to London in the mid-1930s and was one of the co-founders of the London Theatre Studio in Islington which was the first drama school in England to teach theatre design as well as acting. In 1939 he also directed Alec Guinness' stage-adaptation of *Great Expectations* which later became the basis of David Lean's stunning film version in 1946. Incidentally, Guinness had been a student at the London Theatre Studio as had a young Peter Ustinov.

After spending part of the war in Burma, Devine returned to England and founded the Old Vic Theatre School in Dulwich which was to produce alumni such as Prunella Scales and Joan Plowright. He also founded the Young Vic Theatre Company whose mission was to perform the classics to a young audience.

By 1954 Devine, alongside the young director Tony Richardson, founded the English Stage Society (re-named the English Stage Company in 1955) in order to get 'writers of serious pretensions, back into the theatre' and in order to make the theatre 'part of the intellectual life of the country'. The company took a lease on a bomb-shattered theatre in Chelsea called the Royal Court which had been a home for new writing in the early 1900s under the watch of Harley Granville-Barker and Bernard Shaw. The original plan had been to house the ESC at the Kingsway Theatre in the heart of London's West End but this proved too expensive to re-furbish so Chelsea lucked out.

In January 1955 advertisements were placed in *The Stage* newspaper requesting new plays from new writers - so long as they did not include cocktail cabinets, French windows or a ha-ha. Seven hundred and fifty scripts came in and the first season opened on 2nd April 1955 with *The Mulberry Bush* by Angus Wilson. (The preceding production had been of Brecht's *The Threepenny Opera* which ran from 9th February to 20th March 1955 and then transferred to the Aldwych Theatre in the West End. It was directed by Sam Wanamaker). Arthur Miller's *The Crucible* opened a week later, on 9th April, followed by two verse dramas by Ronald Duncan, *Don Juan* and *The Death of Satan* on 15th May.

The 26th June saw the premiere of *Cards of Identity* by Nigel Dennis (whose uncle's wife, Phyllis Bottome, created James Bond*) followed on 31st October by *The Good Woman of Setzuan*. This first season ended on 12th December with a revival of William Wycherley's *The Country Wife*. Actors in the repertory company of 1956 included Rachel Kempson, Joan Plowright, Joan Greenwood, Nigel Davenport, Alan Bates and Robert Stephens.

Another unknown actor, who had three bit-parts in *Cards of Identity*, also had a play he had written included in this first season. One week before he took on the roles of Dr Scavenger, Custodian and Second Aunt in Nigel Dennis' play his own work opened on 8th May. It was called *Look Back in Anger*.

John Osborne sidled into the world on 12th December 1929. He was born in the Crookham Road, Fulham, then a drab corner of west London, to Nellie Beatrice, a sharp-tongued barmaid who he detested and Thomas Godfrey, a copywriter who he adored. When he was seven years old the family moved to the even drabber suburb of Stoneleigh which Osborne hated even more than his mother and desrcibed as 'a Byzantium of pre-war mediocrity'. In 1941 Osborne's father died of tuberculosis and two years later, funded by a Benevolent Society, twelve-year-old John was sent to a very minor pseudo-public school, Belmont College in Devon. He was duly expelled in 1945 for punching the headmaster in the face thereby having to find himself work in his father's old trade by providing copy for such riveting titles as *Nursery World, Gas World* and *The Miller*.

Once he was back in Stoneleigh with his mother sheer boredom drove him first to dancing classes and then to a small drama school in Leatherhead where he bashed his way through the plays of J. B. Priestley and Noel Coward. Enjoying the attention the stage provided he was hooked. By 1948 he had joined a mediocre touring company alternating as stage manager, understudy and tutor to the child actors as it dragged a tired old pot-boiler *No Room at the Inn* around Sunderland, Southport, Norwich and Grimsby. The antithesis of a glamorous life.

By 1951 he was touring in a company run by a RADA-trained actor called Anthony Creighton who had slept with Terence Rattigan whilst in the RAF. Osborne and Creighton schlepped their way around Hayling Island, Ilfracombe and Sidmouth parading their tawdry theatrical wares through the faded repertory theatres of post-war England. As an antidote to the drudgery of bit-part acting, Osborne turned to writing fantastical roles that he would only ever play in his imagination. He also collaborated with Anthony Creighton on two plays, *Personal Enemy* and *Epitaph for George Dillon,* which were both produced in the late 1950s following the success of *Look Back in Anger.* By 1955 the two were sharing an old barge on the river Thames by Chiswick Bridge. As to whether they were lovers at this time is a point of contention. Creighton claimed yes; Osborne claimed no. Consequently we shall never really know. What we do know is that whatever Osborne got up to when the barge hatch was down he had been married to fellow actress Pamela

Lane since 1951 and was to squeeze in four more heterosexual marriages before his death.

Between 4th May and 3rd June 1955 Osborne was stuck on Morcambe Pier playing in the unpromisingly named *Seagulls Over Sorrento*. In between shows, he bashed out *Look Back in Anger* on an Olivetti typewriter he had liberated from his now estranged wife, Pamela Lane. Originally titled *Farewell to Anger* it morphed through *Angry Man, Man in a Rage, Bargain From Strength, Close the Cage Behind You* and *My Blood is a Mile High*. However, it was a manuscript with the title *Look Back in Anger* that George Devine received at the Royal Court in response to his advertisement for ha-ha free plays in *The Stage*.

The opening night of *Look Back in Anger* on 8th May 1956 was rather like the Mayflower. If all the people who claimed to be descended from passengers on the latter had truly had ancestors on board the Mayflower would have sunk in the harbour at Plymouth. Equally, as Osborne himself quipped throughout his life, all those who later claimed to be at his opening night would have in fact filled the Albert Hall.

Two men who definitely were in the audience that night were Binkie Beaumont and Terence Rattigan. Beaumont left at the interval but Rattigan was persuaded to stick it out until the end. Unimpressed, as he left the theatre he was asked by a waiting journalist from the *Daily Express* what he thought of the play. Terence's ill-considered, conceited and superior reply was that Osborne was merely shouting 'Look, Ma, I'm not Terence Rattigan'. Not for the first time Rattigan had misjudged the mood of the moment.

The public found an attractive and exciting dynamism in the ragings of Jimmy Porter whilst Rattigan in their mind was starting to resemble the elderly Colonel in Osborne's play who is 'one of those sturdy old plants left over from the Edwardian wilderness that can't understand why the sun isn't shining anymore'. The tsunami that had begun offshore way back in Lilian Baylis' Old Vic in the 1930s had finally hit land and Binkie and Terry and Noel were suddenly all looking very washed up indeed.

Look Back in Anger's popularity reached further afield than the London metropolitan audience. Within twelve months productions had been staged at the Cambridge Arts Theatre, the Bristol Old Vic (starring Peter O'Toole), the Nottingham Playhouse and the Theatre Royal, Bath. The Angry Young Men were in the ascendant, although this label originated by accident. The press officer at the Royal Court, George Fearon, disliked *Look Back in Anger* and dismissed Osborne by saying 'I suppose you're really - an angry young man'. The phrase made its way to the ears of arts journalists and the soubriquet stuck.

And now the Fates began tugging at Rattigan's wings. He had adapted his Coronation year play *The Sleeping Prince* for the screen as *The Prince and the Showgirl* and by 1956 was in his element as he feted his celebrity cast - Laurence Olivier, Vivian Leigh, Marilyn Monroe and Arthur Miller - through lavish parties at his country house, Sunningdale, in Berkshire (throughout his life he would collect further properties in London, Brighton and Bermuda). When Monroe and Miller arrived in London on 14th July 1956 it was the obvious and courteous thing for their chum Olivier to offer to escort them to any play in town they wished to see. Annoyingly for Olivier they chose *Look Back in Anger* since he loathed the play, finding it to be brutal and unpatriotic.

Even more annoyingly, Miller loved the play and told Olivier so. Never one to miss a trick and suddenly realising that there might be some theatrical future for this 'travesty on England' Olivier sought Osborne out at the post-show drinks. He asked him: "Do you suppose you could write something for me?"

Laurence Olivier's 1957 appearance, against type, as the washed-up music-hall hoofer Archie Rice in the almost Brechtian *The Entertainer* was as much a theatrical landmark as Osborne's debut the previous year. Olivier suddenly made the avant-garde respectable, and he would not be the last West End actor to make the jump to the Royal Court.

Osborne had grown-up with and loved the old vaudevillian Max Miller and he had never forgotten the rusting old Victorian piers and dilapidated Edwardian theatres he had toured in the early 1950s. What a wonderful metaphor for post-war Britain in the grip of the Suez Crisis! Later, in 1962, Dean Acheson, President Truman's Secretary of State, would opine in a speech at West Point that 'Great Britain has lost an empire but not yet found a role'. With the plaster falling off the theatre walls and Archie Rice's jokes and routines clearly well beyond their sell-by date, modern Britain was shown up for what it was - an out-of-date fantasy desperately trying to punch above its weight. Within a few short years Osborne had manoeuvred himself from jobbing actor in end-of-the-pier shows to celebrity playwright and screenwriter. It was Osborne who won the Oscar in 1963 for the movie of *Tom Jones* and now it was Osborne who had the flat in Chelsea, the country house and the smart cars to convey him between the two. Working class made very good.

However, in many ways Osborne's career was a short one since his talent simply failed to truly develop. The splenetic energy of *Look Back in Anger* declined into long, ranting tirades against the world; more monologues than dramas. Also, like Rattigan, he could often wilfully alienate his own public. His vitriolic letter to his fellow countrymen in 1961, *Damn you England,* opened with the lines:

> This is a letter of hate. It is for you, my countrymen ... the men with manic fingers leading the sightless, feeble, betrayed body of my country to its death. You are its murderers. And there's little left in my own brain but the thoughts of murder for you.

The letter might have had more moral clout if it had not been written from Valbonne in the south of France.

Osborne was a mass of contradictions. A radical class-iconoclast who ended his days as a country squire in Shropshire campaigning for the reinstatement of the Anglican Book of Common Prayer. He was a genial and generous host who could, when minded, drunkenly demand that house guests stay up and entertain him until the very early morning. He was also a five times married husband whose bullying behaviour drove two wives to suicide and one to drink whilst his last wife, Helen Dawson, clearly adored him – and they had all loved him once! He was an actor who could return to the screen in 1971with a perfect cameo in the crime thriller *Get Carter* but make a rather less successful appearance as an Arborian Priest in *Flash Gordon* in 1980. For as many people who have described him as a monster there are an equal number who tell of his capricious charm, wit and kindness; clearly he was all these things. Osborne's liver crashed in 1987 and he died in 1994 at the age of sixty-five.

Britain in the 1950s might have been drab but the theatre most certainly wasn't. In London's East End at the Theatre Royal, Stratford East, Joan Littlewood was running her innovative Theatre Workshop. Cut from similar cloth to Lilian Baylis, Littlewood was a theatrical force of nature and took few, if any, hostages. When Irish navvies were re-painting the venue they complained about *her* language. Her theatre opened in 1953 with a production of *Twelfth Night* and was committed to presenting a mixture of classic and modern plays which had socially relevant themes. By the end of the decade, it was specialising in improvisational 'workshopped' theatre. *The Quare Fellow* and *The Hostage* by the guttural Brendan Behan appeared in 1957 and 1958 respectively. In 1958 Littlewood also presented a much-finessed version of Shelagh Delayney's *A Taste of Honey*.

Delayney, who had left school at sixteen and was living in Salford in Northwest England, had been inspired to put pen to paper after seeing a touring production of one of Rattigan's plays *Variations on a Theme*.

"What on earth has this got to say to me?" she asked herself, and decided to create something more relevant, contemporary and gritty. Focussing on the life of a seventeen-year-old girl, Jo, the play overtly addresses illegitimate pregnancy, inter-racial relationships and homosexuality. This was rich fare for 1958 and very un-Rattigan. The play went to Broadway in 1960 starring Joan Plowright and Angela Lansbury; as with Olivier in *The Entertainer*, mainstream actors were now embracing the new 'kitchen sink' drama.

Variations on a Theme was based on the 1848 novel *La Dame aux Camelias* by Alexander Dumas fils. It was directed by John Gielgud, and the best *The Observer's* critic Kenneth Tynan could produce by way of praise was flattery for the costumes by Norman Hartnell who usually designed dresses for the Queen and her mother.

In 1958 another new voice smashed its way onto the English stage in the form of Harold Pinter's *The Birthday Party*. His unique writing style was inspired partly by his life as a young Jewish boy growing up in Hackney in London's East End where anti-Semitic violence could bubble up at any moment and partly by the waspish menace of Jacobean tragedy which Pinter adored from his schooldays onwards.

When the curtain goes up on many of Pinter's plays, we see an innocuous-looking room as realistic as any of those in which Ibsen's central dramas unfolded. It could be your kitchen or your study. The characters in these rooms seem equally part of the real world until, after a while, we begin to wonder if we know who they actually are. As the plays unravel, we begin to sense that the characters themselves might not be quite sure who each other is let alone, in fact, having any real certainty about who they are themselves. In such an unsettling universe it is perhaps understandable that they devise a variety of desperate coping mechanisms whilst wielding the weapons of language, territory, status and class in order to withstand the onslaughts of a dangerous and disconcerting world.

There is way more to this confusion than mere absurdist game-playing. Pinter is dealing with something much more profound. When Deborah, the central character in his 1981 one-act play *A Kind of Alaska,* wakes up after spending thirty years in a coma her first words are 'Something is happening'. The doctor by her bedside replies 'Do you know me?'. This is real life in all its puzzling confusion. Things do indeed happen but what or whom do we really know?

We all live our lives through the prism of our perceptions and our self-analysis of those perceptions. Yet, in daily reality, we know that four people in the same room might all interpret the same shared event differently. Most marital disputes are founded on this principle and in a 'woke' world where 'my truth' can trump 'your truth' Pinter's observations are no longer even that wildly theatrical.

The only true identity that many of Pinter's characters possess is that which they create for themselves in each momentary action within the play. This identity is then re-made (or contradicted) by the next action and so on and so on. Moment A provokes moment B which elicits moment C. There is no overarching purpose or authorial devised plot. One line simply instigates a response which becomes the next line.

"I have usually begun a play in quite a simple manner," Pinter explained. "… found a couple of characters in a particular context, thrown them together and listened to what they said, keeping my nose to the ground."

Explaining the origins of his first play *The Room* he said:

I went into a room one day and saw a couple of people in it … I started off with this picture of two people and let them carry on from there…I went into another room and saw two people sitting down, and a few years later I wrote *The Birthday Party*. I looked through a door into a third room and saw two people standing up and I wrote *The Caretaker*.

Pinter declines the privilege of possessing a greater knowledge of his characters than his audience. And he further resists the temptation to divine any significant scheme or pattern of meaning in their actions. We are all, playwright and audience alike, merely eavesdroppers on other people's moments.

If Pinter is not in direct control of his characters, then what he does provide them with is 'shape, structure and overall unity'. In 1961 he said: "My characters and I inhabit the same world. The only difference between them and me is that they don't arrange and select." With clarifications like this it is easy to see why the great Broadway critic, Walter

Kerr, observed that Pinter is 'the only man working in the theatre today who writes existential plays existentially'.

As characters interact (or fail to interact) a sense of unease arises within the plays - 'the weasel under the cocktail cabinet' as Pinter himself put it when responding to the question 'what are your plays about?'. Characters try to discover how to survive as themselves in a Kafkaesque world where everyone else is also trying to survive as themselves. But in Pinter's world all shall most certainly not have prizes. The cold-war era with its ever-present threat of nuclear annihilation is also reflected in the plays through the unsettling feeling Pinter creates that violence could erupt at any moment (an idea Sarah Kane developed in her play *Blasted* in 1995). In the recently post-war world in which Pinter was working the fear of unknown outside forces invading someone's private space was all too familiar. The over-riding tone of Pinter's plays is that of an unbearable tension building up whilst you sit, alone or with others, anticipating the knock at the door.

All that said, as with Beckett, some people take a contrary view and perceive Pinter as a pretentious peddler of plotless piffle. This school of thought is pithily represented by the English satirist and stalwart of Private Eye Craig Brown in his Pinteresque parody of the children's nursery rhyme *Polly Put the Kettle On*:

Polly, put the kettle on.
Polly put the kettle on.
Polly put the kettle on.
Polly, PUT THE KETTLE ON.
Not here Polly?

How many more fucking times do I have to fucking tell you to put that fucking kettle on!

A second working class Hackney-Jewish voice emerged at the end of the fifties with Arnold Wesker's Royal Court productions of *The Kitchen* and *Chicken Soup with Barley* - unflinchingly realistic plays that sympathetically explore the contrast between socialist idealism and un-idealised human reality. "You have to start with love," says Sarah in *Chicken Soup*. "How can you talk about socialism otherwise?".

Beckett in 1955; Osborne and Brecht in 1956; Delaney, Pinter and Wesker in 1958. Extraordinary times. 1960 saw the legal, unexpurgated publication of *Lady Chatterley's Lover* and the rise of the satire boom with *Beyond the Fringe*. Where was deference? Where was beauty? Where were the ha-has when you needed them? Rattigan was increasingly bothered and bewildered finding himself to be a man out of his times. As he confessed to an interviewer shortly before his death almost twenty years later, he could no longer contend with the critics who dismissed his work as 'just the old effete theatre' that has 'nothing to do with the ongoing movement of the time'. By the mid-1960s the English Chekhov decided to move abroad.

He began to rattle restlessly around Italy and France until he settled on a home in Bermuda where he would live on-and-off as a tax exile until his death. He continued writing plays to little critical acclaim whilst his work on lucrative movies such as *The VIPs* in 1963 and *The Yellow Rolls-Royce* in 1964 and the sentimental and nostalgic *Goodbye Mr Chips* in 1969 made him one of the highest paid screen-writers in the world. The discrepancy was clear for all to see.

Rattigan was honoured with a knighthood in 1971 but booze, leukaemia and bone cancer eventually caught up with him in 1977. He died at home in Bermuda at around noon on 30th November. A few short months earlier he had made a final trip to London having arranged to have his collected plays luxuriously bound and presented as a gift to the Queen. He then hired a car to drive him through theatreland where he could see as plain as day that *Separate Tables* from 1954 was being performed at the Apollo on Shaftesbury Avenue and his last play, *Cause Celebre,* which had opened on 4th July, was defiantly still on at Her Majesty's on the Haymarket. Unfashionable maybe - but still playing.

Fast-forward to 2011 and, on the anniversary of his birth, there was a revival of interest in Rattigan's work in the UK. A series of well-crafted productions of *Flare Path, The Browning Version, The Deep Blue Sea, After the Dance* et al suddenly revealed to a new theatre audience just how perceptive and compassionate towards all those thwarted, half-lived lives his best plays are and how much truth they reveal about the plight of the quieter human heart. Even the critics were impressed.

Rattigan's ashes were quietly placed with his mother, father and brother in the family tomb in Kensal Green cemetery in north-west London. His name was never carved on the tombstone but round the side are the words of the Scottish poet Thomas Campbell - 'to live in hearts we leave behind is not to die'.

* Phyllis Bottome was the pen name of the American wife of MI6 head of station Ernan Forbes Dennis. In 1924 they founded a language school in Austria and one of their students was a young Ian Fleming. Observing this suave, handsome, well-connected, old-Etonian lover of alpine sports Bottome was inspired to write a spy novel called The Lifeline. It was published in 1947, six years before Casino Royale. Her lead character was one Mark Chalmers who just happened to be a suave, handsome, well-connected, old-Etonian lover of alpine sports. Later in life Fleming clearly felt that if Bottome could plagiarise his life he could plagiarise her novel.

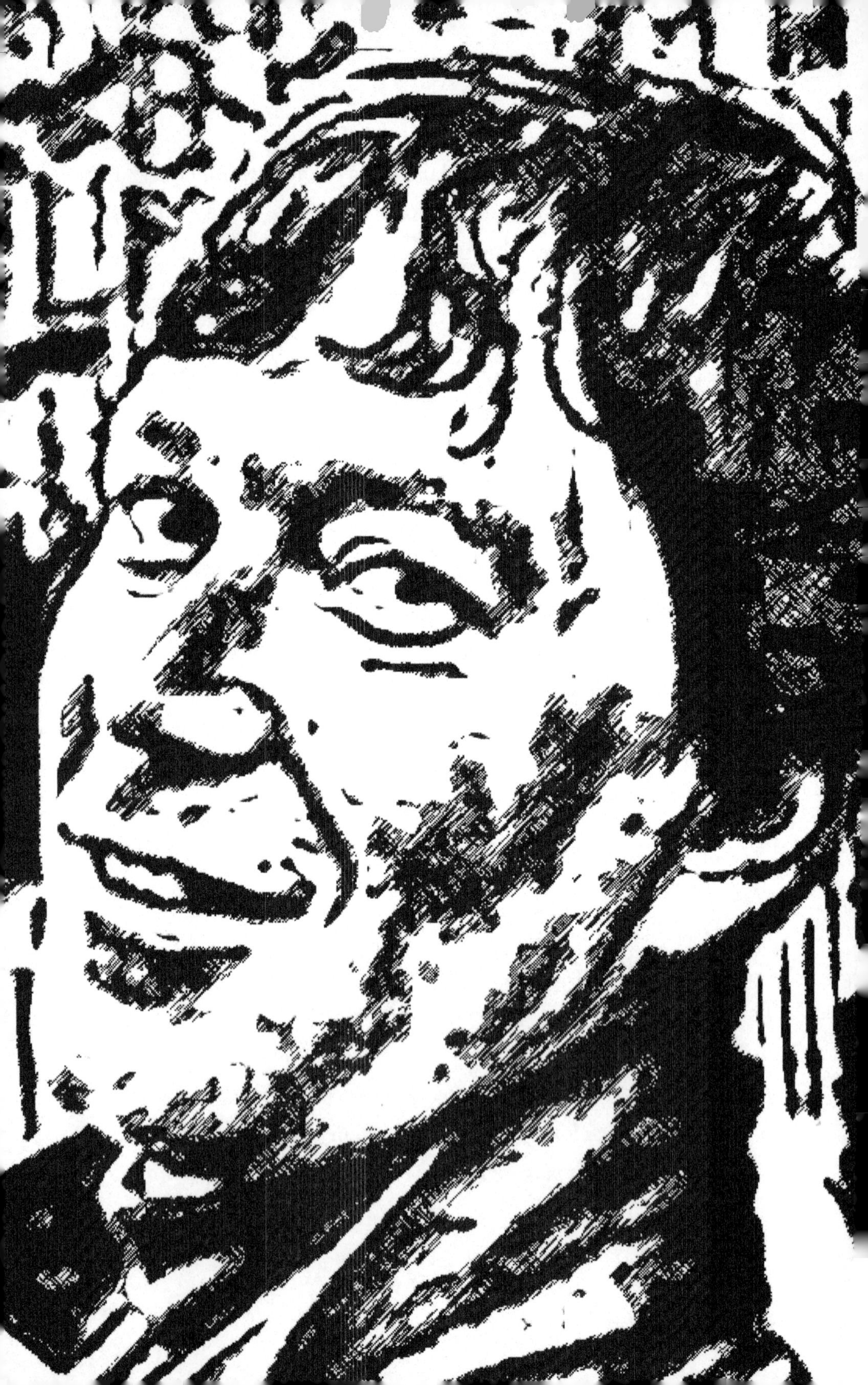

JOE ORTON
Part One - Bring on the Bad Boys

The 1960s were when everything changed. Whatever had been simmering away in the decades following the Second World War boiled over in an explosion of energy and creativity. Old shibboleths were torn down and new icons for a new age erected in their place. For many it was a time pregnant with possibility as the barriers that had formerly blocked their artistic ambition were removed and men and woman from across the whole social spectrum were able to take their places on the stage. In this chapter I want to look at the careers of two men, one a playwright the other an actor, whose private lives and public careers came to epitomise the very essence of the swinging sixties. Neither would have had a voice in earlier times and both were to blaze brightly before burning out far too soon.

Born in 1933 in Leicester, John Kingsley Orton grew up in one of the cities sprawling and monotonous council developments that had been put up in the early 1920s. Uniformly drab and depressing all theses estates could inspire were dreams of escape. Orton's parents were poor and pathetic, living sterile, loveless lives. His father, William, was a council gardener and his censorious mother was a machinist in one of Leicester's many clothing factories. It was not a happy home.

School was no better and young Joe, as he became known, left school in 1944 after failing the eleven-plus exam. From 1945 to 1947 he attended the local secretarial college and after that drifted through a series of dead-end jobs, most of which he was fired from for an overt lack of interest. The one ray of joy in his tedious life was the local amateur dramatic society.

The Little Theatre had been founded in 1922 and was the best equipped and most prestigious amateur dramatic society in the city, boasting Richard Attenborough as an old boy. Clearly not *all* welcoming, the Little Theatre only actually cast Orton in one production over two years and he resigned in 1949. Undaunted, his application to the Royal Academy of Dramatic Art went in on November 6th 1950 and, after a short delay due to appendicitis, he began his training there on May 15th 1951. In his diary on that day he wrote: "Started at RADA. O bliss!". He had successfully broken free from the pebble-dashed conformity of both the East Midlands and his family.

Within weeks Orton had met a fellow student, Kenneth Halliwell, and they clearly had more in common than just acting. By the 16th June they were lovers and Joe moved into Ken's shared flat in west Hampstead. Halliwell was seven years older than Orton and had received a grammar school education before becoming a conscientious objector during the Second World War. He clearly considered himself to be the senior partner in the relationship and rapidly cast himself in the role of mentor as well as lover - a position he would desperately try to maintain for the rest of his life. Halliwell was intensely insecure and emotionally unstable having been deeply scarred after seeing his mother die in front of him from a wasp sting when he was eleven. As if this was not enough, at the age of twenty-three he found his father dead with his head in the gas oven. He stepped over the body and made a cup of tea before calling the authorities.

Following their graduation from RADA the ill-suited pair frittered the next decade away collaborating on a series of un-publishable novels and un-performable plays. They ignored the post-war world of shabby old England as much as they could, becoming drop-outs way before it was fashionable to do so. They lived as happy hermits, joined at the hip, shunning any excessive social life. Instead, they lived hand-to-mouth, taking temporary jobs and enjoying the small bounty of the new welfare state.

The collectivist ideals that held sway in Britain after the war and led to the foundation of the welfare state were generally embraced by all political parties until the late 1970s. The belief was that we were all in this together. Within the arts this world-view was best exemplified in Scotland with the creation of the Edinburgh International Festival of Music and Drama in 1947. Of course it took an Austrian, an earl and a racehorse to get that show up and running!

The Austrian was called Rudolph Bing. He had fled Nazi Germany in 1934 and became a naturalised British citizen in 1946. He then helped to develop Glyndebourne Festival Opera in Sussex in 1949 before moving to New York where he ran the Metropolitan Opera for twenty-two years. In between he established the Edinburgh Festival on the premise of using the universality of the arts (particularly the common language of classical music) to heal the wounds of war.

The original plan was to base this venture in Oxford but unaccountably the worthy city fathers failed to turn up to the meeting. Bath was considered too small and London had sustained too much bomb damage. So all eyes turned north to Edinburgh to 'provide a platform for the flowering of the human spirit'.

Finances were made available from the newly-formed Arts Council of Great Britain (whose first Chairman was John Maynard Keynes) and Edinburgh Town Council were shamed into matching a very public donation of £10,000 from a Scottish aristocrat, the Earl of Rosebery. The Earl's motivation was more than a little mixed being largely inspired by the desire to stop his wife nagging him about his duty to support the putative festival that was extremely close to her heart. When his racehorse Ocean Swell won his own race, the Rosebery Stakes, the winnings were donated to his wife's campaign and peace was duly restored to his home, Dalmeny House. The Festival opened on 22nd August 1947 with a repertoire of predominantly German music. Quite daring only two years after the war.

In his introduction to the first programme, the Lord Provost of Edinburgh wrote:

> I hope you will believe that in the organisation of the many attractions, we have had ever before us the highest and purest ideals of art in its many and varied forms. May I assure you that this festival is not a commercial undertaking in any way. It is an endeavour to provide a stimulus to the establishing of a new way of life centred round the arts.

'Not a commercial undertaking in any way'. For many working in the arts, such elevated sentiments held sway throughout the thirty years of the post-war consensus. After the carnage of Normandy, Stalingrad and Auschwitz-Birkenau, a new world of classless optimism was being forged – a world filled with shared dreams and equal opportunities. It may always have been a chimera but it nonetheless provided the backdrop to Joe Orton's adolescence and early manhood. Except he didn't really feel part of this brave new world in lack-lustre Leicester. To him the world was a disappointment and people in authority were gatekeepers, spitefully barring him from entry to the beautiful garden. Out of this resentment Orton fermented revenge and turned it into laughter.

An early example of Orton's light-hearted pulling down of establishment pillars was his habit of stealing books Halliwell and he disapproved of from local libraries. In their view 'libraries might as well not exist; they've got endless shelves for rubbish and hardly any space for good books'. And so, they would carefully remove book covers or fly-leaves or replace them with surreal or semi-pornographic content and then place the books back on the library shelves. Who knows what the maiden aunts of Islington thought when they opened the adapted fly-leaf of Dorothy L. Sayers' latest novel and read:

"READ THIS BEHIND CLOSED DOORS! And have a good shit while you are reading."

But we do know what the police thought.

In 1962 both of these mischievous hijackers of literature and books on etiquette were sentenced to six months in prison for theft and malicious damage. Of course they both knew that the harshness of their sentences was really due to their sexuality. Orton later commented:

"It affected my attitude towards society. Before I had been vaguely conscious of something rotten somewhere, prison crystallised this. The old whore society really lifted up her skirts and the stench was pretty foul."

More importantly they were sent to separate prisons and for the first time in almost ten years Orton was out of the controlling orbit of the increasingly paranoid Halliwell. He began to write un-mentored. "Being in the nick brought detachment to my writing. I wasn't involved any more. And suddenly it worked." Also, as he wistfully recalled in

1967 when appearing on The Eamonn Andrews Television Show with Zsa Zsa Gabor, "I had a marvellous time in prison".

Two years before being imprisoned another sensational court case might have also helped convince Orton of the doubtful sincerity of society. If he had jumped on the tube to Temple underground during the autumn of 1961 he would have encountered high drama unfolding in the Number One Court at the Old Bailey. The Crown was prosecuting Penguin Books - clearly an upstart publisher and general peddler of filth - for daring to publish an unexpurgated edition of D. H. Lawrence's novel *Lady Chatterley's Lover*.

When old Etonian John Mervyn Guthrie Griffith-Jones opened for the prosecution he began by asking the jury the following question:

Would you approve of your young sons, young daughters - because girls can read as well as boys - reading this book? Is it a book you would have lying around your own house? Is it a book that you would even wish your wife or your servants to read?

The jury spent three hours deliberating what planet Griffith-Jones was living on before returning a unanimous verdict of 'not guilty'. This enabled Penguin to publish the book and prompted Philip Larkin's later comment:

Sexual intercourse began
In nineteen sixty-three
(Which was rather late for me) -
Between the end of the Chatterley ban
And the Beatles' first LP.

A wit in the House of Lords also made the observation that the only person he would keep from reading this book was his gamekeeper.

News about the Profumo scandal and the aristocratic orgies at Cliveden, (home of the Astors) also broke in the 1960s; another spectacular kick in the teeth to the age of deference. It was becoming increasingly hard for the great and good to maintain the moral high ground when everyone had seen their knickers. Many people now had their doubts about 'society', many people were starting to snigger at the 'establishment' and Joe Orton was going to become their voice.

As a sign of the changing times, it should be remembered that in 1963, across the river in Lilian Baylis Land, Laurence Olivier was boldly bashing a new National Theatre into shape from a small hut erected next to the Old Vic. The germ of this idea had been planted in 1848 when the Comedie Francaise had played in London and the theatrical cabal of London got jealous and began to wail 'we want a national theatre too'. After a multitude of committees came and went, (wasting vast amounts of time and public money) Olivier was finally able to put these plans in motion.

Whilst builders laboured and unions and artists fought Olivier's first season of plays began to be staged at the Old Vic, starting with Peter O'Toole's *Hamlet*. Other members of the company included Robert Stephens, Maggie Smith, Joan Plowright, Michael Gambon, Derek Jacobi, Lynn Redgrave, Michael Redgrave, Colin Blakely and Frank Finlay. William Gaskell and John Dexter decamped from the Royal Court to help and alongside revivals of the classics such as *Oedipus, Othello, Hedda Gabler* and *Long Day's Journey into Night* these early years also saw the nurturing of new young writers such as Tom Stoppard and Peter Shaffer.

To the west of London at the end of the King's Road the Royal Court spent the 1960s trying to keep up with its own formidable reputation as a 'cutting-edge' theatre forged through productions such as *Look Back in Anger*. From George Devine's time onwards, it saw itself as a comforting but avant-garde theatre that wanted to change the way drama was done. The Court despised the Royal Shakespeare Company with its faux leather costumes and chrome furniture and instead aimed to create something grittier and more authentic. Such aspirations led to the permanent exclusion of Tom Stoppard for being far too much of a university wit - despite the fact he hadn't been to university whilst most of the Court had; a classic case of the English panicking in the face of intellect. In the Royal Court's ideal world, all productions would have been cast with a mixture of John Gielgud and Arthur Lowe (as they achieved in 1974 with Edward Bond's *Bingo*) mixing the smooth with the rough; classical and cutting-edge combined.

The dynamic of the Court was bustling, bitchy, creative and ground-breaking. Except, of course it wasn't always like that. As the director and writer John McGrath who worked at the theatre throughout the fifties and sixties observed about the Royal Court:

> Its greatest claim to social significance is that it produced a new 'working-class' art, that it somehow stormed the Winter Palace of the bourgeois culture and threw out the old regime and turned the place into a temple of worker's art. Of course, it did nothing of the kind.

On 15th April 1966, the *Spectator* carried an article with the title 'Angry Middle Age' and described the Court as:

> touchy, lugubrious, embattled, inflexible, middle-aged in outlook if not in years – aren't the company's attitudes precisely those of an establishment, and not so very different from the ones attacked so gaily all those years ago?

Hey ho! You clearly can't please everyone. Let's just agree that the Royal Court at this time was where exciting things were happening - even if occasionally they weren't.

Royal Court directors in the 1960s were also very keen on the idea that actors should always 'start from scratch'. This meant that the new generation of actors who had not come through the Binkie Beaumont finishing school continuously had to prove themselves, putting them all under immense competitive pressure. "The actors were all a bit wild," the director Jane Howell observed with calculated understatement. Jane Howell was one of very few women to succeed at the Court at this time. She would later run the Northcott Theatre in Exeter as well as direct for the RSC and the BBC. "Life at the Court in the sixties was an explosion of hearts and minds," she recalled in 2021. "After the dreariness of the fifties there was a great sense of release. Life was better and could be better still. Censorship was going. Hockney was painting. There were police vans outside the theatre arresting us - for putting on plays. It was exciting. Life was ours."

Energy and invention were all in this theatre without cocktails and tennis-whites and the new rough-edged kids on the block were clearly going to rise to the occasion and become household names. Turning up to work in Sloane Square in the mid-sixties were performers such as Anthony Hopkins, Jack Shepherd, Claire Bloom, Jill Bennett, Dennis Waterman, Diana Quick, Ken Cranham, Paul Scofield, Sarah Miles, Glenda Jackson, Edward Fox, Penelope Wilton, Marianne Faithful, John Thaw, Bob Hoskins, Alan Bates, Albert Finney and Victor Henry.

Victor who? Well, Victor Henry merits a digression. Why? Firstly because I want to and I'm the one writing the book and, secondly, because in post-post-modern, post-Thatcherite Britain he epitomises a type of actor who is now utterly extinct. Completely forgotten today there were many at the time who thought he was the most exciting and dangerous actor of his generation. The man most likely to succeed.

Along with Joe Orton, Victor Henry was one of the many new working-class voices, now unapologetically being heard on the British stage. Born in 1943 to Margaret and Alexander Henry in Leeds Victor received a high school education and by 1960 had arrived at RADA to train as an actor - presumably on a scholarship. Graduating in 1963 he decamped to the Farnham Repertory Company and took the lead role in Nina Warner Hooke's new play *The Striplings* which looked at the world of big business through the eyes of rebellious youth. While at Farnham he also played Trofimov in *The Cherry Orchard* and the director, Jean Knight, was clearly impressed enough to take Henry with her to the Royal Court when she went there to direct William Corlett's *The Gentle Avalanche* in November 1964. Coming into the Royal Court every day must have been unbearably exciting and terrifying for this young man from Yorkshire.

The King's Road was buzzing in the sixties. Along the mile or so between Sloane Square and World's End pub Mary Quant and Kiki Byrne were slugging it out for fashion supremacy while the gilded people sipped their kitsch and shameless lives away at Club dell' Aretusa. The Chelsea Drugstore had replaced the old White Hart and became the new chic place to eat, drink, dance and shop whilst Moroccan barber brothers, Joseph and Maurice, snipped smart mod-locks at Salon 33. Jazz rang out from Trogs above the Six Bells and lesbians scuttled in and out of the Gateway Club.

On the corner of Sloane Square itself squatted the King's Arms (today a chic French restaurant) with its sticky carpets and fug of smoke, whisky and beer. Frequented by soldiers from the nearby barracks and elated and depressed actors preparing for or recovering from auditions or productions, The King's Arms was an unofficial annex of the Royal Court and the scene of multiple dramas equal to those acted out on the stage a few yards away. One of the more regular drinkers at the bar was Victor Henry, who was not to survive what everyone who did survive described as a hard drinking culture.

Following *The Gentle Avalanche*, in 1964 Henry spent a season at the newly-built Phoenix Theatre in Leicester. There he was spotted by a BBC producer named Peter Duguid whilst playing Dodger in Arnold Wesker's play examining the English class system, *Chips With Everything*. Duguid recommended Henry to John McGrath who was collaborating on a new television series with another young writer, Troy Kennedy Martin, who would go on to create *Z-Cars*, *Edge of Darkness* and write the screenplay for *The Italian Job*.

Diary of a Young Man was directed by Ken Loach and is a five-part tale of two young northern blokes who go south and seek a roof, a girl and a job in London in no particular order. The series was broadcast in the August and September of 1964 and after having already played the war correspondent Jefferson Brick in the TV adaptation of Dickens' *Martin Chuzzlewit* earlier that same year, Henry was well on his way to being noticed.

He had also been noticed by the police. The summer of 1964 saw Henry in court being fined £15 for taking and driving away a motorcycle. He and an actor chum, David Lowe, with whom he shared digs at Belitha Villas in Islington, had been spotted by the police on the Avonmore Road, West Kensington at two o'clock in the morning. A drunken Henry was astride the bike with an equally inebriated Lowe desperately pushing it. Exactly the sort of crazy caper that two young northern blokes who had come south to seek a roof, a girl and a job in London might be expected to get up to. Well, it was the sixties!

A revival of John Arden's 1959 *Serjeant Musgrave's Dance* opened at the Royal Court on 16th December 1965. This tale about deserters from a colonial war in the late nineteenth century paralleled contemporary controversies regarding actions taken by British troops in Cyprus in 1958. With Arden's signature combination of prose and verse, this ballad-like play provided ample scope for young actors to test their mettle. The cast included Iain Cuthbertson, Jack Shepherd, Ronald Pickup and Dennis Waterman. Henry played the volatile, drunken, doomed Private Sparky.

The production was directed by Jane Howell, who would become one of Henry's champions throughout his career at the Court. Howell was a bright-eyed, tough, smart young director with long dark hair and a cigarette permanently clamped in her left hand (lit from the large box of household matches she forever carried around with her). Howell directed Henry a great deal in his heyday at the Royal Court and found him to be 'exciting .. always dangerous …he would take risks and there was always the feeling that something might explode'. However, she never had any trouble with him in rehearsal or performance. "Victor was incredibly focused when working and wild when not." From Anne Jellicoe's *The Knack* in 1962 to *Serjeant Musgrave's Dance* in 1965, and from *The Vosey Inheritance* in 1966 to the semi-political pantomime for adults and children *The Dragon* in 1967, Howell always found Victor to be 'very good at finessing fine details'. "He was a bit like an art student - always finding small gestures," she said.

Peter Gill directed him in a ground-breaking and revelatory production of D.H. Lawrence's *The Daughter in Law* in 1968 (alongside *A Collier's Friday Night* and *The Widowing of Mrs Holroyd*). This mining town trilogy reintroduced Lawrence to the English stage and established Gill as a major English director. Lawrence might have remained in the public consciousness as a novelist following the Chatterley trial but his reputation as a playwright was non-existent at this time. Gill's meticulously directed, ultra-naturalistic tales of working life designed by John Gunter took London by storm.

The actor Edward Peel recalled:

Whatever the crises, the hardships, the dramas encountered by these working-class people, the practical, everyday duties still had to be performed and were the cornerstone around which these plays were built. Water steamed when it came from the hob, meals steamed and there was a wonderful smell of freshly baked bread and Yorkshire pudding.

Henry played the moody younger brother Joe Gascoigne in *The Daughter in Law* as he had done in the Sunday evening try-out of the play in 1967. His performance was judged by *The Stage* to be 'richer, more natural, more broodingly alive' and his 'homework scene' was regarded by Peter Gill as one of the finest pieces of acting he had ever seen. Gill further recalled Henry's 'intense frail passion' and described him as 'the bad boy with a book'. This image of Victor Henry as some sort of 1960s Trofimov from *The Cherry Orchard* is one that lingers. He had played the role back in 1963 at the Farnham Repertory Company and in 1966 Lindsay Anderson wanted to replace Tom Courtenay with Henry in the role of Chekhov's tortured, eternal student since Tom 'is a nice lad but he doesn't develop imaginatively, isn't too convincing talking in terms of ideas - intellectual terms that is'. Clearly Henry did tick those boxes.

One Friday over Easter in 1966 a young Scottish-born actor graduated from RADA. On the next Monday he started work at the Royal Court and became the general understudy for Victor Henry. His name was Kenneth Cranham and in 2016 he would win the Olivier Award for Best Actor in *The Father* by Florian Zeller in a version translated by Christopher Hampton. From that early Easter onwards Cranham was a close friend, colleague and observer of Henry.

One night they stayed up late working on lines at Henry's flat near Regent's Park in the company of Henry's then girlfriend, the actress Liz Bell. The line learning was well lubricated and by four o'clock in the morning it had descended into a fight. Punches were thrown and Cranham ended up putting Henry into a firm and serious headlock - much to Henry's delight. Victor Henry, it seems, liked to be hurt. Liz Bell observed that he actively wanted to be hit, to be beaten up. Ken Cranham thought that he wanted to be killed.

This aspect of his life is referenced by almost everyone who knew him. He was a short man (Jane Howell affectionately described him as 'a small, runty little chap') with extremely thick, bottle-lens glasses. Another very close friend, actor Jack Shepherd, wrote in his book *Impossible Plays*:

> He was small - his parents were even smaller - short-sighted, red-faced, and thin, with a frizzy mop of red hair and a terrible wiry strength. Nor was he good-looking, boasting that he had 'a mouth like a dog's arse'. Victor's power to attract lay in his personality and, above all, his energy. He once told me that he saw himself as the reincarnation of Eric Bloodaxe, the Viking war leader and 'first king of Yorkshire'. He was only half-joking.

What Cecil Beaton made of this man when he photographed him for the National Portrait Gallery in 1968 is anyone's guess. The image as recorded is coy, almost winsome, Henry's hand partly obscuring his mouth and his soft, intelligent eyes focusing straight forward. He is wearing the boot-lace tie of an old cowboy, a grizzled gunslinger - a wannabe Doc Holliday in repose.

This juxtaposition of the sweet and the deadly seems to encompass the fundamental essence of both Henry's acting and his life - the bad boy with the book. The director and writer Nick Wright thought that, as an actor, 'his best performances were those that revealed a sweetness and innocence not much seen in other circumstances such as in *The Daughter in Law*. At other times, his whiney self-righteousness could be annoying'.

But Henry liked being annoying. He would go out of his way to provoke fights, particularly with authority figures or with men who were considerably stronger than himself such as policemen or soldiers from the barracks drinking alongside the actors at the King's Arms. Jack Shepherd observed that Henry's vocabulary would go up a notch or two on these occasions - "I find your verbosity rather …offensive …and bereft of any coherent content." Friends knew trouble was afoot when Henry, having actively stirred up a confrontation, discreetly placed his spectacles in his top pocket in anticipation of the first delicious thump in the face.

The same gesture accompanied his acting. Before stepping onto the stage the opaque specs would be removed rendering Henry semi-blind on stage. But, as Cranham commented, 'by being semi-blind he became lost in his own world, his own unique energy field'.

This 'excess of energy' was much noticed by the playwright Christopher Hampton who also knew Henry extremely well. Their paths had first crossed in June 1966 when the twenty-year-old Hampton had been catapulted from Oxford University to the Royal Court through the success of his play about adolescent homosexuality - *When Did You Last See My Mother?* Henry was cast as the lead Ian and the part of Linda went to a young Lucy Fleming - daughter of Peter Fleming (brother of Ian) and the actress Celia Johnson.

It must have been around this time when Henry and Lucy, having decided to spend the afternoon rehearsing horizontally, were disturbed in bed by the sound of Celia Johnson coming in the front door. Henry dashed into the wardrobe to hide but when the star of *In Which We Serve*, *This Happy Breed* and *Brief Encounter* suspiciously opened the door she came face-to-face with Victor standing bolt upright and stark naked. Attempting to defuse the situation he opted to impersonate an elevator bell-boy, looked the grande dame in the eye and said 'Going-up?'.

During the run of *When Did You Last See My Mother?* Hampton was so bowled over by Henry's performance that he gave up any dreams of his own to become an actor and decided instead to focus full-time on writing. "The reviews of the play…were full of stuff about Victor being the most exciting new actor since Albert Finney," he said. "When I saw Victor do this play I thought, move on from acting. Leave it to people who know how to do it."

The production began as a Sunday night 'upstairs without décor' but was rapidly moved to the Comedy Theatre by producer Michael Codron, making Hampton the youngest playwright in modern times to have a play on in the West End. It was Henry's West End debut as well.

The Theatre Upstairs at the Royal Court is an interesting tale in itself. As early as 1957 the team of George Divine and Tony Richardson had introduced Sunday night performances 'without décor'. These cheap staged readings (no sets or costumes) allowed for a significant expansion of experimentation and created a plethora of opportunities for writers, directors and actors alike. Poor old designers! It was through this system that a new generation of directors began to make their mark such as William Gaskell, John Dexter, Lindsay Anderson, Jane Howell and Anthony Page, to name just a few.

Up until 1963 the garret rooms above the theatre had been run as a restaurant and bar by Sigmund Freud's witty, bon viveur nephew, the now discretely disgraced Clement. However, once the lease expired, the space was taken over by Bill Gaskell and in 1968 the English Stage Company used it to stage private club performances of new works. Lindsay Anderson dismissed the new venture as a one-man showing-off shop by dubbing it 'The Gaskill - a self-glorifying ghetto'. However, something clearly worked because, by 1969, the Arts Council gave the Court a grant to open the space as a public venue under the directorship of a young man from South Africa called Nicholas Wright. This thirty feet by forty feet attic would, over the next few decades, be home to playwrights as varied as Caryl Churchill, Howard Brenton, Heathcote Williams, Sam Shepherd, Joe Penhall and Sarah Kane. It was also the cramped and confined womb from which sprang the Rocky Horror Show.

Early 1967 was a good time for Victor Henry. In January he attended a dinner at The Savoy hosted by the Chairman of the English Stage Company, Neville Blond, and was awarded a bursary for 'exceptional work' in the previous year's season. The other recipients were the playwrights Edward Bond and David Cregan. In July he went on tour to Canada with two young directors from the Court, Peter Gill and Robert Kidd, and played Napoleon at the Vancouver Festival. He also made an appearance in a new TV series (*The Gamblers* on Rediffusion) and tucked three small parts in movies under his belt.

Privilege was a cult-sixties-rock-music-meets-political-paranoia romp, starring Manfred Mann's lead singer Paul Jones and the supermodel Jean Shrimpton. In the schlock horror *The Sorcerers* he appeared with Susan George, Ian Ogilvy and Boris Karloff and in *The White Bus* (written by Shelagh Delaney and directed by Lindsay Anderson) he shared the screen with his drinking buddy Anthony Hopkins who was making his movie debut. Not bad company for a young actor still on the make.

Christopher Hampton and Victor Henry worked together again in 1968 on Hampton's *Total Eclipse* which charted the tempestuous affair between the nineteenth century French poets Verlaine and Rimbaud. Directed by Robert Kidd the production, in full solidarity with the sixties-fashionista-mood of the King's Road, had a set designed by Patrick Proctor and was lit with lamps borrowed from the shop of the man credited with inventing the 'swinging sixties' - Christopher Gibbs. The Royal Court was painted pink and pierced Moroccan lamps revolved in the middle of the auditorium, spinning shards of light over the whole theatre, whilst Verlaine (played by John Grillo) and Rimbaud drowned each other in passion, poetry and absinthe. It was also during this production that Henry decided to take a live, loaded revolver onto the stage and fire real bullets at his fellow actors.

Victor Henry's 'escapades' became legendary:

- Drunk in a lavatory stall pontificating loudly to Simon Ward in the stall next door on the benefits of a good shit!

- Taking pot-shots with a starting pistol at fellow drinkers from behind the slot-machine in Clement Freud's bar above the Royal Court.

- Attempting to assault Ian McKellen in 1966. During rehearsals for Arnold Wesker's *Their Very Own and Golden City* the decision was made to replace Henry and his acting and drinking chum Dennis Waterman with Ian McKellen. (Henry and Waterman had appeared together earlier that year in Middleton's 1620 play about sex and cash, *A*

Chaste Maid in Cheapside). Henry had always resented McKellen who learned his newly allocated lines with indecent haste, provoking Henry and Waterman to enact their revenge. They turned up at the Court's stage-door late one evening armed with broken bottles and waited for McKellen to leave the theatre. Tipped off by actress Gillian Martell who was also in *Golden City,* McKellen had to make a furtive and undignified exit over the rooftops under cover of night. Waterman was fired from the Royal Court for this 'prank' but Henry survived to act another day.

- Turning up drunk at the stage-door in Zurich during the brief tour of *Serjeant Musgrave's Dance* covered in blood having been beaten up. He went on stage as if nothing had happened.

- Punching Dustin Hoffman in New York in 1966. Whilst Hoffman was performing at Circle in the Square in a play called *Eh?* by Henry Livings and directed by Alan Arkin, Henry was in the city to perform in *Hail Scrawdyke* the American version of David Halliwell's *Little Malcolm and His Struggle Against the Eunuchs*. While attending a performance of *Eh?* Henry took umbrage at Hoffman's performance and felt it had let down the play. As he explained later while throwing his punch, 'I'm a friend of the author'.

- Getting Anthony Hopkins briefly barred from the Royal Court stage. The two were great drinking buddies (and apparently shared digs in a greenhouse for a period). One evening a drunken Hopkins decided he needed to see his playmate and was not to be deterred by the stage-hands even though Henry was performing on the stage at the time.

- Pulling a gun on Arnold Wesker during rehearsals for *The Friends* at the Roundhouse in May 1970. Wesker, who was known to be a rather pompous bore, was directing his own play and attempted to give a note to Henry who was having none of it. He pulled out a revolver and laid it calmly on the table. "If you talk as much as yesterday, I'll have to blow your brains out," snarled Henry. The rehearsal moved on. There seems to be a back-story to this event since (a) Henry hadn't forgotten or forgiven being removed from Wesker's play *Golden City* (b) Like many others, Henry thought Wesker was massively overrated and that his plays were only made presentable through the skilled direction of John Dexter (c) Henry was anti-Semitic, (d) Henry had gone off Wesker when he had made them all rehearse in the Welsh countryside where there were no pubs within walking distance. Henry had to go on enormous night-time treks to get a drink. An unforgivable inconvenience.

- Driving over the limit in 1971 'after his car was stopped travelling at a fast speed having been seen swerving from side to side in Fulham Road', reported Inspector Colin Richmond. At the police station Henry was found to have 142 milligrams of alcohol in 100 millilitres of blood and was fined £20. He had previous convictions for careless driving and for having a defective tyre. In court Henry said he could not remember driving fast or swerving in the road.

- Crashing the car of actress Jocelyne Sbath; smashing up the bathroom of actress girlfriend Diane Fletcher; viciously spitting in the face of Deborah Norton during a 1970 production of *AC/DC* by Heathcote Williams.

- Going AWOL from rehearsals at the Court. A scouting team was sent out to all the usual places where Henry might drink - primarily the Antelope or the King's Head. He was found at the bar of the latter, drunk as a skunk with a large glass of whisky in his hand. As they poured coffee down his throat and tried to sober him up for the stage, one well-meaning innocent pointed out 'you haven't been eating!'. Clearly not a man who appreciated unsolicited advice Henry picked up his whisky glass, bit firmly into it and began to chew. As he grinned the blood poured out over his chin.

In 1968 Henry was cast as Jimmy Porter in the first major revival of Osborne's *Look Back in Anger* that played at the Royal Court between October and December before transferring to the Criterion on Piccadilly Circus. The critics observed that: "Victor Henry reaches beyond Jimmy's rage and anguish into deeper realms of the sadness of the world of no-man's land occupied so hazardously by Jimmy and Alison" and "Victor Henry catches the rage in Jimmy expressing it best in his gleeful chuckles and sense of immediate wrecking of any sign of harmony."

Anthony Page, who directed the production, recalled in 2021 Henry's performance to be 'absolutely magnificent' but Jane Asher who played Alison, in a 2018 interview in *The Telegraph* stated:

> The only problem with our production was Victor Henry, who played Jimmy. He was one of the most brilliant actors I've ever worked with, but also an alcoholic. The play famously starts with Jimmy reading the newspaper and Alison ironing. As Victor lowered the newspaper some nights his eyes would be small and bloodshot, and I would know he'd been drinking and that it would be a terrible night. Some actors can get away with a drink but Victor couldn't. He thought he was being wonderful but he was mumbling and incoherent and it was disastrous.

Despite landing the leading role in the film *All Neat in Black Stockings,* Henry was clearly coming off the rails. The movie, starring Henry, Susan George and Jack Shepherd, was part of the British New Wave movement and followed the life of an easy-going, chirpy-chappie window cleaner called Ginger who falls in love with a young girl in swinging sixties London. What should have been a quirky British sex-comedy (and box-office hit like Michael Caine's 1966 triumph *Alfie*) instead drifted into darker realms and the end of the movie is startling, depressing and irredeemably bleak.

The film failed to be the breakthrough that Henry had hoped for and over the next few years he began to bagatelle about the board lurching between triumph and carnage. Nick Wright recalled that working with him on Heathcote Williams' play *AC/DC* in 1970 'was awful'.

"He was drinking all day and pretty maudlin. He was pretty well gone into alcoholism by then."

The show sounds pretty crazed itself. The Royal Court publicity described it as 'the weirdest play the Royal Court has ever produced…Your brain has no toilet facilities. *AC/DC* shows you how to flush it. And it gives you four tastes of Utopia en route'. However, *AC/DC* was also the first play in the Court's history to enjoy an internal transfer, moving from the theatre upstairs to the main house in November 1970. *The Evening Standard* awarded it the prize for most promising play. A psychedelic critique of the mental health industry, Ken Cranham described it as 'Timothy Leary meets black magic' and recalls that it was during this run that Henry carved the sign of a cross into his forehead. It was also at this time that Henry begged his friend Christopher Hampton if he could attend the opening preview of his new play *The Philanthropist* at the Royal Court. In the darkness of the theatre, Hampton remembers Victor holding onto his hand throughout the entire performance. Violence and fragility made flesh.

Henry continued working though, directing Ian Holm in a double bill of Chekhov's (adapted by Hampton) above north London pubs and his last role at the Royal Court was as Bosola in Webster's *The Duchess of Malfi*. Directed by Peter Gill this pared down production consisted of 'a few wooden doors, a kitchen table and a chair or two' so that the characters would dominate, not the period or the gore and melodrama. In this production Webster's blood-stained world was washed clean, at least outwardly, so that the audience could get closer to the leading characters as instruments in a mighty web of intrigue.

At one point, Henry took a position on the stage and looked up from under his monk's cowl. He held the look, fixing the audience with his stare - and then he spoke. It was transfixing. Simon Callow remembers: "Victor's Bosola was one of the most terrifying performances I ever saw in my life. He terrified his fellow actors too."

Henry was fired from the production after one week. No-one can quite remember why but I suspect we can guess.

However, as luck would have it, John McGrath who had co-written *Diary of a Young Man* for Ken Loach and Henry back in 1965, was running a new theatre company in Scotland - "7:84" (statistic: in 1966 7% of the population of the UK owned 84% of the country's wealth). In August 1971 he persuaded Victor to appear as an 'invading and sexually predatory' young revolutionary called Joe in his new play at the Edinburgh Festival - *Trees in the Wind*. Jack Shepherd went to see the production. "He [Victor] seemed to be a true embodiment of William Blake's archetypal creation Orc, the flame-headed demon of energy, the spirit of ungovernableness." This was Henry in a nutshell.

On 4th November 1971 *Trees in the Wind* made an appearance at the Gardner Centre at Sussex University where Henry was observed to have acted with 'diverse and polished brilliance'.

In early to mid-April 1972, the director Michael Wearing and Henry had adapted Gogol's *The Diary of a Madman* as a one man show for the stage. The one man, the clerk, was played by Henry and the show was put on at the Arts Lab in Birmingham where it was reviewed by Judith Cook: "Victor Henry sits shaven-headed, king of a barrel, musing on the fact that the human mind is not contained in the head but floats on the wind. He weeps 'Sadly there is no place in the world for me'."

The show went on to Sheffield where it was seen by a young television director, David Rose (who was to go on to become Head of Drama for Channel 4) and who asked if he could film it and turn it into a piece for television. Wearing agreed and filming took place in a studio for an intensive four full days.

While preparing *Diary of a Madman,* Henry moved into Wearing's spare room - a step up from the abandoned car he had been living in at the bottom of Dartmouth Park Hill in north London - and he began to get his act together. His drinking had not stopped but was certainly now under control and he was keeping his demons at arm's length. Nick Wright remembers bumping into him during the period and noted that Henry was 'in a comparatively good state'.

It was in November 1972 that Henry was taking a sober stroll, either through Sloane Square as some people report it or elsewhere in west London, after having picked up some bottles of beer to take round to a friend. At some point on his walk a car mounted the pavement and crashed into a lamp-post which snapped off at the base and slammed down onto the back of Henry's skull.

None of Henry's friends thought he would make old bones any more than Henry did. Jack Shepherd wrote about 'the romantic death we'd all envisioned'. Jane Howell remembers him saying 'if I'm not famous by the age of 27 that'll be the end of me'. She thought that in some ways Henry viewed his talent to be a burden, something that might overwhelm him. Jane Asher recalled that 'he always thought he would die a dramatic, wild, drink-fuelled death'.

Instead of going out gloriously in some dazzling Western gunfight, Henry was rendered into a semi-coma caused by a lesion of the middle brain.

Peter Gill organised a benefit performance at the Royal Court of D. H. Lawrence's *The Merry Go Round* in November 1973 and in July 1974 a colour television was placed at the foot of Henry's hospital bed. The plan was to play a recording of *Diary of a Madman* in the hope that this would jog Henry back into consciousness. His mother, Margaret, had previously tried to awaken him by playing tape-recordings of his theatre and TV successes. "He said Goodnight to us a few weeks ago," she tragically told *The Daily Mirror* who ran the story. "He can move his left arm from the elbow and make signals with his fingers. His eyes follow us everywhere and he can signal with them. His friends and I will be at his bedside watching the TV play and hoping for some new sign from him."

The sign never came and both of Henry's parents were to die in 1980. Jack Shepherd visited him on two separate occasions at Pindersfield hospital in Wakefield. The first time he was convinced that Henry was able to understand him and was trying to convey the hell he was in. (Jane Howell told me that 'Jack really understood Victor; he *knew* him'). On the second visit Henry looked up from his bed, saw who it was and fell asleep.

Christopher Hampton was also a regular visitor and used to read to him by his bedside. One day he looked up and caught such a look of hatred in Henry's eyes that he stopped reading and left. He never went back again.

Disturbingly, in 1969 Henry was the narrator on a Thames Television documentary called *A Life Worth Living*. The synopsis for the programme in The British Film Institute archive makes for harrowing reading:

> The life of victims of brain and head injuries following road accidents. Filmed at the Birmingham Accident Hospital. A road accident leading to head injuries. The procedures followed in caring for the patient, especially in the case of long-term unconsciousness; the importance of helping the patient breathe and helping to feed the patient. Recovery and re-education, including learning to walk, speech therapy and occupational therapy, working with patients in the gym. A number of case studies are examined: a girl severely disabled and in hospital; a young man who was previously a bright apprentice and is now nearly incapacitated; a man who had a motorbike accident, which led to severe disability but who went on to have a son; a man who also had an accident, but which led to the departure of his wife, who is interviewed. Part two deals with the ethical questions raised by keeping alive a severe head injury victim whose quality of life is severely diminished. The work of the Head Injuries Club which provides companionship. The need of patients to work, and the provision of special workshops. Problems of care and where the patients are housed; some head injury patients have been put into mental hospitals. The problem of serious brain damage caused by road accidents, showing a number of cases at the Birmingham Accident Hospital including people who have been in comas for months and those whose personalities have changed completely.

Locked inside his semi-coma there is a horrifying probability that Victor Henry, the bad boy with a book, the boy with an excess of energy, knew exactly the condition he was in. As with Marlowe's Mephistopheles he would have been all too aware of the bleak reality that 'this is hell, nor am I out of it'. Henry remained in this state for thirteen years until he finally died on 20 November 1985. By which time those lazy, hazy days of summer were a long distant memory and the rebellious optimism of the sixties had faded into the anxious avarice of the eighties where audiences were being converted into customers and the musical was king.

JOE ORTON
Part Two - Bad Boys Blazing

After leaving prison Orton got down to business writing a radio play for the BBC which was eventually broadcast in 1964. It was called *The Ruffian on the Stair*. This comedy of menace owed a lot to Pinter but also introduced Orton's unique tone of absurdist black humour that amused as much as it undermined. The play features a couple who are living in a bedsit. Joyce is a Protestant ex-prostitute and Mike is a Roman Catholic former boxer from Donegal. An eighteen-year-old man called Wilson joins them but, apart from the fact that he had been having an incestuous affair with his now deceased brother Frank, we learn little about him. His sole desire is to be shot by Mike – and Mike dutifully obliges. As Wilson lies dying it is also revealed that the bullet has smashed the goldfish bowl killing the resident fish. Both Joyce and Mike are mortified and grief stricken - about the fish.

There is a distinct lack of propriety or moral order in Orton's world. Moral compasses are turned into crazed spinning tops as everybody screams for help only to find that no-one is listening; largely because they are too busy screaming for help themselves. Orton delighted in pricking the bubbles of the great and good, drawing attention to the shocking possibility that we are *all* for sale, the only true question being, when and how much?

Orton described himself as being 'broad minded to the point of obscenity' and in his plays, as in his life, no taboo is left untouched. Instead he promotes the disarmingly charming image of man as a fallen innocent living in a society that is nasty and brutish and run by madmen and hypocrites. Orton's work is extravagantly sexual and blasphemous and he did with perversion what Feydeau did with adultery during the Belle Epoque - he treated it as normal. With a schoolboy delight in his own cleverness and dexterity Orton created breakneck plots riddled with black humour. His characters reflect a cheerfully cynical world through the dizzyingly low moral expectations they have of each other as well as of themselves. "There must be hundreds of innocent people in the country," Caulfield says in *Funeral Games* and, when McLeavy protests that 'the police are there for the protection of ordinary people' in *Loot* Inspector Truscott replies with bemused calm: "I don't know where you pick up these slogans Sir. You must read them on hoardings."

And then there is Orton's distinctive use of language. While often categorised as the epitome of the iconoclastic swinging sixties Orton actually slots rather honourably into the tradition of heightened, epigrammatic wit that runs from the Restoration dramas of Congreve and Wycherley through to Wilde and Coward. How the line sounded was as important to Orton as the thought it carried.

In May 1964 Terence Rattigan was over from Bermuda and he and Vivian Leigh went to see a new play being presented at the Arts Theatre. It was Joe Orton's first full-length play for the stage called *Entertaining Mr Sloane* and it was haemorrhaging money. Rattigan, however, noticed at once the pithiness of the dialogue and the dexterity of the plotting and recognised that 'what Orton had to say about England and society had never been said before'. Acting on this impulse, Rattigan connected Orton with the producer Donald Albery, and invested £3,000 of his own money in the West End transfer of Sloane to the Wyndham's Theatre. There is a case to be made that, without Rattigan, Orton's voice might never have been heard at all. At one point soon after, Rattigan invited Orton and Halliwell to stay for the weekend at his house in Brighton. The occasion was a disaster. A rouge wearing Halliwell was determined to prevent Orton from speaking at all, deciding instead to dominate all conversation himself; even when Laurence Olivier and Joan Plowright joined the party. Rattigan recalled afterwards that Halliwell was 'desperately trying to give the impression that he wrote all Joe's plays' and was clearly 'a bit round the bend'.

Ever ambitious, Orton rapidly followed up *Sloane* with *Loot* in 1965; a dark hybrid of farce and detective whodunnit. While it initially flopped the play was revived in 1966 with a new cast and a re-written script. The public and the critics gave it their approval and by November 1966 it had transferred to the Criterion on Piccadilly and would go on to win the *Evening Standard* Drama Award for 'best play of the year'. That same year Orton sold the film rights of *Loot* for £100,000.

In June 1967, whilst Orton was enjoying a bit of sex-tourism in Morocco, Peter Gill was at the Royal Court rehearsing a short play by him called *The Erpingham Camp* (a very loose re-writing of Euripides' *The Bacchae* set in a holiday camp run by a lunatic). This was to be performed in the Theatre Upstairs alongside a revival of *The Ruffian on the Stair* as part of a double bill called *Crimes of Passion*.

Whilst the production received luke-warm reviews, the first part of 1967 was a fantastic period for Joe Orton, not least because he was also then working on a screenplay for the Beatles called *Up Against It*. The second half of the year was cancelled.

On 9th August 1967 Kenneth Halliwell, depressed, jealous and clearly mad, took a hammer to his lover and bludgeoned him to death. He then killed himself with an overdose of barbiturates having just silenced one of the most original voices of the age.

A few days before his death, Orton gave a revealing interview to the BBC in which he likened the career of the playwright to that of a boxer. He stated that after about ten years they get 'punchy' and go off. "A playwright's career is very short … I only have so much inspiration … I shan't always be young." He also quipped: "I hope I've never written anything as bad as some of the early Shakespeares."

At the time of his death Orton was working on *What the Butler Saw*. This play was posthumously produced at the Queen's Theatre in 1969 by none other than Binkie Beaumont. The play is set in a psychiatric hospital where all the characters are deranged, amoral and suffering from over-active libidos. As Dr Prentice says of his wife: "You were born with your legs apart. They'll send you to the grave in a Y-shaped coffin." The plot revolves around incest, cross-dressing and Winston Churchill's penis and the play ends with the entire cast climbing up a ladder into a blazing, divine light with the parting line of 'let us put our clothes on and face the world'.

Orton's death is one of those watershed moments - much like the deaths of Garrick, Sheridan and Wilde. Somehow they all mark a crossing of a rubicon, a passing from one age into another. Born in the low dishonest decade of the 1930s, Orton died in the Summer of Love and by 1968 the world, from London to Paris to Washington DC, would be in a frenzy of revolt and reform. 1968 was also the year that censorship was finally abolished in Britain. Since Robert Walpole's Theatre Licensing Act of 1737 all new plays had been forced to jump through hoops held by government watchdogs. But after ground-breaking work at the Royal Court such as Osborne's *A Patriot for Me* with its drag ball, and Edward Bond's *Saved*, with its shocking scene showing the stoning of a baby, such control had become untenable. The right of the Lord Chancellor to red-pen scripts was revoked and public morals were suddenly left in the hands of the public.

Orton missed this revolution - and all that came after. *Hair* and *Oh! Calcutta!* were just months away. And who were the creators of this latter nude review? One was Kenneth Tynan, the Literary Manager of the National Theatre of Great Britain' and the first person to say 'fuck' on British television (I was eleven days old at the time and was most offended). Others were John Lennon, Samuel Beckett and Sam Shepard. The Wannabes were now running the asylum; they were the new establishment.

When Orton's coffin arrived at Golder's Green crematorium the attendant was heard to ask the family 'Is this the 2.30 or the 2.45?'. A very Ortonesque sort of line to go out on. Later, when Orton's sister Leonie came to scatter his ashes it was, rather strangely considering events, decided to mix them with those of Kenneth Halliwell. She began spooning them out with the incantation of 'One of Joe; one of Ken. One of Joe; one of Ken'. Peggy Ramsay, Orton's formidable agent, was heard to mutter 'It's a gesture, not a recipe'.

There is a line from Christopher Marlowe's *Doctor Faustus* that seems particularly applicable to Joe Orton: 'cut is the branch that might have grown full straight'. Like Marlowe himself one can ponder forever how such a vibrant and iconoclastic writer as Orton might have developed over the ensuing decades: but in vain. That particular promiscuous, playful playwright had prematurely left the stage; even though he'd made one hell of a journey from the unwelcoming Little Theatre in Leicester. The motto of Orton's hated home city is 'Semper Eadem' which translates as 'Always the Same'. Thanks to playwrights like Joe Orton, and all those who came before and after him, the world of theatre isn't.

Giles Ramsay is an independent theatre producer who specialises in creating new work with artists in developing countries. He is the Founding Director of the charity Developing Artists, a former Fellow of St. Chad's College, Durham University and a Course Leader in Theatre at The Victoria and Albert Museum in London.

Giles has run theatre projects in Botswana, Cape Verde, Equatorial Guinea, Kenya, Kosovo, Palestinian Territories, Mexico, Thailand and Zimbabwe. He has also produced international work in the UK at venues ranging from The Traverse Theatre in Edinburgh to Ronnie Scott's Jazz Club and The British Museum in London.

He lives in London and Northumberland.

Printed in Great Britain
by Amazon